ENTERPRISE LIABILITY AND THE COMMON LAW

Theories of enterprise liability have, historically, had a significant influence on the development of various aspects of the law of torts. Enterprise liability has impacted upon both statutory and common law rules. Prime examples would include laws on workmen's compensation and products liability. Of late, in a number of jurisdictions, enterprise liability has been a powerful catalyst for change in the employer's responsibilities towards third parties by prompting changes to the law on vicarious liability. The results have been seen most dramatically where the employer's responsibility for the intentional torts of employees is concerned. Recent common law reforms have not been without controversy and have raised difficult and challenging questions about the appropriate scope of an employer's responsibility. In response to this, Douglas Brodie offers a critique of the employer's common law obligations, both in tort and under the law of contract of employment.

DOUGLAS BRODIE is one of the UK's leading labour lawyers. He is Professor of Employment Law and Head of School at Edinburgh University's School of Law.

ENTERPRISE LIABILITY AND THE COMMON LAW

DOUGLAS BRODIE

CAMBRIDGE
UNIVERSITY PRESS

CAMBRIDGE
UNIVERSITY PRESS

University Printing House, Cambridge CB2 8BS, United Kingdom

One Liberty Plaza, 20th Floor, New York, NY 10006, USA

477 Williamstown Road, Port Melbourne, VIC 3207, Australia

314-321, 3rd Floor, Plot 3, Splendor Forum, Jasola District Centre, New Delhi - 110025, India

79 Anson Road, #06-04/06, Singapore 079906

Cambridge University Press is part of the University of Cambridge.

It furthers the University's mission by disseminating knowledge in the pursuit of education, learning and research at the highest international levels of excellence.

www.cambridge.org
Information on this title: www.cambridge.org/9780521762014

First published 2010
First paperback edition 2013

A catalogue record for this publication is available from the British Library

Library of Congress Cataloging in Publication data
Brodie, Douglas, 1960–
Enterprise liability and the common law / Douglas Brodie.
p. cm.
ISBN 978-0-521-76201-4 (Hardback)
1. Enterprise liability. 2. Common law. I. Title.
K957.B76 2010
346.02–dc22

2010017659

ISBN 978-0-521-76201-4 Hardback
ISBN 978-1-107-63010-9 Paperback

In Memoriam
Bill Stewart

CONTENTS

PREFACE

The sexual abuse cases of *Bazley v Curry* and *Lister v Hesley Hall* led to considerable changes in the law of vicarious liability in Canada and the UK. In *Bazley* this expansion of liability was legitimised by reference to the doctrine of enterprise liability. In the author's view recourse to enterprise liability is of particular significance given contemporary concern over the proper extent of corporate social responsibility; the invocation of enterprise liability can be seen as the common law's response. Leaving aside changes to the law of vicarious liability, how else might the common law respond and how pivotal is enterprise liability likely to be? This book seeks to provide a critique of recent developments and an assessment of the further changes that are likely to take place where the employer's common law obligations are concerned (whether in tort or under the law of contract of employment). The author hopes that the book will have considerable appeal to scholars of both tort and labour law in the UK, Australia and Canada, all being jurisdictions where enterprise liability has been invoked.

ABBREVIATIONS

AJLL	Australian Journal of Labour Law
Ariz. St. L.J.	Arizona State Law Journal
Can. J. L. & Soc'y	Canadian Journal of Law and Society
CLJ	Cambridge Law Journal
Colum. L.R.	Columbia Law Review
Conn. L. Rev.	Connecticut Law Review
Edin. LR	Edinburgh Law Review
Harv. L.R.	Harvard Law Review
ILJ	Industrial Law Journal
Ind. L.R.	Indiana Law Review
JBL	Journal of Business Law
J. Legal Studies	Journal of Legal Studies
LQR	Law Quarterly Review
Man. L.J.	Manitoba Law Journal
Me. L. Rev.	Maine Law Review
MLR	Modern Law Review
Mich. L. Rev.	Michigan Law Review
Minn. L. Rev.	Minnesota Law Review
QUTLJJ	Queensland University of Technology Law and Justice Journal
SAcL	Singapore Academy of Law Journal
S. Cal. L. Rev.	Southern California Law Review
S. Cal. Rev. L. & Women's Stud.	Southern California Review of Law and Women's Studies
Syd. L. Rev.	Sydney Law Review
Tenn. L. Rev.	Tennessee Law Review
TLJ	Tort Law Journal
TLR	Tort Law Review
U. Chi. L. Rev.	University of Chicago Law Review
U. Colo. L. Rev.	University of Colorado Law Review

UNSWLJ	University of New South Wales Law Journal
UTLJ	University of Toronto Law Journal
Vand. L. Rev.	Vanderbilt Law Review
WMLR	William and Mary Law Review
Yale L.J.	Yale Law Journal

1

Introduction

Theories of enterprise liability have, historically, had a significant influence on the development of various aspects of the law of torts.[1] Enterprise liability has impacted upon both statutory and common law rules. Prime examples would include laws on workmen's compensation and products liability. Of late, in a number of jurisdictions, enterprise liability has been a powerful catalyst for change in the employer's responsibilities towards third parties by prompting changes to the law on vicarious liability. The results have been seen most dramatically where the employer's responsibility for the intentional torts of employees is concerned. Whilst enterprise liability has been widely influential and, whilst the policy issues faced by the courts have been very similar, the solutions adopted have varied in different jurisdictions, some displaying a greater debt to enterprise liability than others. Recent common law reforms have not been without controversy and have raised difficult and challenging questions about the appropriate scope of an employer's responsibilities. It seems timely to both review whether recourse to enterprise liability has provided an appropriate basis upon which to justify an expansion of legal responsibilities and to assess the merits of the specific reforms that have occurred. It is also timely to consider what further developments are likely and the ways in which different jurisdictions may respond. The potential for such developments is not confined to the law of torts but also exists at the level of the contract of employment: a major question is whether enterprise liability will be as influential in prompting changes to the duties owed by employer and employee.

Two of the most significant decisions concerning the employer's responsibilities for the intentional torts of employees have been those of the Canadian Supreme Court in *Bazley v Curry*[2] and *Jacobi v*

[1] G. C. Keating, 'The Theory of Enterprise Liability and Common Law Strict Liability' (2001) 54 Vand. L. Rev. 1285.

[2] (1999) 174 DLR (4th) 45.

Griffiths.[3] Vicarious liability was said to be justified on the basis of enterprise liability: 'the employer puts in the community an enterprise which carries with it certain risks. When those risks materialise and cause injury to a member of the public despite the employer's reasonable efforts, it is fair that the person or organisation that creates the enterprise and hence the risk should bear the loss.'[4] In the UK in *Lister v Hesley Hall*,[5] Lord Steyn warmly endorsed the Canadian jurisprudence: 'Wherever such problems are considered in future in the common law world these judgments will be the starting point.' Prior to *Lister* an employer would have been vicariously liable for some instances of intentional wrongdoing but by no means all. *Bazley* prompted a radical reappraisal of the extent of an employer's responsibilities and, as discussed below, led to the claimant succeeding in *Lister*. It should be noted at the outset that the Australian courts have been much less taken with *Bazley*.

Historical influences

Theories of enterprise liability have, of course, been hugely influential in the development of both statutory and common law rules in a variety of jurisdictions over many years. In the UK an early example is constituted by the workmen's compensation legislation. The enactment of the Workmen's Compensation Act 1897 meant that henceforth, irrespective of fault, employers would be obliged to pay accident compensation to their employees. The 1897 Act compelled the employer to pay compensation in respect of some of life's vicissitudes and was an extremely important piece of legislation. It provided for compensation for industrial injuries where the injury was caused by an 'accident arising out of and in the course of employment'.[6] The compensation was to be paid by the employer but there was a complete defence where the injury was attributable to the serious and wilful misconduct of the injured employee.[7] Where the employer was liable at common law the rights of employees were preserved but an employer was not liable to pay compensation both independently of and under the Act.[8] The Act did not apply to all employments but only to railway, factory, mine, quarry or engineering work and some forms of construction work,[9] the underlying rationale

[3] (1999) 174 DLR (4th) 71. [4] Ibid., 60. [5] [2002] 1 AC 215.
[6] Workmen's Compensation Act 1897, s. 1(1).
[7] Ibid., s. 1(2)(c). [8] Ibid., s. 1(2)(b). [9] Ibid., s. 7(1).

for the selection being that priority for inclusion should be given to the more hazardous enterprises. The Act was a remarkable piece of social legislation and imposed a form of strict liability on employers. Compensation for industrial injuries was now seen as the responsibility of the enterprise: 'Where a person, on his own responsibility and for his own profit, sets in motion agencies which create risks for others, he ought to be civilly responsible for the consequences of what he does.'[10] Uncertainty was expressed as to who would ultimately bear the cost of the scheme: 'whether in the ultimate allocation of that burden the larger share will fall upon profits or upon wages, or whether it will be possible to transfer under existing economic conditions any appreciable portion of that burden upon the consumer in the shape of an added price of goods, are questions upon which opinions may very well differ'.[11]

Numerous US states also adopted similar statutes[12] and the radical nature of the legislation prompted one US commentator to ask whether fundamental changes in the common law might emerge: 'the time-honoured principles of the law of torts have been cast aside, a wider rule of responsibility has been framed, and no man can now say what will be the ultimate effects of the new doctrine'.[13] One reason for supposing that this was a realistic possibility was the incongruity between the position of the worker injured in the course of his employment by a 'pure accident' and that of a third party. The former was able to recover because of the statutory scheme whilst the latter could not in the absence of fault.

Theories of enterprise liability have also driven key common law developments. In the case of products liability in the US, for example, the impact has been dramatic as the respective rights and obligations of manufacturers and consumers have changed very significantly,[14] two landmark cases being *Henningsen v Bloomfield Motors*[15] and *Greenman v Yuba Power Products*.[16] In the latter the plaintiff was injured while using a power tool which had been given to him by his wife who had purchased it. He brought an action against the retailer and the manufacturer. The Supreme Court of California held that a manufacturer is strictly

[10] Parl. Deb., 3.5.1897, Vol. 48, H.C., Col. 1427. [11] Ibid., Col. 1441.

[12] W. G. Cowles, 'Workmen's Compensation in the United States' (1912–13) 6 Me. L. Rev. 283.

[13] J. Smith, 'Sequel to Workmen's Compensation Acts' (1913–14) 27 Harv. L.R. 235. And see E. R. Thayer, 'Liability Without Fault' (1915–16) 29 Harv. L.R. 801, 814.

[14] G. L. Priest, 'The Invention of Enterprise Liability' (1985) 14 J. Legal Studies 461, 462.

[15] 161 A.2d 69. [16] 377 P.2d 897.

liable in tort when an article he places on the market, knowing that it is to be used without inspection for defects, proves to have a defect that causes injury to a human being. Strict liability is very much the exception within the common law of tort and Traynor J looked to his earlier opinion in *Escola v Coca Cola*[17] in explaining why this position was justified. Imposing strict liability on the manufacturer is an effective means of deterring dangerous behaviour: 'Even if there is no negligence, however, public policy demands that responsibility be fixed wherever it will most effectively reduce the hazards to life and health inherent in defective products that reach the market. It is evident that the manufacturer can anticipate some hazards and guard against the recurrence of others, as the public cannot.'[18] The results in terms of loss distribution were also desirable: 'Those who suffer injury from defective products are unprepared to meet its consequences. The cost of an injury and the loss of time or health may be an overwhelming misfortune to the person injured, and a needless one, for the risk of injury can be insured by the manufacturer and distributed among the public as a cost of doing business.'[19] Crucially, such a position was fair because the creation of the risk was attributable to the manufacturer: 'However intermittently such injuries may occur and however haphazardly they may strike, the risk of their occurrence is a constant risk and a general one. Against such a risk there should be general and constant protection and the manufacturer is best situated to afford such protection.'[20] *Henningsen* was a decision of the Supreme Court of New Jersey in an action brought by a car owner's wife against the manufacturer to recover damages on account of injuries sustained by her while she was driving the car (which was said to be defective) shortly after its purchase. It was held that the defendant was liable irrespective of whether negligence had occurred and even though privity of contract was absent. Justifications of loss distribution and deterrence again came to the fore:

> where the commodities sold are such that if defectively manufactured they will be dangerous to life or limb, then society's interests can only be protected by eliminating the requirement of privity between the maker and his dealers and the reasonably expected ultimate consumer. In that way the burden of losses consequent upon use of defective articles is borne by those who are in a position to either control the danger or make an equitable distribution of the losses when they do occur.[21]

17 150 P.2d 436. And see R. J. Traynor, 'The Ways and Meanings of Defective Products and Strict Liability' (1964–5) 32 Tenn. L. Rev. 363.

18 Ibid. 19 Ibid. 20 Ibid. 21 *Henningsen*, n. 15 above.

These decisions proved to be extremely influential and led to many states in the USA adopting rules of strict liability for defective products.[22] Indeed this body of jurisprudence was codified, in the form of the revised section 402A, when the second Restatement of Torts was published in 1965.[23] It is important to note at this stage that a number of different meanings can be attributed to the concept of enterprise liability. This is a point of some significance because recourse to different definitions can determine which policy factors are promoted by the outcome in any particular case.

Reforming the law on the basis of enterprise liability gives rise to challenging questions for the judiciary, as the case of *Goldberg v Kollsman*[24] (decided shortly after *Greenman*) demonstrates. There a damages action was brought after a passenger died in a plane crash. The operator was sued in negligence but the plane manufacturer and the manufacturer of the plane's altimeter were also sued. The claim against the latter was regarded as irrelevant on the basis that adequate protection for the passengers arose from the obligations of the manufacturer. The minority suggested that the plane operator rather than the manufacturer was the enterprise with which the court should be concerned: 'the dominant enterprise and the one with which the plaintiff did business and relied upon was the airline'. The case is of interest as it illustrates that identifying the responsible enterprise may involve contentious value judgements. The minority saw their task as one of placing the risk on the enterprise in the course of whose business it arose.

Where tort is concerned the influence of enterprise liability is not confined to questions of duty but may impact on other key questions such as causation. In the notable US case of *Sindell v Abbott Laboratories*[25] the claimants brought claims against drug manufacturers seeking to hold them individually and jointly liable for unlawfully manufacturing, marketing and promoting a drug (DES) which was said to have carcinogenic effects. It was held that the claims could succeed on the basis that the defendants could be jointly liable on the concerted action theory of causation. The fact that some of the defendants may not

[22] C. J. Peck, 'Negligence and Liability Without Fault in Tort Law' (1971) 46 Washington Law Review 225, 237.

[23] S. P. Croley and J. D. Hanson, 'Rescuing the Revolution: The Revived Case for Enterprise Liability' (1992–3) 91 Mich. L. Rev. 683, 701.

[24] 12 N.Y.2d 432.

[25] For a critique of *Sindell* see D. Fischer, 'Products Liability – An Analysis of Market Share Liability' (1981) 34 Vand. L. Rev. 1623.

have manufactured the DES ingested was irrelevant in the light of that theory. The claimants would be successful if they could show that the defendants had acted jointly and in concert in the testing, marketing and promoting of DES. The court went on to indicate that had the concerted action theory been inapplicable they might well have adopted an 'enterprise liability' theory of causation and the discussion in an academic article by Sheiner was commended.[26] There might be thought to be a close correlation between the approach adopted in the case and one based upon enterprise liability.[27] The application of Sheiner's theory would result in the joint and several liability of all the members of an industry who marketed the same defective product. The theory would be applicable where a number of elements were satisfied, including a pattern of inadequate standards across an industry.[28] Such an approach, whereby a group of enterprises was viewed as a single collective entity, was appropriate on classic enterprise liability grounds: 'The employer, who derives a profit from the enterprise, is the party best able to absorb and distribute its foreseeable costs to the public. He is also in the best position to take preventative measures.'[29] A collective approach was called for: where 'an entire industry, engaged in a predictably dangerous enterprise and following similar safety practices, places an identically defective product in the stream of commerce, the industry rather than the individual manufacturer should be the focal point for liability because it can best allocate risks, distribute costs and take preventive measures'.[30]

Invoking enterprise liability as a justification for vicarious liability also has a considerable pedigree. In a seminal article in the *Yale Law Journal* in 1929, Douglas reasoned that the 'hazards of a business should be

[26] N. Sheiner, 'DSS and a Proposed Theory of Enterprise Liability' (1977–8) 46 Fordham Law Review 963.

[27] J. Stewart, 'Beyond Enterprise Liability in DES Cases – Sindell' (1981) 14 Ind. L.R. 695, 704.

[28] The elements of enterprise liability were said to be: (1) Plaintiff is not at fault for his inability to identify the causative agent and such liability is due to the nature of the defendants' conduct. (2) A generically similar defective product was manufactured by all the defendants. (3) Plaintiff's injury was caused by this product defect. (4) The defendants owed a duty of care to the class of which the plaintiff was a member. (5) There is clear and convincing evidence that plaintiff's injury was caused by the product of one of the defendants. For example, the joined defendants accounted for a high percentage of such defective products on the market at the time of plaintiff's injury. (6) There existed an insufficient, industry-wide standard of safety as to the manufacture of this product. (7) All defendants were tortfeasors satisfying the requirements of whichever cause of action is proposed.

[29] Sheiner, n. 26 above, 1001. [30] Ibid., 1002.

borne by the business directly'.[31] Loss distribution was thereby facilitated in that the costs would be borne by the consumers of the products of the business. The opinions in *Bazley*, in this very area, would prove to be hugely profound.

Contemporary judicial thinking

Whilst the Canadian decisions referred to above may have pride of place, the earlier US decision in *Ira S. Bushey v US*[32] has been highly influential. Cases such as *Greenman* placed great store on deterrence and loss distribution, policy considerations which have long held sway in vicarious liability cases. Indeed they continue to do so in some versions of enterprise liability. The vicarious liability case of *Bushey* brought questions of equity centre stage. The case was decided on the basis of enterprise liability which was said to reflect 'a deeply rooted sentiment that a business enterprise cannot justly disclaim responsibility for accidents which may fairly be said to be characteristic of its activities'. The case concerned a coastguardsman who was living aboard a coastguard vessel while it was in dry dock. Whilst intoxicated he opened the dry dock's floodgate valve, thereby causing the dry dock to sink. The decision to impose vicarious liability was justified on the basis of equitable considerations; the court was not convinced, for example, that imposition of liability would lead to a more efficient allocation of resources. Indeed, denial of liability 'might induce drydock owners, prodded by their insurance companies, to install locks on their valves to avoid similar incidents in the future, while placing the burden on shipowners is much less likely to lead to accident prevention'.[33]

The possibility of such drunken misbehaviour arising was seen as a risk of the enterprise and it was therefore fair to hold the employer responsible. What happened was on a par with what might have been expected: it was foreseeable that crew members crossing the dry dock might do damage, negligently or even intentionally. Other risks which might have materialised would have been too far removed from those generated by the enterprise:

> If Lane had set fire to the bar where he had been imbibing or had caused an accident on the street while returning to the drydock, the Government would not be liable; the activities of the 'enterprise' do not reach into

[31] W. O. Douglas, 'Vicarious Liability and Administration of Risk', 38 Yale L.J. 584, 586.
[32] 398 F.2d 167 (2d Cir. 1968). [33] Ibid., 170–1.

> areas where the servant does not create risks different from those attendant on the activities of the community in general . . . if the seaman upon returning to the drydock, recognized the Bushey security guard as his wife's lover and shot him, vicarious liability would not follow; the incident would have related to the seaman's domestic life, not to his seafaring activity, and it would have been the most unlikely happenstance that the confrontation with the paramour occurred on a drydock rather than at the traditional spot.[34]

The significance of the decision becomes apparent when it is recalled that the fact that a particular form of harm is characteristic of an activity does not, in tort as a whole, lead to strict liability: 'the harm of knife cuts are in some sense "characteristic" of the distribution of knives; adverse side effects are "characteristic" of the manufacture of prescription drugs . . . yet our tort system shows no interest in imposing automatic liability on the companies that produce knives and drugs'.[35] The reasoning in *Bushey*, along with some highly creative Californian jurisprudence (see Chapter 3), played a big part in shaping the decision in *Bazley*. The linkage of risk creation and responsibility in law came to be seen as an eminently equitable nexus.

The significance of enterprise risk in determining the extent of vicarious liability came to the fore in the Canadian Supreme Court in *Bazley v Curry*.[36] In that decision, which was very much policy driven, the court elected to modify the Salmond test;[37] as formulated it failed to give adequate weight to the principal policy factors. At the level of practical application *Bazley* allowed a finding of liability on the basis of a 'close connection' between the employee's tort and the employment in question, some such formulation being seen as necessary to ensure that there is adequate linkage between the employee's behaviour and the risks inherent in the employer's enterprise. Justifying such a modification of the existing law involved an articulation of the key policy concerns. It has long been accepted that vicarious liability is a creature of policy, but establishing the precise nature of the relevant policy concerns has been very much a matter

34 Ibid., 172.

35 G. T. Schwartz, 'The Hidden and Fundamental Issue of Employer Vicarious Liability' (1995–6) 69 S. Cal. L. Rev. 1739.

36 (1999) DLR 174 (4th) 45.

37 Salmond said that a wrongful act is deemed to be done by a 'servant' in the course of his employment if 'it is either (a) a wrongful act authorised by the master, or (b) a wrongful and unauthorised mode of doing some act authorised by the master': J. W. Salmond, *The Law of Torts* (London: Stevens and Haynes, 1907), p. 83; and R. F. V. Heuston and R. A. Buckley (eds.), *Salmond and Heuston on the Law of Torts*, 21st edn (London: Sweet & Maxwell, 1996), p. 443.

for debate. The Supreme Court dealt with these matters with some vigour. Not only were the principal policy concerns fully articulated and appraised but, crucially, they were also ranked. Ultimately, *Bazley* puts forward a justification for the imposition of vicarious liability which might be styled 'enterprise liability'. This, the author would suggest, is a matter of some importance where future development of the law is concerned. Henceforth, it should be easier to determine, in any given context, what judicial policy requires. We learn that, most fundamentally, vicarious liability is justified given that 'the employer puts in the community an enterprise which carries with it certain risks. When those risks materialise and cause injury to a member of the public despite the employer's reasonable efforts, it is fair that the person or organisation that creates the enterprise and hence the risk should bear the loss.'[38] Such a stance also has the merit of facilitating loss distribution. Vicarious liability is, therefore, seen as the corollary of the creation of risks by an enterprise. Equity dictates that the enterprise, which stands to profit from the running of those risks, should be obliged to compensate in the event of harm materialising. Whilst equitable considerations provided the principal justification, the role of vicarious liability in promoting deterrence was seen as the second principal justification. This is not altogether surprising since one function of strict liability is to reinforce fault liability.[39] In a negligence action the burden of proof is on the plaintiff to demonstrate the actual steps that the reasonably careful employer should have taken. This may be far from easy. For instance, in the UK decision in *Lister v Hesley Hall*,[40] which dealt with similar issues, the complaints that the employers were careless in their care, selection and control of the warden were not accepted. However, if the employer cannot hope to avoid liability, simply by defeating the particular allegations of fault that the plaintiff puts forward, it must look to doing so through taking measures beyond that required by the law of negligence. Strict liability compels innovation in that, if the enterprise cannot find a means of averting the risk, it will be liable for the consequences. In *Bazley* it was said that 'beyond the narrow band of employer conduct that attracts direct liability in negligence lies a vast area where imaginative and efficient administration and supervision can reduce the risk that the employer has introduced into the community'.[41] This requires not only that suitable

[38] *Bazley*, n. 36 above, 60.
[39] P. Cane, *Responsibility in Law and Morality* (Oxford: Hart Publishing, 2002), p. 48.
[40] [2002] 1 AC 215. [41] *Bazley*, n. 36 above, 61.

precautions are introduced to meet specific risks but that questions of organisational 'culture' are addressed. For instance, incentive schemes should not function in such a way as to undermine the impact of health and safety measures. However, it must be recognised that, at the end of the day, there may be nothing that could have been done by the most imaginative and enterprising employer. This does not present a problem for enterprise liability. It holds that the employer should be vicariously liable given that the employer is obliged to accept responsibility for managing the risks it has created. It is seen as equitable that, having introduced a risk, you are taken to warrant that you will manage that risk effectively. At this point the two principal justifications converge in that it is regarded as fair that breach of that warranty leads to liability on the part of the enterprise to pay compensation. It might also be the case that strict liability would lead to an enterprise extending their insurance coverage.[42]

In conclusion, *Bazley* holds that enterprise liability justifies the doctrine of vicarious liability because, on grounds of equity, an enterprise should compensate when risks it has introduced materialise. Equity also demands that the enterprise must accept full responsibility for managing those risks. The intellectual debt to *Bushey* is readily apparent.

Given the obvious desire to compensate children who had been the subject of abuse, the outcome in *Bazley* is not unduly surprising. However, that outcome was greatly facilitated by enterprise liability. It had long been recognised that such a theoretical perspective suggested that 'all injuries caused by workmen which arise out of and in the course of their employment should result in the master's liability – whether or not the injury resulted from some activity which benefited the employer or was authorised by him, and whether it occurred through the servant's wilfulness or through his negligence'.[43]

The significance of profit

In a stimulating article Neyers[44] draws attention to the fact that some theories of enterprise liability stress the significance of profit: 'if, in seeking to secure financial profit, an enterprise causes certain types

[42] See G. L. Priest, 'The Current Insurance Crisis and Modern Tort Law' (1986–7) 96 Yale L.J. 1521, 1538.

[43] G. Calabresi, 'Some thoughts on risk distribution and the law of torts' (1960–1) 70 Yale L.J. 499, 544.

[44] J. W. Neyers, 'A Theory of Vicarious Liability' (2005) 43 Alberta Law Review 287.

of loss, it should be legally obliged to pay compensation to the victim.'[45] Neyers questions how enterprise liability can justify a finding of vicarious liability against a non-profit-making body such as a charity. By way of rejoinder it might be said that charities still run risks for the benefit of the organisation. The criticism only has merit if profit is viewed in a purely financial sense. Neyers also points out that damages for vicarious liability are not restricted by the profitability of the business. The absence of any such correlation is not surprising. Enterprise liability reflects the moral sentiment that those who undertake activities in the pursuit of profit should compensate those damaged as a result. It is the pursuit that is the key – not the realisation or the amount. In any event Neyers himself concedes that not every theory of enterprise liability regards the pursuit of profit as significant. Most pertinently, the seminal decision in *Bazley* is predicated on the element of reciprocity: the enterprise which created the risk should bear the losses. Nevertheless Neyers has qualms here too. He argues that enterprise liability fails to explain why vicarious liability is not strict in that the employer is not liable where the employee causes the harm accidentally. It must be admitted that enterprise liability cannot explain this without reference to the fundamental aims of the law of tort. Tort seeks to strike a balance between an individual's interest in security and in freedom of action. Modern tort law favours the latter to the extent that, in general, liability should not exist without fault. When set against that backdrop it becomes apparent why vicarious liability does not extend to accidental damage. Were matters otherwise, enterprise liability could certainly be invoked to justify the imposition of strict liability.

Even if it is accepted that enterprise liability can in principle encompass charitable organisations, should it? In *Bazley* the defendants argued that they should be placed outwith the clutches of enterprise liability on the basis they were a charity. Three arguments were put forward in favour of this proposition:

(1) that it is unfair to fix liability without fault on non-profit organisations performing needed services on behalf of the general public;
(2) that non-profit organisations are less able to control and supervise the conduct of their agents, many of whom are volunteers, which enhances the unfairness of imposing vicarious liability and diminishes its deterrent effect; and

[45] J. Stapleton, *Product Liability* (London: Butterworths, 1994), p. 186.

(3) that the practical effect of making non-profit organisations vicariously liable for the misconduct of their agents will be to make it difficult or impossible for such organisations to carry out their important work.

The Supreme Court rejected such an exemption. With regard to the first argument the public interest in work done by charitable organisations was not in dispute. It was also accepted that, in some instances, unless an activity was undertaken by a charity no one else would perform it. In *Bazley* itself 'the Children's Foundation took in the respondent when no one else seemed ready or able to do so and undertook the difficult task of providing him with the love and guidance that other children receive from their parents'.[46] Nevertheless, the defendant's contention was outweighed by the belief that, as between two innocent parties, the victim of the tort should win out. This was so even though it was maintained that loss distribution is more problematic in the case of a charity as they cannot pass additional costs on to the public by way of higher prices for goods or services. They may also be unable to obtain insurance in respect of intentional torts. The conduct of charitable organisations was also seen as susceptible to improvement through the imposition of strict liability beyond that which could be expected from a regime of fault-based liability: 'It may also deter other incidents of sexual abuse by motivating charitable organizations entrusted with the care of children to take not only such precautions as the law of negligence requires, but all possible precautions to ensure that their children are not sexually abused.'[47] The final argument was that non-profit charitable organisations often work with volunteers and are thus less able than commercial enterprises to supervise what such individuals do. This was rejected as it was said to be based on the false premise that an employer has less control over volunteers than employees. In any event, the acts of volunteers who are not employees do not give rise to vicarious liability.

The position of charities was viewed with more sympathy in *Jacobi*.[48] Without departing from the position in *Bazley* the court took the view that a number of the policy factors that underpin vicarious liability might have less weight where a non-profit organisation is concerned. For instance, the imposition of liability might lead to over-deterrence:

[46] *Bazley*, n. 36 above, para. 48. [47] Ibid., para. 50. [48] *Jacobi*, n. 3 above.

> the *rational* response of such organizations may be to exit the children's recreational field altogether. This is particularly the case with unincorporated groups, whose key members may find themselves personally responsible as the "employer" for the unforeseen criminal acts of a deviant employee; children's recreation is not a field that offers monetary profits as an incentive to volunteers to soldier on despite the risk of personal financial liability.[49]

The conclusion drawn was that a measure of caution might be called in applying the close connection test where a charity is concerned. It may be that in this regard *Jacobi* may prove to be the more influential decision. *Jacobi* indicates that an 'all or nothing' approach is not required and that judicious application of the close connection test may provide welcome flexibility.

Competing formulations

On occasion references in the literature or the case law to enterprise liability are simply descriptive of a context where an enterprise has been found liable. All that has occurred is that the law of tort has impinged on the running of the enterprise: 'To adopt "enterprise liability" is to combine rules of liability and agency in such a way that accountability is sought by threatening corporate profits.'[50] To invoke the term in this way tells us nothing more than that a court has thought that the imposition of liability should take place. Far greater interest and concern stems from the fact that multifarious definitions of enterprise liability exist.[51] Were one to frame matters widely the following definition might be adopted: 'losses to society created or caused by an enterprise or, more simply, by an activity, ought to be borne by that enterprise or activity'.[52] It is striking that there is no reference to risk creation; for the court in *Bazley* this provided not simply an equitable basis but also a means of limiting liability. The Supreme Court was adamant that causal connection was not enough. A multitude of alternative definitions can be produced with great ease. The decision by a court to adopt any particular formulation is an important one because different definitions

[49] Ibid., para. 75.

[50] C. D. Stone, 'The Place of Enterprise Liability in the Control of Corporate Conduct' (1980–1) 90 Yale L.J. 1, 8.

[51] See Keating, n. 1 above.

[52] H. C. Klemme, 'The Enterprise Liability Theory of Torts' (1975–6) 47 U. Colo. L. Rev. 153, 158.

promote a range of policy considerations. Decisions as to the selection or weighting of policy factors can lead to very different outcomes in individual cases and the substantive rules which emerge might be decidedly different.

Some theories stress the importance of placing liability on an enterprise which was in the best position to prevent harm arising. The issue of whether a potential defendant is in a position to deter effectively careless behaviour then becomes central in determining the responsibilities of the enterprise. Matters are particularly problematic where vicarious liability for intentional torts such as assault is concerned:

> if deterrence of criminal behaviour is regarded as a reason for imposing tortious liability upon innocent parties, three things need to be remembered. First, the problem only arises where there has been no fault, and therefore no failure to exercise reasonable care to prevent foreseeable criminal behaviour on the part of the employee. Secondly, it is primarily the function of the criminal law, and the criminal justice system, to deal with matters of crime and punishment ... Thirdly, by hypothesis, the sanctions provided by the criminal law have failed to deter the employee who has committed the crime.[53]

Theories of enterprise liability may also have regard to considerations of distribution of loss: 'though the entrepreneur himself is relatively blameless, his enterprise entails a certain amount of risk, and it is proper to place the burden of this risk upon him in the first instance, because he can pass it on to his customers. They benefit from the risky endeavour and should therefore suffer the burden of the more or less inevitable accidents which arise from that activity.'[54] Accordingly in identifying the enterprise which should be held responsible the ability to spread losses across appropriate groups (e.g. those who benefit from the enterprise's activities) is a key factor. An enterprise may be a highly efficient mechanism for spreading losses by way of insurance policies held or by an ability to pass the costs on to consumers by way of higher prices. The availability of insurance also helps to determine which loss-distribution channels are the most effective. The rise in reported incidents of child abuse, for example, may mean that bodies caring for children find it much more difficult to obtain insurance. This will point against liability should one's conception of enterprise liability place a strong emphasis on loss distribution. Equally, where an enterprise is viewed as an efficient

[53] *New South Wales v Lepore* [2003] 212 CLR 511, 534.

[54] C. R. Morris, 'Enterprise Liability and the Actuarial Process – The Insignificance of Foresight' (1960–1) 70 Yale L.J. 554, 584.

loss distributor an expansive view may be taken of acts for which the employer is vicariously liable and which are held to be within the 'scope of the employment'.[55]

Sometimes, as with *Bazley* itself, a theory of enterprise liability may also place great store on appropriate allocation of risk. Liability rules will seek to apportion the true costs to the enterprise of the conduct of that type of business. Imposing the costs of an activity on the enterprise can be defended on economic grounds: 'not charging an enterprise with a cost which arises from it leads to an understatement of the true cost of producing its goods; the result is that people purchase more of those goods than they would want if their true cost was reflected in price. On the other hand, placing a cost not related to the scope of an enterprise on that enterprise results in an overstatement of those goods, and leads to their underproduction.'[56]

In this book the focus will be on the definition put forward in *Bazley*. This is because the author's aim is not to review enterprise liability in the abstract but rather to analyse its current impact on the common law. Given this aim it seems clear that the dominant contemporary decision is that of the Supreme Court in *Bazley*. It has become the first point of reference for courts in other Commonwealth jurisdictions which, in determining outcomes in cases before them, are considering an enterprise liability approach. In appraising where the common law stands, and where it might go, the formulation in *Bazley* would appear to provide the ideal base. It is the aim of this book to explore a number of questions that the decision triggers, with particular reference to the case law of the UK, Australia and Canada.

[55] Calabresi, n. 43 above, 501. [56] Ibid., 541.

2

The reception of *Bazley v Curry*

Bazley v Curry[1] has proved to be very influential but its reception has been far from uncritical in jurisdictions outside Canada. For example, it has provoked a very mixed response amongst the members of the High Court of Australia. Initially, in *Hollis v Vabu*,[2] the High Court embraced the reasoning in *Bazley*. Contemporary Australian conditions dictated that 'the conduct by the defendant of an enterprise in which persons are identified as representing that enterprise should carry an obligation to third persons to bear the cost of injury or damage to them which may fairly be said to be characteristic of the conduct of that enterprise'.[3] The key issue in *Vabu* was whether the employer was responsible for the activities of a courier whose employment status was in issue. The case centred upon the composition of the employer's enterprise. The subsequent case of *New South Wales v Lepore*[4] displayed great diversity of opinion and, more significantly, only minority endorsement of *Bazley*. The context was very different to *Vabu*; *Lepore* concerned the sexual assault of a pupil by a teacher. The facts, for a case of this type, were all too familiar. The claimant maintained that he was sexually assaulted on a number of occasions by his primary school teacher. The sexual assaults were said to have occurred after he was sent to a storeroom attached to the classroom on account of his misconduct in class. Only three of the seven judges who sat were of the view that vicarious liability would arise where an employee committed a criminal act of this nature.[5] Of those three Gleeson CJ found it helpful to consider the power and authority conferred by employment in determining the risks at stake: 'where the

[1] (1999) 174 DLR (4th) 45. [2] [2001] 207 CLR 21. [3] Ibid., 40.

[4] [2003] 212 CLR 511. And see S. White and G. Orr, 'Precarious liability: The High Court in Lepore, Samin and Rich on school responsibility for assaults by teachers' (2003) 11 (2) TLJ 101.

[5] Gummow and Hayne JJ do not favour the analysis of risk adopted by the Supreme Court of Canada in *Bazley*. Callinan J rejects the application of vicarious liability to situations of intentional wrongdoing by employees. McHugh J decided the case with reference to the law on non-delegable duties and did not need to address the issue.

teacher-student relationship is invested with a high degree of power and intimacy, the use of that power and intimacy to commit sexual abuse may provide a sufficient connection between the sexual assault and the employment to make it just to treat such contact as occurring in the course of employment'.[6] Whilst this stance was clearly heavily influenced by *Bazley*, only Kirby J[7] was wholly persuaded by the enterprise liability analysis advanced by the Supreme Court. In language reminiscent of *Bazley* he accepted that 'profit-making enterprises, which derive financial benefits from an operation, must bear the cost of any particular risks which such operation introduces into the community or exacerbates'.[8] The rationale was also said to be applicable to non-profit organisations.[9] Whatever the merits of enterprise liability in general it was clear that Kirby J applauded the desire to frame the law in such a way as to facilitate the protection of children. This was of course also the case in *Lister v Hesley Hall*.[10] The law had long recognised that vicarious liability might arise where crimes such as fraud were concerned.[11] This is despite the fact that it might be thought to be a misuse of language to say that such criminal behaviour was a mode of performing the employment in

6 *Lepore*, n. 4 above, 546.

7 Gaudron J introduces an analysis based on the law of estoppel. Gaudron J was clearly troubled by the extension of vicarious liability to include intentional criminal acts and modifications to the test for scope of employment were not seen as assisting. In the author's opinion, resort to estoppel points to a more restrictive approach than that advanced in *Bazley*. The employer must do something beyond employment of the worker in a risky occupation before responsibility for an intentional act will arise. It was said that the crux of the matter is whether the person whose acts or omissions are in question was acting as the servant, agent or representative of the person against whom liability is asserted. This is somewhat circular as the difficulty is then to establish when the employee was so acting. Gaudron J also said that a person will not be estopped from denying that a person was acting as his or her servant, agent or representative unless there is a close connection between what was done and what that person was engaged to do. Given the language used it may be that *Bazley* is being recognised, to some extent, after all but that the true juridical basis is estoppel. It was also said, at 561, that on that basis, 'vicarious liability is not necessarily limited to the acts of an employee, but might properly extend to those of an independent contractor or other person who, although as a strict matter of law, is acting as principal, might reasonably be thought to be acting as the servant, agent or representative of the person against whom liability is asserted'.

8 *Lepore*, n. 4 above, 613.

9 Kirby J observed at 613 that 'schools undoubtedly benefit the community, with the education and development services they provide for students. In that way, the broader tax-paying community that "profits" from the enterprise should also bear the cost of any particular risks which evidence establishes would be closely associated with the functioning of such an institution.'

10 [2002] 1 AC 215.

11 *Lloyd v Grace Smith* [1912] AC 716.

question.[12] It would be regrettable if the law were to be less willing to facilitate recovery by children who were the victims of sexual abuse. The common law should not place greater store on protection of wealth. Kirby J saw the move to the 'close connection' test as an instance of incremental development rather than a radical departure from the traditional approach to vicarious liability for intentional acts. Salmond was quoted to the effect that '[A] master, as opposed to the employer of an independent contractor, is liable even for acts which he has not authorised, provided they are *so connected with* acts which he has authorised, that they may rightly be regarded as modes – although improper modes – of doing them.'[13] The links with the past notwithstanding, it was anticipated that liability might be much wider by virtue of adopting *Bazley*. An extensive range of both voluntary workers and professionals were seen as potential defendants in cases brought by children. The range of potential claimants might also be considerable in cases of physical and sexual abuse and one might expect to see claims brought by, for example, the old and the mentally ill. In *Lepore* itself Kirby J took an expansive view of the risks involved in teaching.[14] Sexual abuse of children in the care of a school was an undoubted enterprise risk: the risk being 'inherent in close intimacy between adults and vulnerable children that may arise in the specific circumstances of a school setting'.[15] On the other hand, risks of sexual assault would not normally be introduced to the community by a company involved in engineering or accountancy.

Gummow and Hayne JJ were not attracted to the approach in *Bazley* and in espousing this stance offer an interesting critique. It was accepted that before the decisions in *Bazley* and *Lister* there would have been little argument that a teacher who sexually assaulted a pupil, whether at school or out of school, was not acting in the course of employment: 'Such an assault is the antithesis of the central task confided to a teacher

[12] *O'Keeffe v Hickey* [2008] IESC 72.

[13] *Lepore*, n. 4 above, quoting J. W. Salmond, *The Law of Torts* (London: Stevens and Haynes, 1907), pp. 83–4.

[14] Kirby J observed at 621 that: 'In the case of an educational authority, involving immature and vulnerable pupils, the risk, although small, is one that may be inherent in the conduct of the particular employer's enterprise. This may be so especially in the case of a "one teacher" school in a remote area where the restraints of supervision and school community are reasonably limited. However regrettable it may be, in certain circumstances, sexual and physical abuse can "fairly be said to be characteristic" of such enterprise in a small minority of cases.'

[15] *Lepore*, n. 4 above, 621.

which is to care for and teach the child. It could in no way be said to be a part of what a teacher is held out as being employed to do.'[16] Both this position and reasoning were regarded as correct; a conclusion fortified by reference to the writings of Pollock. The latter believed that the underlying rationale of cases concerning vicarious liability was that legal responsibility arose where 'a man has for his own convenience brought about or maintained some state of things which in the ordinary course of nature may work mischief to his neighbours'.[17] Reliance upon Pollock's rationalisation has a number of consequences. Applying that rationale to the employment context one would say that where an employer employed staff to conduct its business, it brought about a state of things in which, if care was not taken, harm would arise. It is appropriate to hold the employer responsible in law because it is inevitable that in conducting any business carelessness will occur. However, intentional assaults do not arise in the normal course of things and on the Pollock formulation liability on the part of the employer would be unlikely. Invoking Pollock to deny that *Bazley* should be followed is not wholly persuasive. The cogency of the Pollock view turns on the identification and ranking of the governing policy factors. If one takes the same view of policy as the court in *Bazley* one would not arrive at the sort of restrictive formula promulgated by Pollock. Criticism based on the Pollock approach really says little more than that *Bazley* does not adhere to traditional thinking on vicarious liability.

Of greater interest was the criticism of Gummow and Hayne JJ of the key concepts that lie at the heart of *Bazley*. In deciding whether the employer was vicariously liable the 'close connection' test was not seen as making adjudication any easier than the application of the traditional course of employment formula. Recourse to issues of risk creation and enhancement was problematic. Clearly entry into employment gave the opportunity for wrongdoing but the court in *Bazley* was adamant that did not suffice. It was though seen as nigh on impossible to decide when the *Bazley* threshold was met. How can one tell when an employment creates or increases a risk that an employee would commit an intentional tort?

> Conducting a school may certainly provide the occasion or the opportunity for a teacher to assault a pupil. But in what other sense can it be said that the school authority creates (let alone enhances) the risk that a

[16] Ibid., 583.

[17] Ibid., 582, quoting F. Pollock, *Essays in Jurisprudence and Ethics* (London: Macmillan and Co., 1882), p. 122.

> pupil will be sexually assaulted? The teacher is given authority over the pupil; the pupil is, inevitably, vulnerable to abuse of that power. According to the nature of the duties to be undertaken by the teacher there may be greater or lesser opportunity for assault. If the duties are intimate there may be greater opportunity than if they are not, but experience dictates that sexual assaults on young people are not confined to assaults by those who are required to perform intimate tasks for, or with a child.[18]

The inability of the courts to furnish a means of distinguishing between a situation where the employer merely provided an opportunity for harm to arise and one where the risk of harm was created meant that the moral authority of *Bazley* was undermined. It also meant, on the assumption that this critique was well founded, that the impact on defendants of the adoption of *Bazley* was potentially very considerable:

> it would seem that a test which is cast in terms of creating or enhancing the risk of sexual assault leads inexorably to a conclusion that a school authority will always be vicariously liable for sexual assault by a teacher if the assault occurs on school premises or during school hours. That is a large conclusion. But in every school, teachers exercise power or authority, and in every school, no matter what may be the duties of the teachers, there is the opportunity for abuse, no matter whether the duties which the teacher is required to perform will inevitably require intimate contact with the child.[19]

The two learned judges also doubted whether deterrence would be furthered by enterprise liability in contexts where the criminal law had no impact.

The ultimate difficulty with the analysis in *Bazley* was:

> founded in the general proposition that those who conduct a business or other venture, and employ staff for that purpose, receive the benefits of the enterprise and should therefore also bear its burdens. Where the analysis made in *Bazley* departs from the proposition identified by Pollock is that the risks to be considered are not confined to those risks which attend the *furtherance* of the venture but include the risks of conduct that is directly antithetical to those aims.[20]

[18] *Lepore*, n. 4 above, 586. Callinan J rejected the application of vicarious liability to situations of intentional wrongdoing by employees. However, he too was concerned that liability would be imposed simply on the basis that the employment provided the opportunity for wrongdoing.

[19] *Lepore*, n. 4 above, 587. [20] Ibid., 588.

This approach does not involve antipathy towards enterprise liability in general but indicates a preference for a different formulation. In the eyes of Gummow and Hayne JJ equity dictated that the extent of the employer's responsibilities be more narrow. *Bazley* imposes liability on enterprises to an extent that is inequitable. This element of the reasoning is strongly linked to the scepticism that one can in fact distinguish between creation of a risk and provision of an opportunity.

Vabu and *Lepore* demonstrate very different attitudes to *Bazley*. This can be explained in part by the differently constituted courts in the two cases. The author would suggest that the very different contexts were far more determinative. *Vabu* concerned, in effect, contracting out of obligations traditionally assumed by employers (an area of law that has provoked much judicial concern). The employer in *Vabu* had chosen to set up working arrangements in a particular way with a number of aims in mind, one of them being avoidance of liability in tort.[21] *Lepore* deals with the very different question of the employer's responsibility for behaviour that he had not authorised and which the criminal law (including the likelihood of a custodial sentence) could not deter. The behaviour concerned is also behaviour that could not have been anticipated in respect of that particular employee otherwise the employer would be liable in negligence (though on the assumption it was a risk characteristic of that type of enterprise it could be predicted that an unidentified member of staff might behave in this way).

Up until recently, in the UK, an employer would have been vicariously liable for some instances of intentional wrongdoing but by no means all. A significant barrier in the path of a plaintiff was the fact that any action raised would be determined on the basis of the Salmond test, which rendered the employer liable for acts 'which he has not authorised, provided they are so connected with acts which he has authorised that they may rightly be regarded as modes – although improper modes – of doing them'.[22] This could render litigation a daunting prospect as more extreme acts could be portrayed as the very antithesis of what the employee was employed to do and, therefore, unconnected with his/her employment. A prime example was the Court of Appeal decision in *Trotman v North Yorkshire County Council*[23] where it was observed that 'in the field of serious sexual misconduct, I find it difficult to visualise

[21] See Chapter 7.

[22] R. F. V. Heuston and R. A. Buckley (eds.), *Salmond and Heuston on the Law of Torts*, 21st edn (London: Sweet & Maxwell, 1996), p. 443.

[23] [1999] LGR 584.

circumstances in which an act of the teacher can be an unauthorised mode of carrying out an authorised act'. The accuracy of this application of the Salmond test was acknowledged in the Lords: 'It is stretching language to breaking-point to describe the series of deliberate sexual assaults on them on which he embarked as merely a wrongful and unauthorised mode of [performing that duty].'[24] The test looks to the individual bargain between employer and employed and focuses on what the employee was hired or authorised to do. Acts beyond this may render the employer vicariously liable by reason of analogy. Such a stance might be felt to be deficient in that it focuses, very specifically, on the particular employment relationship to the exclusion of the nature of the employing enterprise. As a corollary tortious behaviour is seen as the 'random consequences of discrete acts' rather than the 'inevitable by-products of planned activities'.[25]

The jurisprudence of the Canadian Supreme Court proved to be hugely influential in persuading the House of Lords to depart from the traditional approach in *Lister*. *Lister* was another case concerning child abuse. The claimants were resident in a boarding house attached to a school owned and managed by the defendants. The warden of the boarding house, unknown to the defendants, systematically sexually abused the claimants. The claimants claimed damages against the defendants on the basis that they were vicariously liable for the torts committed by him. The Court of Appeal allowed an appeal by the employer, holding that the warden's acts could not be regarded as an unauthorised mode of carrying out his authorised duties. The House of Lords held for the claimant; there was a sufficient connection between the work that the warden had been employed to do and the acts of abuse committed. The replacement of the Salmond test by the 'close connection' test, put forward by their Canadian counterparts, was accepted by the Lords. The court chose not to justify the decision in terms of the sorts of general policy arguments which underpin vicarious liability. As a consequence, it is not entirely clear how firmly wedded the House of Lords is to enterprise liability as conceptualised in *Bazley*. In particular, when it comes to questions relating to policy factors, it is unclear to what extent the reasoning of the two courts converge. In arriving at judgment Lord Steyn acknowledged the intellectual debt owed to the Supreme

[24] *Lister*, n. 10 above, 244.

[25] G. Keating, 'The Idea of Fairness in the Law of Enterprise Liability' (1997) 95 Mich. L.R. 1266, 1267.

Court: 'I have been greatly assisted by the luminous and illuminating judgments of the Canadian Supreme Court in *Bazley v Curry*, 174 DLR (4th) 45 and *Jacobi v Griffiths*, 174 DLR (4th) 71. Wherever such problems are considered in future in the common law world these judgments will be the starting point.'[26] However, he was somewhat reticent about explicitly endorsing their stance on policy: 'it is unnecessary to express views on the full range of policy considerations examined in those decisions'.[27] However, the author would submit that, when subsequent decisions are taken into account, the position in the UK is reasonably clear. It should be said at the outset that *Lister* is utterly consistent with the ultimate justification for the imposition of vicarious liability being the creation of enterprise risk. It is highly significant that the one judge (Lord Millet) who does address policy issues quotes Fleming to the effect that the most important policy justification for vicarious liability is that 'a person who employs others to advance his own economic interest should in fairness be placed under a corresponding liability for losses incurred in the course of the enterprise'.[28] Indeed Lord Millet went on to say that 'if the employer's objectives cannot be achieved without a serious risk of the employee committing the kind of wrong which he has in fact committed, the employer ought to be liable'.[29] The House of Lords adopted an approach consistent with *Bazley* in the later case of *Dubai Aluminium v Salaam*.[30] Lord Nicholls, in giving the judgment of the majority, observed that:

> the underlying legal policy is based on the recognition that carrying on a business enterprise necessarily involves risks to others. It involves the risk that others will be harmed by wrongful acts committed by the agents through whom the business is carried on. When those risks ripen into loss, it is just that the business should be responsible for compensating the person who has been wronged.[31]

[26] *Lister*, n. 10 above, 230.

[27] Lord Hutton agreed with this speech. Lord Hobhouse appeared to view the case as concerning non-delegable duties.

[28] *Lister*, n. 10 above, 243. Lord Millet goes on to quote from P. S. Atiyah, *Vicarious Liability in the Law of Torts* (London: Butterworths, 1967), where it is said, at 24, that: 'The master ought to be liable for all those torts which can fairly be regarded as reasonably incidental risks to the type of business he carries on'. He adopts a similar approach in *Dubai Aluminium v Salaam* [2003] 2 AC 366, 395, though in that case he also draws attention to vicarious liability's loss distribution attributes.

[29] *Lister*, n. 10 above.

[30] [2003] 2 AC 366.

[31] Ibid., 377. It is also worth noting that in *Bernard v A-G* [2005] IRLR 398 the Privy Council appeared to endorse the reasoning in *Bazley*. It was accepted at 402 that the 'employer ought to be liable for a tort which can fairly be regarded as a reasonably

The recent decision of the House of Lords in *Majrowski v Guy's & St Thomas's NHS Trust* is though more equivocal, Lord Nicholls merely summarising the policy factors that have long been regarded as relevant to the imposition of vicarious liability.[32] Nevertheless, when the House of Lords decisions which have been decided since *Bazley* are viewed in the round it is reasonable to conclude that there has been firm though not overwhelming support for the Canadian approach.

Acceptance of the analysis of policy in *Bazley* does not make it inevitable that the close connection test will be equally influential. Deakin has commented that the test can be depicted as merely replacing 'one verbal formula (the distinction between "authorised duties" and "unauthorised modes") with another ("sufficient connection") which in the long run may prove no more adequate to the task in hand'.[33] The author agrees. In the author's opinion, it fails to provide a meaningful test but merely offers a form of wording to describe situations where vicarious liability arises. The real question is, what is the proper extent of the employer's responsibility? And that is very much a matter of policy. The outcome in any particular case will owe far more to the judicial assessment and ordering of policy considerations than to the semantics of competing tests. Thus we find that, in *Lepore*, whilst Kirby J favoured the adoption of the close connection test he was less clear as to how much in the way of guidance it would offer and echoed Deakin's concerns:

> In saying this, I do not overlook the fact that determination of the 'connection', necessary to establish legal liability, will itself involve value judgments and policy choices. Ultimately, these oblige the decision maker to answer the question whether, in the particular circumstances, it is just and reasonable to impose on the enterprise in question legal liability for the particular civil wrong done by its employee. Try as verbal formulae and specific rules might, they cannot ultimately escape the necessity to answer this basic question.[34]

The Australian case of *Sprod v Public Relations Oriented Security*[35] demonstrates that there is little point in becoming overly concerned with semantics. There the claimant had been brutally assaulted by bouncers and sustained brain damage. The severity of the assault prompted the

incidental risk to the type of business he carried on'. See also *Brown v Robinson* [2004] UKPC 54.

32 [2007] 1 AC 224.

33 S. Deakin, '"Enterprise-Risk": The Juridical Nature of the Firm Revisited' (2003) 32 ILJ 97, 105.

34 *Lepore*, n. 4 above, 619.

35 [2007] NSWCA 319.

trial judge to hold that the employer was not vicariously liable: 'That brutal and vicious assault was not for the purpose of subduing him. It was so severe and unnecessary that it was motivated by the blood lust of the security officers involved. I would therefore hold that the assault upon the [appellant] by the security guards was not done in the course of their employment but was an independent "frolic" of their own.'[36] Prior to *Bazley* such a conclusion would not have seemed surprising. Yet on appeal it was held that the predominant motive was to discharge the duties under the employment contract and, therefore, the employer was vicariously liable. A conclusion justified, not by the language of the close connection test, but on the traditional basis that the behaviour was an improper mode of doing what the staff were employed to do: 'the conduct of the guards was so connected with acts that the respondent authorised them to perform that they may be regarded as modes – although highly improper modes – of doing them'.[37] The authority invoked in support of this analysis was the old Australian High Court case of *Deatons v Flew*[38] rather than any of the contemporary decisions. The New South Wales Court of Appeal took the view that their conclusion could also be justified in terms of the close connection test. The decision in *Sprod* evidences a desire to take a more expansive view of an employer's responsibilities though the test deployed is somewhat incidental; Deakin's scepticism is wholly borne out. Atiyah's view that more emphasis should be placed on risk has come to the fore: 'is there a substantial risk that, in doing what he has been authorised to do, the servant will commit torts of the kind which he in fact has committed?'[39] In 1977 Rose had commented that 'Courts within the British Commonwealth have demonstrated a persistent reluctance to hold that an employee's assault has been committed within the course of his employment so as to make his employer vicariously liable for the tort'.[40] *Sprod* suggests that this view is no longer valid. This would appear to be the case in the UK as well as in Australia. I would suggest

[36] Ibid., para. 37. In *Lepore*, n. 4 above, 540, Gleeson CJ observed that: 'Where acts of physical violence are concerned, the nature and seriousness of the criminal act may be relevant to a judgment as to whether it is to be regarded as a personal, independent act of the perpetrator, or whether it is within the scope of employment. A security guard at business premises who removes a person with unnecessary force may be acting in the course of employment. On the other hand . . . extreme and unnecessary violence, perhaps combined with other factors, such as personal animosity towards the victim, might lead to a conclusion that what is involved is an act of pure personal vindictiveness.'

[37] Ibid., para. 83. [38] (1949) 79 CLR 370. [39] Atiyah, n. 28 above, 183.

[40] F. D. Rose, 'Liability for an Employee's Assaults' (1977) 40 MLR 420.

that what we are seeing is, on policy grounds, a decision to expand the scope of an employer's responsibility for the intentional wrongs of employees. This is by no means confined to cases of intentional assault on children. In this regard it is helpful to compare the 1960s case of *Daniels v Whetstone*[41] with the much more recent decision in *Mattis v Pollock.*[42] In *Daniels* the claimant had been assaulted by a steward as he was being ejected from a nightclub. Not long after the ejection was accomplished the steward committed a further, and more serious, assault on the claimant. The employer was held to be vicariously liable for the first assault but not the second, the latter being categorised as an act of private retaliation. The facts in *Mattis* were broadly analogous. In *Mattis* a bouncer had been forced to flee following an altercation in the nightclub where he worked. He went home but, having armed himself with a knife, decided to return to the nightclub. As he approached the club he stabbed one of the customers who had been involved in the altercation. The trial judge found that the lapse of time and intervening events culminating in the stabbing did not amount to one incident. He concluded that there was not a sufficiently close connection between the doorman's employment by the defendant and the claimant's stabbing for it to be fair and just to hold the defendant vicariously liable for the consequences of the attack. The Court of Appeal disagreed and held that the employer was vicariously liable. The court found that where an employee is expected to use violence while carrying out his duties, the likelihood of establishing that an act of violence fell within the broad scope of his employment is greater than it would be if he were not.[43] It did not help the employer's case that the bouncer was encouraged and expected to perform his duties in an aggressive and intimidatory manner, which included physical manhandling of customers.

I would submit that *Bazley* has been highly influential in increasing the extent of an employer's obligations to third parties. In particular, victims of sexual abuse are much more likely to be able to recover than they were before. The utility of the close connection test is, though, very much in question. It is also not entirely clear whether the UK courts have fully accepted the analysis of policy in *Bazley.* Subsequent cases will no doubt assist in clarifying matters. Most fundamental of all has been the questioning of the pivotal concept of enterprise risk by some of the judges in the High Court. The next chapter will explore the concept at length and appraise those concerns.

[41] [1962] Lloyd's Rep 1. [42] [2003] ICR 1335. [43] And see *Brown,* n. 31 above.

3

Enterprise risk

The concept of enterprise risk is absolutely central to the body of jurisprudence emanating from *Bazley*. The equitable basis of enterprise liability demands that the risks of the enterprise be identified before liability questions can be determined:

> The policy purposes underlying the imposition of vicarious liability on employers are served only where the wrong is so connected with the employment that it can be said that the employer has introduced the risk of the wrong (and is thereby fairly and usefully charged with its management and minimization). The question is whether there is a connection or nexus between the employment enterprise and that wrong that justifies imposition of vicarious liability on the employer for the wrong, in terms of fair allocation of the consequences of the risk and/or deterrence.[1]

The appeal to fairness proclaimed by enterprise liability is predicated on the capacity of the courts to render an enterprise responsible for the risks engendered by it. The requirement to demonstrate the existence of the requisite nexus could not be more fundamental as it goes directly to the moral claim of enterprise liability. It is one thing to say that the enterprise should be responsible for the risks it has created; it is quite another to say that it remains responsible when the existence of the risk is entirely coincidental or where the employment has merely furnished the opportunity for the commission of the tort. This is explained with great clarity in *Bazley*:

> *any* employment can be seen to provide the causation of an employee's tort. Therefore, "mere opportunity" to commit a tort, in the common "but-for" understanding of that phrase, does not suffice ... The enterprise and employment must not only provide the locale or the bare opportunity for the employee to commit his or her wrong, it must

[1] *Bazley v Curry* (1999) 174 DLR (4th) 45, 62. It may be noted that in *Lister v Hesley Hall* [2002] 1 AC 215 Lord Millett stated (at 244) that the employer 'is liable only if the risk is one which experience shows is inherent in the nature of the business'.

> *materially* enhance the risk, in the sense of significantly contributing to it, before it is fair to hold the employer vicariously liable.[2]

For example, 'if two employees, neighbours perhaps, who have a confrontational relationship outside and unconnected with their work, continue the confrontation at work so that one harasses the other, there would be no sufficient close connection between the nature of their employment and the harassment'.[3] Cane's hypothetical example is also helpful: 'an engineering company would not be vicariously liable where, without more, an employee sexually assaulted another employee on the employer's premises; carrying on an engineering business does not (as far as we know) materially increase the risk of assault on the employer's premises'.[4] When can we say that a risk has been created or increased by the conduct of an enterprise?

The Californian courts

Much of the pioneering jurisprudence emanated from the Californian courts.[5,6] The courts in that jurisdiction have taken the view for a considerable period of time that the modern justification for vicarious liability rests upon allocation of risk.[7] More particularly in *Hinman v Westinghouse Elec. Co.* the Supreme Court stated that:

> the losses caused by the torts of employees, which as a practical matter are sure to occur in the conduct of the employer's enterprise, are placed upon that enterprise itself, as a required cost of doing business. They are placed upon the employer because, having engaged in an enterprise which will, on the basis of past experience, involve harm to others through the torts of employees, and sought to profit by it, it is just that he, rather than the innocent injured plaintiff, should bear them; and

[2] Ibid., para. 40.

[3] *Majrowski v Guy's & St Thomas's NHS Trust* [2005] IRLR 340, 353. This example may have been inspired by *Bazley*, n. 1 above, where it was said at 61 that 'if a man assaults his wife's lover (who coincidentally happens to be a co-worker) in the employees' lounge at work, few would argue that the employer should be held responsible'.

[4] P. Cane, 'Vicarious Liability for Sexual Abuse' [2000] 116 LQR 21, 24.

[5] And on the US jurisprudence in general see R. R. Weber, 'Scope of Employment Redefined: Holding Employers Vicariously Liable for Sexual Assaults Committed by Their Employees' (1991–2) 76 Minn. L. Rev. 1513.

[6] For a review see M. E. Roszkowski and C. L. Roszkowski, 'Making Sense of Respondeat Superior: An Integrated Approach for both Negligent and Intentional Conduct' (2004–5) 14 S. Cal. Rev. L. & Women's Stud. 235.

[7] *Hinman v Westinghouse Elec. Co.* 2 Cal.3d 956, 959–960.

> because he is better able to absorb them, and to distribute them, through prices, rates or liability insurance, to the public, and so to shift them to society, to the community at large.[8]

The court went on to explain that the risks for which it was appropriate to hold the employer responsible were those which were inherent in or created by the enterprise. Determining whether such a state of affairs exists is hugely problematic and, in *Perez v Van Groningen*, the Supreme Court suggested that a risk may be attributed to the employer where 'in the context of the particular enterprise an employee's conduct is not so unusual or startling that it would seem unfair to include the loss resulting from it among other costs of the employer's business'.[9] This refinement was derived from the judgment of the California Court of Appeal in *Rodgers v Kemper Construction*.[10] There the court had made clear that foreseeability would assist in determining whether conduct was 'unusual or startling'. Certainly if a risk was highly foreseeable it might seem axiomatic that it was a characteristic of an enterprise of the type in question. However, the degree of foreseeability required is in fact very low and it suffices that the occurrence is 'not so unusual or startling' as to make it unfair to attribute responsibility to the employer. The bar is set lower than it would be in the case of negligence.[11] Once this is understood it becomes apparent that what is advanced is much more akin to a presumption; which will be very difficult for the employer to overturn. The test adopted in *Perez* provides very little assistance in identifying enterprise risks and, more particularly, distinguishing them from risks which are merely background risks. By background risks the author means those where the employment has done no more than provide an opportunity for harm to arise. The difficulty is illustrated by the case of *Rodgers*, where the harm that occurred was the result of fighting between employees. This was seen as a risk of employment:

> it was reasonably to be expected that Kemper's employees would come in contact with employees of other contractors on the same project. The risk of such association ... extends to expressions of normal human traits which, unhappily, include occasional emotional flare-ups and propensity for violence ... It was manifestly an outgrowth of the employment relationship and a risk which may fairly be considered as typical of, or incidental to, the employment. The incident which led to the plaintiff's

[8] The court was quoting from W. L. Prosser, *Handbook of The Law of Torts*, 3rd edn (St Paul: West Publishing Co., 1964), p. 471.

[9] 41 Cal.3d 962. [10] 50 Cal. App.3d 608.

[11] *Farmers Insurance Group v County of Santa Clara* 906 P.2d 440.

> injuries was such as might normally be expected to occur during the course of a major construction job.[12]

One might cavil with this. It is far from clear that the employment created or enhanced this risk. Behaviour which can be properly described as an 'expression of normal human traits' could presumably arise in any forum where people interact. It would not be 'startling' to discover that adults who engage in fighting in the workplace behave in this way when not at work.

The foregoing reveals real difficulty in translating the concept of enterprise risk into a practically applicable test. Against that backdrop, in the 1989 case of *John R. v Oakland Unified School*[13] the Supreme Court began to wrestle with many of the contemporary controversies that have plagued the law of vicarious liability. There a school pupil alleged that he had been sexually molested by his mathematics teacher while he was at the teacher's home participating in an officially sanctioned, extra-curricular programme. It was held that vicarious liability did not arise, but the case is significant in that it anticipated many of the arguments that were to prove influential in subsequent cases.[14] In particular the unsuccessful plaintiff argued that the conferring of authority was important because of the consequent possibility of abuse. Liability should arise it was said where there is an official, job-created, hierarchical relationship by which the employee is given authority over a certain, and possibly limited, class of persons. In addition there should be a sufficient nexus between the exercise of that authority and the commission of the tort that it was foreseeable that the authority so conferred might be abused to the detriment of the victim.[15] The court was not persuaded by this analysis and, in any event, the imposition of

[12] *Rodgers*, n. 10 above, para. 13. [13] 48 Cal.3d 438.

[14] In the subsequent case of *Kimberly M. v Los Angeles Unified School District* 215 Cal. App.3d 545, it was acknowledged that there was a case for taking a different approach where younger children were concerned: 'John R. was fourteen years old, Kimberly M. only five years old at the time of molestation. Anyone who has been a parent knows an adult has vastly greater dominion over a five-year-old than over a fourteen-year-old. Most five-year-olds told to undress will comply without hesitation and would submit to most forms of sexual abuse without objection, indeed without even knowing at the time they were being abused. On the other hand, a teacher's – or indeed a parent's – ability to order or otherwise compel a fourteen-year-old to engage in activities he or she does not want to engage in is problematical at best. Thus the authority the teacher exerted over the five-year-old victim in the instant case was at least equal to the authority the deputy sheriff exerted over the victim in *White* and far greater than the rather tenuous influence the teacher in *John R.* could expect to wield over the fourteen-year-old in that case.'

[15] *John R.*, n. 13 above, para. 5.

vicarious liability was seen as inappropriate in the light of the policy factors underpinning that doctrine. Over-deterrence might arise: the imposition of liability 'would be far too likely to deter districts from encouraging, or even authorizing, extracurricular and/or one-on-one contacts between teachers and students or to induce districts to impose such rigorous controls on activities of this nature that the educational process would be negatively affected'.[16] It was also the case that the natural tendency to further the compensatory aim of the law of tort was outweighed by the nature of the defendant; liability might lead to the diversion of scarce resources from a public body. Clearly, placing liability upon the shoulders of the education authority would allow losses to be distributed across the community who benefit from the work of teachers, and it was arguably equitable that that enterprise bear the risk because it could distribute most effectively across the most appropriate constituency.[17] However, this was rejected on the basis that the risk which had materialised could not be viewed as pertaining to the enterprise since the way in which the harm arose was too far removed from the scope of authority conferred.

However, only a few years later a very different stance was taken by the same court in *Mary M. v City of Los Angeles*.[18] It was held that a jury was entitled to find that a police officer was acting within the scope of his employment when he raped a woman whom he had detained whilst on duty. After she had asked not to be arrested for driving while intoxicated, he drove her to her home, threatened to take her to jail, and raped her. The imposition of vicarious liability was justifiable on policy grounds. The aim of deterrence was furthered; unlike the decision in *John R.* there were not perceived to be concerns in respect of over-deterrence. A powerful dissent drew attention to the fact that no evidence was advanced to demonstrate that the employer would be encouraged to put in place better preventive measures which did not undermine law enforcement. Indeed given that someone committing rape has shown that the prospect of criminal sanctions does not deter, it would be surprising if vicarious liability would have any effect whatsoever:

16 Ibid.

17 In *Whitson v Oakland Unified School District* 123 Cal. App.3d 133 the employer was held not responsible for a sexual assault committed on a school student by a janitor. The connection between the employee's duties and the tort committed was not sufficiently close: 'Sexual molestation is in no way related to mopping floors, cleaning rooms, or any of the other tasks that are required of a school custodian'.

18 814 P.2d 1341. For a similar approach see *Applewhite v City of Baton Rouge* 380 So.2d 119.

'Rape, of course, is no accident. It results from an individual's conscious decision to commit the outrageous act despite all moral and legal sanctions. Hence, it cannot be prevented in the way a city might train its officers in safe driving. Rape is a serious crime punishable by imprisonment ... and a compensable civil wrong as well.'[19] It was also questionable whether there was anything more that the employer could have done. There was no suggestion that negligence had arisen in the course of the selection process or in the training and supervision of the officer concerned. Clearly recovery would further the compensatory function but, as was pointed out by Baxter J, if ensuring compensation were the only goal, vicarious liability should apply against all employers in all cases. It was also said to be appropriate that the loss be distributed over the local community because of the benefits that the community gains from policing. Such a loss distribution mechanism could be viewed as equitable on the basis of the risk created by the enterprise of policing. Such an argument had, of course, been refuted in *John R.* The latter decision was distinguished on the basis of the role of authority. By joining the police an officer was viewed as gaining a great deal of authority over his fellow citizens; as a corollary the scope for abuse was considerable. By contrast, in *John R.* the authority possessed by the teacher did not present concerns of anything like the same magnitude. This is highly questionable; Weber has pointed out that the authority possessed by a teacher allows him to isolate and manipulate pupils.[20] In a similar vein, in his dissenting judgment in *Mary M.*, Baxter J said that: 'A schoolteacher alone at his home with an impressionable child has as much power and opportunity to commit a sexual assault against the child, especially one of tender years, as a police officer has to commit an assault against a citizen'.[21] Indeed some would argue that if anyone is to be liable it should be the teacher: 'students may feel the teacher's authority to a greater extent than citizens feel the police officer's authority during an encounter, because students interact with their teachers on a daily basis in a way that continually reinforces the authoritarian relationship. In marked contrast, police officers generally interact with citizens on a one-time basis.'[22]

[19] Baxter J (dissenting).

[20] R. R. Weber, 'Scope of Employment Redefined: Holding Employers Vicariously Liable for Sexual Assaults Committed by their Employers' (1991–2) 76 Minn. L. Rev. 1513, 1538 n. 56.

[21] Baxter J (dissenting).

[22] Recent case, 'California Supreme Court Holds Police Department Vicariously Liable for Rape Committed by On-Duty Police Officer' (1992) 105 Harv. L. Rev. 947, 952.

At the time of decision *Mary M.* could readily be depicted as a highly successful exercise in creative jurisprudence. Since then the reluctance of the Californian courts to apply the reasoning in other contexts has made the decision appear anomalous. How has this come about? The concept of 'job-created authority' has not proved appealing in subsequent cases. For example, the decision in *Lisa M.* (discussed below), where a hospital technician sexually abused a patient in the course of carrying out a medical examination, might seem a little surprising given the significance of job-created authority.[23] Even where, as with a teacher and a very young child, the scope for abuse of authority would seem significantly greater than in *Mary M.*, the courts have declined to apply it. For instance, in *Farmers Insurance Group v County of Santa Clara* the Supreme Court said that *Mary M.* did not 'suggest that an employer may be vicariously liable for an employee's misconduct whenever there is an abuse of a job-created, hierarchical relationship in which the employee is afforded a high degree of authority over the victim'.[24] The key attribute of *Mary M.* was said to be the 'unique authority' vested in police officers. The more restrictive approach displayed by the more recent Californian cases may, in part, reflect a belief that the burden on employers has become too severe. It may also suggest dissatisfaction with the concept of 'job-created authority' itself. Many employments confer a degree of authority on the employee and thereby facilitate the commission of an intentional tort. One might well be able to say that but for the existence of authority the tort would not have taken place. The difficulty is to decide at what point on the spectrum the extent of that authority creates a risk of a magnitude that attachment of blame on the employer is equitable.[25] This task is now seen as highly problematic

[23] 907 P.2d 358. [24] 906 P.2d 440.

[25] In their article the Roskowskis, n. 6 above, flag up a number of questions that might be thought to go to the issue of job-created authority, including: '... (4) Does the employment require the plaintiff to assume a vulnerable or compromising position that he or she would be unwilling to assume but for the plaintiff's good faith belief that such a position is required by the employment? For example, is the plaintiff required to be sedated or partially or completely undressed? ... (6) Does the employment provide access to instrumentalities capable of restraining or confining the plaintiff? For example, a police officer's or security guard's gun, handcuffs, mace, nightstick, or access to a locked space, such as a jail cell or back seat of a squad car. (7) Does the employee possess indicia of authority, however created, over the plaintiff, that is inherent in the employment? Examples of such employees might include police officers, security guards, elementary and grade school teachers, and clergy members. (8) Can the employee use the employment relationship to achieve psychological domination over the plaintiff, or induce dependence by the plaintiff on the employee, which the employee exploits in

and the Californian courts have shown great reluctance to develop this dimension of vicarious liability. They have not sought, for example, to develop a set of more detailed criteria that would facilitate the application of the concept of job-created authority in specific contexts. Instead the position has been reached such that arguments based on job-created authority are unlikely to be successful. *Lisa M.*[26] provides a good example. There a pregnant young woman was injured in a fall and sought treatment at a hospital. An ultrasound technician (Tripoli) performed obstetrical ultrasonic imaging examinations. In the course of doing so he sexually molested the plaintiff. The majority took the view that this behaviour did not reflect the risks of employment. The case to the contrary had considerable force: 'This intimate contact, inherent in the job, put plaintiff in a vulnerable position and permitted Tripoli to dupe plaintiff into believing that his sexual assault was actually part of a standard medical procedure, thereby giving Tripoli a basis to hope that his misconduct would remain undetected. Moreover, it is not unreasonable to infer that the intimate contact inherent in the job contributed to Tripoli's sexual arousal and incited him to engage in the misconduct.'[27]

The Canadian Supreme Court takes over

Despite the fact that the expansive approach to liability discussed in the preceding section appears to have ground to a halt, the Californian jurisprudence has proved to be highly influential in Canada. The concepts of enterprise risk and job-created authority were seized upon in the seminal case of *Bazley* where the Canadian Supreme Court built on the pioneering work of their Californian counterparts.[28] In determining whether the risks created by the enterprise meant that there was a close connection between the tort committed and the nature of the employment it was said to be helpful to have regard to a number of criteria. Where intentional torts are concerned the criteria might include the following:

injuring the plaintiff? Examples of employees who have abused such power include psychological counselors, and staff members of residential mental health care facilities.'

26 *Lisa M. v Henry Mayo Newhall Memorial Hospital* 907 P.2d 358.

27 Ibid., Kennard J dissenting.

28 See n. 1 above.

(1) the opportunity that the enterprise afforded for the employee to abuse his or her power;
(2) the extent to which the wrongful act may have furthered the employer's aims (and hence be more likely to have been committed by the employee);
(3) the extent to which the wrongful act was related to friction, confrontation or intimacy inherent in the employer's enterprise;
(4) the extent of power conferred on the employee in relation to the victim; and
(5) the vulnerability of potential victims to wrongful exercise of the employee's power.[29]

In sexual abuse cases (and indeed in a good number of instances where an intentional tort has been committed) factor (2) might be thought to be less than helpful. The very reason why such cases are legally controversial is that the behaviour of the employee is the very antithesis of what he was hired to do and, as a corollary, in conflict with the aims of the employer. Factor (1) might also be thought to be of questionable significance given that it does not suffice that employment has conferred the opportunity for wrongdoing (though it may assume significance when taken with factor (4)). It is much more apparent why the application of the last three factors is likely to be determinative in sexual abuse cases. Mindful of this the court in *Bazley* sought to elaborate on why those criteria were significant. Relationships involving power and dependency were seen as involving particular risk: 'Because of the peculiar exercises of power and trust that pervade cases such as child abuse, special attention should be paid to the existence of a power or dependency relationship, which on its own often creates a considerable risk of wrongdoing.'[30] In general it was felt that the more an enterprise requires the exercise of power or authority for its successful operation, the more likely it is that an abuse of that power relationship can be fairly ascribed to the employer. An employment situation which might well give rise to considerable risk was one where the employee had a

[29] *Bazley* was distinguished in the later case of *E.B. v the Order of Oblates of Mary Immaculate* [2005] 3 SCR 45, which also involved a residential situation. The tortfeasor was employed as a baker, part-time motorboat operator and odd-job man. The Supreme Court was clear that holding such posts did not confer the authority or intimacy that would give rise to a risk of harm. The duties and responsibilities involved meant that there was an absence of a strong connection between '*what the employer was asking the employee to do* (the risk created by the employer's enterprise) and the wrongful act'. The employment merely furnished the opportunity and that is not enough.

[30] *Bazley*, n. 1 above, para. 41.

parenting or mentoring role. Again employment which, of necessity, involved physical intimacy carried added risk of sexual touching. Whilst *Bazley* owes a great deal to the Californian jurisprudence it attempts to elaborate upon the features of employment which increase the likelihood of an assault arising. It should be stressed that the criteria were framed with this very specific form of behaviour in mind. Their utility in a wider range of situations requires, at the very least, further exploration.

In *Bazley* itself the appellant, a non-profit organisation, operated two residential care facilities for the treatment of emotionally troubled children. As substitute parent, it practised 'total intervention' in all aspects of the lives of the children it cared for. The appellant's employees were to do everything a parent would do, from general supervision to intimate duties like bathing. They hired Curry, a paedophile, to work in one of its homes and he went on to abuse a child. In holding the appellant vicariously liable it was said that 'the opportunity for intimate private control and the parental relationship and power required by the terms of employment created the special environment that nurtured and brought to fruition Curry's sexual abuse'.[31] An enterprise which necessitated employments of that nature created real risks of harm. Indeed it was claimed that it is difficult to imagine a job with a greater risk of sexual abuse of a child occurring.

The facts in the sister case of *Jacobi v Griffiths*[32] were somewhat different and illustrate that the application of the criteria set out in *Bazley* is highly sensitive to the nuances of the employment in question. In *Jacobi* the respondent children's club, a non-profit organisation, employed the respondent G. as programme director. The employer required G. to supervise volunteer staff and organise recreational activities and the occasional outing. G. was also encouraged to form friendships and a positive rapport with the children at the club. Both of the appellants testified that all of their friends and activities centred on the club. There was essentially a single incident of sexual assault by G. involving the male appellant, and one incident of sexual intercourse involving the female appellant, at G's home outside working hours following several lesser incidents, including one incident of sexual touching in the club van. The Supreme Court was divided as to the outcome. For the majority, who declined to find that vicarious liability arose, the more limited scope of the employer's activities in *Jacobi* was hugely significant. It was noted that the employer provided a recreational, not

[31] Ibid., para. 58. [32] (1999) 174 DLR (4th) 71.

a residential, facility for children and did not purport to offer parenting of any description. The key responsibilities of the tortfeasor were the organisation of recreational activities and the occasional outing. It was acknowledged that any job which places adults in contact with children creates some possibility of abuse. Nevertheless the situation was viewed as being qualitatively different to that in *Bazley*.[33]

In contrast to the ground-breaking Californian jurisprudence, the Supreme Court in *Bazley* and *Jacobi* were at pains to elaborate criteria which would assist in determining where the conferment of authority by employment created or enhanced risks to third parties. After all, many employments bestow a measure of authority and a consequent scope for abuse but, in most cases, the risk will be of a magnitude that can be disregarded. The criteria adumbrated have been faithfully applied in subsequent cases, and it is submitted that the fact of their elaboration helps to explain the influence of the concept of job-created authority. In contrast to the position in California, where the concept has failed to flourish, it has become entrenched in Canadian case law. All that said there is a significant degree of commonality in the outcome of the application of the concept to specific employments. Both jurisdictions have adopted the same position in respect of policemen who commit sexual assaults whilst on duty. In *Evans v Sproule*[34] the facts were remarkably similar to *Mary M.*, as was the outcome and the reasoning. The court drew attention to the power and authority that a police officer has over a motorist who has violated road-traffic legislation. In addition, a person in that position was seen as being particularly vulnerable to intimidation. As in *Mary M.* a decision in favour of the claimant was seen as promoting deterrence:

> the imposition of liability on the employer ... may well serve to prevent a recurrence of the wrongful conduct. It may, for example, provide an

[33] In the minority in *Jacobi*, n. 32 above, McLachlin J observed at para. 14 that: 'An environment into which children are entrusted not just for adult supervision, but for adult *mentoring*, is one highly charged with potential for an abuse of that trust. While Griffiths was hardly a police officer or foster parent, power must be understood in context. Here, as a role model at a club that dealt with vulnerable children, there is little to negate the trial judge's conclusion that Griffiths' position over the children was one of power. By clothing the employee with that power, the employer introduced a risk, small but real, of its abuse. When victims are vulnerable, a heightened risk exists that a predatory employee will exploit the chance to abuse positions of trust or power. It goes without saying that children are vulnerable as potential victims of intentional torts such as sexual abuse. These children, troubled adolescents, were more vulnerable than most.'

[34] 2008 Can. L. II 58428.

> incentive for vigilance and the imposition of preventative measures, such as ensuring that no police officer be on night patrol without a partner and that vigilant reporting measures are in place for suspicious circumstances or infractions involving one of them.[35]

Again, as in California, the courts have declined to hold that approaching vicarious liability on the basis of enterprise risk leads to a finding that employers are inevitably liable where teachers commit sexual assaults.[36] In *S.G.H. v Gorsline*[37] counsel for the claimant drew attention to the influence and authority teachers have over young children, that employers encourage teachers to act as mentors and role models, and that children are taught to obey teachers. In denying that vicarious liability arose it was noted that the teacher's job gave him an opportunity to abuse his authority but his duties did not require anything approaching intimate contact. It was also held that the fact that teachers were encouraged to act as mentors and role models did not substantially increase the risk of harm. This stance gains support from *Jacobi* where Binnie J had said: 'I do not accept that an enterprise that seeks to provide a positive role model thereby encourages intimacy. Nor do I believe that "mentoring", as such, puts one on the slippery slope to sexual abuse.'[38]

Attention has been drawn to the fact that the criteria in *Bazley* were elaborated with particular risks in mind. Further consideration is called for should the close connection test be invoked in other contexts. It is far from clear that the criteria help to make sense of the close connection test outwith the context for which they were derived.

The *Bazley* criteria in other contexts

Bazley drew up criteria to make sense of liability underpinned by enterprise risk in the context of sexual assault. As has been seen, close attention is paid to the capacity for abuse of authority, but how might that factor fare in other contexts? In *Majrowski* the court took the view

[35] Ibid., para. 98.

[36] Similarly, in Australia it was said in the High Court in *New South Wales v Lepore* [2003] 212 CLR 511, that: 'It cannot be said that the risk of sexual abuse ought to be regarded as an incident of the conduct of most schools, or that the ordinary responsibilities of teachers are such that sexual assaults on pupils would normally be regarded as conduct (albeit serious misconduct) within the scope of employment. However, there are some circumstances in which teachers, or persons associated with school children, have responsibilities of a kind that involve an undertaking of personal protection, and a relationship of such power and intimacy, that sexual abuse may properly be regarded as sufficiently connected with their duties to give rise to vicarious liability in their employers.'

[37] [2005] 2 WWR 716.

[38] *Jacobi*, n. 32 above, para. 82.

that not every instance of harassment which occurs at work can be said to be work-related. From the hypothetical example given in the case we learn that quarrelling neighbours who extend their feud into the workplace do not render the employer liable thereby. This is presumably on the basis that the employer has done nothing to enhance or increase the risk. In line with both *Lister* and *Bazley*, the Court of Appeal in *Majrowski* regards the possession of authority by the employee as having the potential to be significant in harassment cases. As has been noted, it was said in *Bazley* that it may be relevant to examine both the extent of power conferred on the employee in relation to the victim and the vulnerability of potential victims to wrongful exercise of the employee's power.[39] Echoing this it was said in *Majrowski* that the:

> reasonably incidental risk criterion may be of particular value when considering whether an employer should shoulder responsibility for, say, harassment by an employee whom he has put in a position of authority over other employees who may, for one reason or another, be vulnerable to such conduct, or in a position to exploit third parties such as needy customers, clients or claimants who may be similarly vulnerable.[40]

It appears that certain forms of abusive behaviour are seen as flowing from the risks which the holding of positions of authority gives rise to. However, the mere fact of possession of authority is not seen as a danger in itself. The risk of abuse arises, in undefined sets of circumstances, where employees so empowered are placed in a position where they acquire the opportunity to exploit those who may be vulnerable. However, under precisely what sorts of circumstances will the enterprise be regarded as creating or increasing a risk of exploitation? In short, when does the possession of authority become problematic? This is a matter of some difficulty. In *Majrowski* the Court of Appeal relied upon the concept of job-created authority in the harassment context; whether this was appropriate is a much more difficult question.[41] The court assumed that the concept of job-created authority was not context specific and readily transferable; whether this is in fact the case remains to be demonstrated.

[39] Again in *Lister*, n. 1 above, it was acknowledged that the possession of authority over vulnerable people may give rise to particular risks.

[40] *Majrowski*, n. 3 above, 350.

[41] In *Faragher v City of Boca Raton* the US Supreme Court (524 US 775) acknowledged that the job-created authority of a supervisor could give rise to a risk of harassment, but they declined to hold that an employer would be inevitably liable should harassment occur. The possibility of a defence was allowed for.

The author would submit that if enterprise risk is to flourish, greater regard must be had to empirical considerations. This will be explored by looking at the position of children's homes. It can be readily accepted that such institutions are likely to contain a number of vulnerable people – by reason of their age if nothing else. Concern that employees in positions of authority may seek to exploit such individuals can also be recognised. However, in the absence of empirical evidence, how can we gauge if these concerns are well-founded? Again, without such evidence, how can we tell what degree of risk exists? Moreover, how can we judge whether the enterprise has increased the risk of children being abused? Children who are not institutionalised may be abused and it is not readily apparent that this is more likely to occur if a child is taken into care. In *New South Wales v Lepore*[42] the state argued that requiring children to attend school did not increase the risk that they would be sexually abused but, in fact, probably reduced it: 'Much would depend on what they might otherwise be doing.' Further pertinent questions readily come to mind, such as what degree of risk is relevant. Does there need, for example, to be a serious risk? In *Lister* it was said by Lord Millett that: 'If the employer's objectives cannot be achieved without a serious risk of the employee committing the kind of wrong which he has in fact committed, the employer ought to be liable.'[43] If such questions cannot be addressed satisfactorily then the equitable basis of enterprise liability is very much in issue. The appeal to equity is only convincing where the scope of the enterprise's liability is actually determined by reference to the risks it has created. The approach of the courts in the jurisdictions under discussion has, at least up until now, been to determine matters without regard to empirical evidence. The identification of enterprise risks has been regarded as very much a value judgement; it is a matter of what 'experience shows'. There is nothing to suggest that any of this is empirically grounded; certainly no evidence of that sort appears to have informed the judgments of the House of Lords in *Lister.* In that decision Lord Millet noted that: 'Experience shows that in the case of boarding schools, prisons, nursing homes, old people's homes, geriatric wards, and other residential homes for the young or vulnerable, there is an inherent risk that indecent assaults on the residents will be committed by those placed in authority over them, particularly if they are in close proximity to them and occupying a position of trust.'[44] The mere fact of

[42] [2003] 212 CLR 511. See n. 36. [43] *Lister,* n. 1 above, 244.
[44] *Lister,* n. 1 above, 250.

employment in such an institution is not enough, per se, to render the employer vicariously liable. Thus the warden's behaviour gave rise to vicarious liability in *Lister* but it appears that the employer might not have been responsible for sexual abuse committed by the groundsman: 'he was employed to look after the grounds, not to have anything to do with the boys'.[45] How do we judge if an enterprise has brought about a particular risk? If one were to say that the risk should be characteristic of the enterprise before liability can be imposed one might expect empirical evidence. Schwartz has written that 'a harm is "characteristic" of business activity in a "strong" sense if in some significant number of cases the activity is the dominant cause of the harm. Hence property damage can be deemed "characteristic" of the activity of blasting.'[46] If this characterisation is accurate one would expect to see a statistical correlation between the operation of a business involved in blasting and damage to neighbouring property which differed from that which arose where businesses in general were involved. There is however no indication whatsoever that courts proceed on the basis of such evidence; instead a variety of assumptions are made based upon judicial knowledge. By way of contrast, Piepmeier has suggested that, where sexual harassment is concerned, industries which are traditionally dominated by one gender are more likely to be affected.[47] She goes on to conclude that 'under such circumstances, an employer could foresee that sexual harassment would occur where hostility toward one sex or the other is most likely already present'.[48] Up until now the courts have not approached matters in this way.

Generic risks

As discussed in the case law, enterprise risk focuses on those risks particular to the defendant enterprise, but what of generic risks such as harassment? The Court of Appeal in *Majrowski* held that harassment in the workplace was a real risk for employees as a class: 'It is the very place where harassment is often encountered and from which its victim is often powerless to escape. It is thus often likely to be a risk incidental

45 *Lister*, n. 1 above, 247.

46 G. T. Schwartz, 'The Hidden and Fundamental Issue of Employer Vicarious Liability' (1995–6) 69 S. Cal. Rev. 1739.

47 K. Piepmeier, 'Employer Liability for Workplace Sexual Harassment Perpetrated by Supervisors' (2000) 36 Willamette L. Rev. 141.

48 Ibid. Piepmeier also flags up the issue of whether the fact that litigation has tended to arise in a number of particular industries is significant.

to employment.'[49] The nature of the risk, therefore, dictated that the employer should, depending upon the circumstances, be obliged to meet the cost of compensation. In addition, the imposition of strict liability may well have been seen as a means of promoting deterrence and encouraging proper risk management: 'Nowadays, employers, whether public or commercial undertakings, are expected to be alert to all sorts of discrimination and exploitation by their employees, which may include harassment, in or from the workplace, whether of fellow employees or third parties, and to establish good working practices and procedures to warn and/or guard against such abuse.'[50] Of course, it would be a question of fact, in any particular case, whether there was a sufficiently close connection between the employee's behaviour and the employment.[51] In *Majrowski* the court drew attention to the dangers posed by an absence of appropriate procedures. In the author's view, such an analysis is predicated on the basis that employees, as a class, are likely to indulge in harassment unless preventive measures are taken. Such an assumption would suggest that it is employment, per se, that is perceived as posing the risk rather than a specific employing enterprise. After all, it could be said that 'harassment is a reasonably foreseeable risk in a workplace, because it is a common and recognised problem in businesses'.[52] However, can a risk be said to be characteristic of a particular enterprise when, in fact, it is generic to employment as a whole? In principle, the answer to this question must be yes. There may be some risks which are inevitably brought about by the very existence of any employing enterprise. However, an apparent readiness to suggest that harassment is an occupational risk may provide a further insight into judicial decision-making. It may indicate that, rather than embark on the difficult task of identifying when an enterprise has created a risk, the courts will be tempted to raise the question of whether the harm would have come about but for the existence of the enterprise. It should be noted that the court in *Bazley* observed that 'reduced to formalistic premises, any employment can be seen to provide the causation of an employee's tort. Therefore, "mere opportunity" to commit a tort, in the common "but-for" understanding

49 *Majrowski*, n. 3 above, 350.

50 Ibid.

51 The decision of the Court of Appeal was subsequently upheld by the House of Lords ([2007] 1 AC 224) by a rather different route. An argument based on the wording of the statute which had not been raised in the courts below, and indeed was identified from the bench by Lord Hope, was to prove decisive. See D. Brodie, 'How Prescient is Parliament?' (2007) 11 Edin. LR 81.

52 See T. Kaesebier, 'Employer Liability in Supervisor Sexual Harassment' 31 Ariz. St. L.J. 203.

of that phrase, does not suffice'.[53] The fear being expressed is that it would be wrong to turn the employer into an 'involuntary insurer'. It is conceivable that the claim to fairness that the equitable basis of enterprise liability seeks to espouse may be undermined by the practical difficulties in its application. The discussion in this chapter has undoubtedly revealed considerable difficulties in translating the concept of enterprise risk into a practically applicable test.

By way of contrast, in *Farmers Insurance Group v County of Santa Clara*,[54] the Supreme Court of California declined to hold that harassment of employees by those in positions of authority was a general occupational hazard. In *Farmers* the claimant pointed to a number of studies and surveys indicating that sexual harassment was pervasive. Evidence of this nature might be thought to have the potential to demonstrate that harassment was an occupational hazard. Indeed the Supreme Court accepted the force of this. The claim still failed because of a lack of evidence that harassment was a risk of the workplace in question: 'evidence of the general prevalence of sexual harassment in workplaces and in newly integrated work environments has little, if any, probative value in determining whether lewd propositioning and offensive touchings of co-workers are typical of or broadly incidental to the particular enterprise here'. Interestingly Mosk J, in the minority, did not rely upon the same body of empirical evidence rejected by the majority. Instead he focused on more specific studies which showed that harassment by co-workers is pervasive in traditionally male workplaces that have recently been integrated by sex, and especially so in employments such as law enforcement: 'Although various explanations for co-worker harassment of members of a female minority have been proposed, there is much support for the view that men employed in a traditionally male setting may perceive women entering their workplace as threatening either their job security or their self-esteem, and may use sexual harassment as a means to resist the intrusion.'[55]

Conclusions

Risk allocation can only take place on an equitable basis where the extent of the connection between the risk and the enterprise is known. I would suggest that this is likely to prove highly problematic as identification of

[53] *Bazley*, n. 1 above, 63. [54] 906 P.2d 440.

[55] B. Lindemann and D. Kadue, *Sexual Harassment in Employment Law* (Washington, DC: Bureau of National Affairs, 1992), p. 235.

the risks, which an enterprise can be said to have created, will present significant difficulties. In *Lister*, as has been seen, judicial experience was drawn upon as a means of identification. However, deciding such matters, in the absence of empirical evidence, runs the risk that all manner of unwarranted assumptions will come into play. It may be noted, in passing, the stark contrast with industrial disease cases. In *McGhee v NCB*,[56] for instance, had it not been for the expert evidence, the court would not have been able to hold that the employer had materially increased the risk of harm arising. It is difficult to accept that continuing to proceed on the basis of enterprise risk will remain acceptable if empirical evidence is not forthcoming.

Bazley indicates that adjudication in vicarious liability cases may be assisted by recourse to the underlying policy factors such as deterrence:

> the test for vicarious liability for an employee's sexual abuse of a client should focus on whether the employer's enterprise and empowerment of the employee materially increased the risk of the sexual assault and hence the harm. The test must not be applied mechanically, but with a sensitive view to the policy considerations that justify the imposition of vicarious liability – fair and efficient compensation for wrong and deterrence.[57]

This seems, at first glance, very sensible. A word of caution is called for. In *John R.*, for example, it was said that the imposition of liability would have led to over-deterrence.[58] Such a conclusion could only have been validated empirically. It was not. Once again adjudication in the absence of such evidence is problematic. Having recourse to the compensatory aim of the law of tort is no more likely to ease the burden on the adjudicator since promoting that aim will always point toward liability. If, on the other hand, loss distribution is the principal issue, the most effective mechanism for achieving this may not be readily apparent.

[56] [1972] 3 All ER 1008.   [57] *Bazley*, n. 1 above.   [58] See n. 13 above.

4

The risk and the individual

As has already been made clear, *Bazley* seeks to achieve equity as between the enterprise and the victim of the tort. In the eyes of the Supreme Court ensuring that this is achieved in a way that is not unfair to the enterprise requires that the trial court focus on the risks flowing from specific employments rather than those which could simply be said to be risks of the enterprise. Again, where intentional torts are concerned, *Lister* requires a close connection between the tort and the nature of the employment. (See Chapters 2 and 3.) Of course, consideration of the risks inherent in an enterprise remains essential if one wishes to be fully appraised of the risks that a particular job, within that enterprise, gives rise to. It is difficult to determine the true nature of a post if it is detached from the context within which it operates. The emphasis on the risks created by a particular post is not without controversy. This is illustrated by the conflict of views between the trial courts and the appellate courts in *E.B. v the Order of Oblates of Mary Immaculate.*[1] There the claimant had attended a residential school run by the Order. He was sexually assaulted by a lay employee (S) who worked as a baker, boat driver and odd-job man and resided in a building located on the school grounds. The trial judge found that vicarious liability arose on the basis that the operational characteristics of Christie Residential School ('Christie') created and materially enhanced the risk of the assaults.[2] These characteristics included the separation of the children from their families, the fact that employees lived in close proximity to the children and the fact that the children were under a regime where they were to respect and obey all staff. An expert witness testified that these characteristics increased the chance of sexual assault. Counsel for the plaintiff had argued that 'in summary, S's living quarters was located in the midst of an overcrowded and understaffed playground populated by especially vulnerable children; and that the closed boundaries of Christie,

[1] [2005] 3 SCR 45. [2] *B.(E.) v Order of Oblates* (2001) BCSC 1783.

its custodial character, its isolation, and the high ratio of students to adult staff members materially enhanced the risk of abuse'.[3] The Court of Appeal set aside the trial judge's decision, holding that he had erred in over-emphasising job-created opportunity and in failing to have sufficient regard to the specific employment duties and responsibilities assigned to S and the connection, if any, between those duties and responsibilities and the wrongs S committed against the appellant. The Supreme Court agreed and drew attention to the absence of a strong connection between the job the abuser was employed to do and the circumstances in which the abuse took place. There was a clear concern that adherence to the approach of the trial judge would significantly increase the burden on employers. An employer in the position of the defendant would be liable for all tortious acts of all of its employees which could be said to be related to risks generated by the enterprise, no matter how remote the wrongdoing was from any position of authority over, or intimacy with, those abused. Instead an examination of the abuser's actual powers, duties and responsibilities was required to determine whether or not there was 'a strong connection between what the employer was asking the employee to do (the risk created by the employer's enterprise) and the wrongful act'.[4] In dissenting Abella J stressed the wider context: the 'events occurred in the context of a residential school, where children were forcibly removed and segregated from their families to facilitate the obliteration of their Aboriginal identity. Few environments could be more conducive to enhancing the vulnerability of children.'[5] With reference to the *Bazley* criteria Abella J observed that:

> the power structure inherent in the employer's enterprise greatly increased the level of friction and confrontation, helping to create the conditions that led to the sexual assault of E.B. He found that the discipline at Christie was strict and harsh, and that order was maintained largely through fear and the threat of punishment. The students' daily life included physical and emotional violence, deprivation, belittling, and intimidation.[6]

The courts insist that the tort must be sufficiently connected to the tortfeasor's assigned tasks, so that it can be regarded as a materialisation of the risks created by the enterprise, before the employer will be held vicariously liable. Thus in *Lister*,[7] whilst the employer was responsible for the warden, the position would have been different had the behaviour of a groundsman been in issue. Simply by establishing an enterprise of

[3] Ibid., para. 118. [4] *E.B.*, n. 1 above, 78. [5] Ibid., 84. [6] Ibid., 87.
[7] *Lister v Hesley Hall* [2002] 1 AC 215.

a particular type an employer does not create risks for which it will be responsible on the basis of vicarious liability. The opening of a children's home, for example, would not be seen as increasing the chances of children being abused. Instead risks may be created depending on the nature of the roles that are given to staff. For the purposes of the *Bazley* analysis the material risks are not those created by the enterprise as such but those which arise from specific roles. In identifying the latter the nature of the enterprise is relevant. The validity of this approach is open to question; returning to concerns raised in the previous chapter, it may well be asked whether it is empirically sound. The expert evidence put forward at trial in *E.B.* would suggest otherwise. A further means of analysis is to examine several reports which have been published of late in different jurisdictions, addressing a number of issues in respect of child abuse. For example, in Queensland the Forde Inquiry[8] examined whether children who had been placed in institutional care had been subjected to any unsafe, improper or unlawful care or treatment. Such reports contain invaluable information on the conditions and circumstances giving rise to the risk of abuse. In the process they offer a number of insights on the wisdom of the judicial approach.

The Law Commission of Canada, in a report entitled 'Restoring Dignity: Responding to Child Abuse in Canadian Institutions',[9] sought to identify why abuse of children had occurred in residential homes. It pointed to the fact that children in those institutions were much more vulnerable than children in general. They were, for example, often from economically disadvantaged sections in society. The children may well have been further disadvantaged by physical or mental disabilities. Their acute vulnerability made it much easier for abuse to occur. The characteristics referred to 'made it easier for officials to discount, disbelieve or deny the children's complaints of the treatment they received or witnessed. They also made it easier for society in general to regard these complaints as unimportant.'[10] The power imbalance that existed between children who were resident in homes and the staff that were in charge was particularly marked because of the nature of the organisations (for example churches) that ran the homes: 'These organisations wield significant social power and are potent symbols of authority today. They were

[8] 'Commission of Inquiry into Abuse of Children in Queensland Institutions' (1999). (Hereafter 'Queensland Inquiry'.)

[9] Law Commission of Canada: 'Restoring Dignity: Responding to Child Abuse in Canadian Institutions' (2000). (Hereafter 'Law Commission of Canada'.)

[10] Ibid., 7.

even more potent symbols of authority in previous decades, when much of the child abuse under consideration took place.'[11] The Law Commission of Canada took the view that the extent of the deference accorded to governments and churches made it difficult for anyone to challenge the way homes were run at the time. They concluded that the 'dynamic thus created within residential institutions – a group of vulnerable children placed under the control of caregivers whose authority was virtually unquestioned – was a recipe for the abuse of power by predators'.[12] A third factor was an inadequate supervision and inspection regime. This was thought to be particularly significant where children were placed in homes as a result of parental abuse or neglect as it would be less likely that members of the family would maintain an interest in the child's welfare.

Beyond specific failings the culture pertaining in a residential home could give rise to risks. The Law Commission of Canada referred to the concept of a 'total institution', which was defined in the following terms:

> Total institutions are not simply places to live; each is a world unto itself. In this world, those who are in charge hold all formal power. Rules govern almost every aspect of daily life and residents have little say about how these rules are administered. More dangerously, life in such institutions may at times be governed more by arbitrary and unpredictable orders than by established rules. In such a situation, the possibility of effective protests or appeals is inhibited. During the period in which the abuse under consideration took place, there was little effective external oversight and usually no independent procedure for handling complaints from children. Contact with the outside world – family, friends, community – was tightly controlled and infrequent.[13]

Those institutions were found to 'impose the following conditions on their residents: disconnection; degradation; and powerlessness. While all children in all institutions did not necessarily experience them, each condition played a part in facilitating and perpetuating the infliction of abuse.'[14] 'Disconnection' might involve a child experiencing a sense of both physical and psychological isolation. A residential home might be located far away from the child's family; indeed more generally it might be in a remote part of the country. 'Degradation' could take a wide variety of forms and need not be physical. The term encompassed the 'harsh reality of months or years of being emotionally beaten down and having one's self-confidence and pride continually undermined, with little or no opportunity for nurturing, support or encouragement.'[15] A child's lack of power ('powerlessness'):

[11] Ibid. [12] Ibid. [13] Ibid., 22. [14] Ibid. [15] Ibid., 25.

> is not reflected in the equitable enforcement of fair and explicit rules. It is reflected in the infliction of suffering on arbitrary grounds, the meting out of punishment disproportionate to the misconduct, or the imposition of rigid and overly harsh rules that make compliance a hardship and punishment a virtual certainty ... Once that sense of the unchecked power of those in authority is firmly established, an atmosphere of insecurity and fear pervades an institution. Children do not have to experience arbitrary or excessive punishment to want to avoid it – they just have to witness enough of it to understand that they could be next.[16]

There was a recognition that abuse can and does occur in a wide variety of settings, e.g. foster homes, group homes, day schools, summer camps, and on educational field trips and sports and exchange programmes. This prompts a questioning of the distinction made by the Supreme Court between the circumstances pertaining in *Bazley* and those in *Jacobi*.[17] Indeed the report throws up a number of questions given the approach of the Supreme Court. It strongly suggests that, in terms of assessing the degree of risk to children, a key determinant is the nature of the institution and the ethos that pervades it. A home which could be categorised as a 'total institution' would present a hazardous environment for a child. The report indicates that the focus should be much more on the type of institution involved, given that institutions with particular characteristics present dangers to children. The role performed by an individual within such a setting is much less pivotal. As Feldthusen points out: 'children do not draw distinctions between adults who work in residential settings based on their job descriptions. The church decided how the duties were to be assigned, not the children. Adults who work in settings where adults control children are perceived by the children, usually quite accurately, to have power over the children.'[18] The archetypal risk for *Bazley* is the employee who performs a parenting-type role in a residential home. Empirical evidence tells us that this is to take an overly narrow view; it leads to discounting both a number of types of employment and various settings (e.g. non-residential ones) which present a material risk. The arguments of counsel[19] and the stance of the trial judge in *E.B.* seem much more attractive in the light of all this.

[16] Ibid., 2.

[17] See 'The Canadian Supreme Court takes over' in Chapter 3.

[18] B. Feldthusen, 'Civil Liability for Sexual Assault in Aboriginal Residential Schools: The Baker Did It' (2007) 22 Can. J.L. & Soc'y 61.

[19] In *B.(E.)*, n. 2 above, 122, counsel placed emphasis on the following operational characteristics of the enterprise and argued that they pointed to vicarious liability arising: '(a) The children were separated from their families and held in custody all

The dangers of the approach adopted by the Supreme Court are confirmed by Australian experience. In Australia a similar inquiry was undertaken by Forde which sought to understand why child abuse took place in institutions.[20] It was hoped that apart from anything else this would allow effective preventive strategies to be developed. The causes of abuse were seen as complex and therefore it would be both misleading and dangerous to focus unduly on individual abusers: 'although there is a commonly held belief that abusers are in some way abnormal or evil, and that child abuse could be prevented by ensuring such people are not employed in institutions, this does not reflect the reality'.[21] Institutional culture was a factor of real importance: 'the dynamics and culture of an institution play an important role in whether or not child abuse is likely to occur. Institutional norms and values lead to certain approaches to child management, work and organisation, power and control, and the openness of the institution.'[22] The norms and values which inform the ethos of an institution influence how children will be treated and impact on the likelihood of abuse taking place. It was found that where carers perceive young people to be 'bad', children become dehumanised or devalued and the usual constraints on abuse and violence are loosened. In those circumstances children are more likely to become victims of abuse. In line with the Law Commission of Canada, Forde recognised that the vulnerability of children in residential settings was a significant factor: 'children will protect their access to adults at all costs, adapting tenaciously to any mysterious conditions an adult places upon them. When in institutional care, it is reasonable to assume that these especially vulnerable children see the relationship with carers as particularly precarious.'[23] The added vulnerability of children in care facilitates

day and every day. Brothers were separated from sisters; older siblings were separated from younger siblings. Christie was geographically isolated, enhancing its closed institutional character and exacerbating the severance of relations with parents and extended family. (b) Christie was chronically overcrowded and understaffed. The number of children held in custody exceeded the capacity of the supervisory staff to effectively supervise. (c) Adult employees of Christie, including Saxey, lived within the closed boundaries of the school, facilitating unrestricted and unsupervised access to the children for prolonged periods of time. There was no effective mechanism to prevent sexually predatory behaviour. Employees of Christie, including Saxey, were permitted to form casual acquaintanceships with the children. (d) The children were conditioned under a regime of education, religion and discipline to demonstrate respect and obedience toward *all* of the adult employees of Christie, including Saxey. The institutional character of Christie was such that Saxey was explicitly or implicitly clothed with power and authority over the resident children.'

20 Queensland Inquiry, n. 8 above. 21 Ibid., 12. 22 Ibid., 16. 23 Ibid., 15.

exploitation by abusers. As with the Law Commission of Canada, Forde asserted that should the running of an institution exhibit particular charactistics, abuse will be more likely to take place. One example given was role dispossession. This may occur should children be stripped of their identity when they enter a home:

> This can happen through compulsory showers, haircuts, the wearing of institutional clothing, or confiscation of personal possessions. Loss of identity can prevent the new inmate from presenting his or her normal self. During the orientation period, the inmate often must endure 'obedience tests' or perhaps will-breaking contests. These are designed to demonstrate that an inmate who shows defiance will receive immediate, visible punishment.[24]

Again Forde drew attention to the dangers in being too fixated with particular settings in which abuse may take place. It was pointed out that children who have been abused, and who are not in residential care, are highly vulnerable to further abuse and neglect. There are a number of reasons for this but these include the fact that a child who has been abused in the past may be reluctant to speak out since their previous complaint did not keep them safe.

Forde also drew attention to the fact that residential accommodation in the period under review was often inadequately resourced. This had obvious implications for the quality of life of the children involved but also had further implications for the possibility of abuse occurring. In the eyes of Forde under-resourcing also conveyed a message to staff about the value of their work and legitimated poor standards of care and behaviour. Features of an institution, other than its ethos, are also relevant. Forde emphasised matters such as hierarchy, composition of the residents and the size of the institution. A residential home which was run on hierarchical lines could be conducive to abuse. Standards of behaviour might be laid down by those running the organisation but, if seen as unrealistic, would not command the respect and allegiance of employees at the operational level of the organisation. Placing too many 'troublesome' children in the same home could lead to abuse: 'In the case of "difficult" children, a modest degree of violence is accepted in dealing with them. These environments allow a culture of violence that quickly leads to more abusive situations.'[25] The size of institutions was also relevant in that large institutions could lead to depersonalisation. Forde also stressed the vulnerability of children in residential institutions

[24] Ibid., 16. [25] Ibid., 17.

and, like the Law Commission of Canada, explained that the authority possessed by staff can, if misused, mean that it is very easy for abuse to occur:

> there is a powerful combination of traditional and charismatic authority vested in the adult carer. For children who enter institutional care there is often pre-existing oppression from their previous social and material circumstances. Therefore these children are already vulnerable to the power of an adult abuser. Furthermore, these children may have already been rejected by the traditional authority of their families, and directed to institutional care by the authority of the welfare system. There is great appeal in the charismatic leader who offers a sense of self-esteem and power not previously experienced.[26]

The isolation, perhaps by reasons of location, of an institution was seen as creating a 'high risk' of abuse occurring. The physical design of a home was also viewed as significant. Forde drew on research on violence in prisons to show that the layout of accommodation within an institution correlated to the chances of abuse taking place. Inadequacies in systems of regulation, supervision and inspection created risks. The value of having effective systems in place for dealing with allegations of abuse was noted, as was the importance of operating such a system in a way that encouraged complainants to come forward and was supportive of staff who dealt with complaints.

The final report that will be considered is the Commission of Inquiry into Child Abuse set up by the Irish Government in 2000 and chaired by a High Court judge (Laffoy).[27] Its findings are particularly helpful in flagging up the fact that the holders of a wide variety of employments within institutions may commit acts of abuse and this should be borne in mind when considering the likelihood of a tort occurring. The Laffoy Commission reported in 2009. In children's homes abusers were said to include religious and lay staff, co-residents and other adults who had access to the homes.[28] The staff said to be involved included those regarded as ancillary workers who were generally involved in building, maintenance or farm work. The parts of the report dealing with sexual abuse make clear that acts of abuse might also be committed by those external to a home such as visitors. A number of witnesses reported that 'abusive behaviour was a way of life in the Children's Homes and that

[26] Ibid., 18.

[27] 'Commission of Inquiry into Child Abuse' (hereafter 'Laffoy Commission'). Ryan J took over from Laffoy J in the course of the inquiry.

[28] Ibid., 275.

they believed staff and residents were powerless to do anything to stop it. Witnesses believed that staff members were afraid of losing their jobs, and co-residents were afraid of being abused or punished themselves if they spoke out against the abuse they observed and experienced.'[29] Lack of supervision in homes led to abuse: witnesses 'reported being physically and sexually abused by staff and co-residents in circumstances where there was no effective supervision. Witnesses also reported being abused by groups of co-residents in circumstances where there was no available protection and where older residents had unsupervised access to younger, vulnerable residents.'[30]

The conclusions reached by the Laffoy Commission suggest that much of the abuse arose because of the culture that pertained in residential institutions: 'the harshness of the regime was inculcated into the culture of the schools by successive generations of brothers, priests and nuns. It was systemic and not the result of individual breaches by persons who operated outside lawful and acceptable boundaries. Excesses of punishment generated the fear that the school authorities believed to be essential for the maintenance of order.'[31] It was found that a climate of fear, 'created by pervasive, excessive and arbitrary punishment, permeated most of the institutions ...'[32] There was found to be a cultural understanding within the system that beating boys was acceptable and appropriate.[33]

The Laffoy Commission also received reports of abuse from children who had been placed in foster care; various forms of abuse were involved. It was noted that the isolation of many foster homes increased the sense of hopelessness in a number of victims. Witnesses reported being physically abused by both foster parents and their biological children.[34] Sexual abuse was also said to have taken place by individuals who were not members of the family such as workmen or a member of the priesthood. Aspects of neglect which gave rise to complaints included: 'the inappropriate placement of children with foster parents who were unable to meet their developmental and social needs, the subsequent lack of supervision of the foster care placements, neglect of bodily integrity, lack of adequate food and clothing, neglect of education and inappropriate work'.[35]

Recourse to empirical findings suggests that the concept of enterprise risk fails to capture the true extent of the hazards generated by the enterprise. The difficulty is that the tort must be sufficiently connected to the

[29] Ibid., 287. [30] Ibid., 248. [31] Ibid., 452 [32] Ibid. [33] Ibid., 453.
[34] Ibid., 308. [35] Ibid., 311.

tortfeasor's assigned tasks, before it can be regarded as a materialisation of the risks created by the enterprise. Were attention to be focused on the enterprise rather than the individual the boundaries of liability might be much more extensive. The recent Irish Supreme Court decision in *Reilly v Devereux*[36] provides an excellent example. There the plaintiff, who had been employed as a member of the Defence Forces, complained that he had been sexually assaulted by his Sergeant Major on various occasions during the course of his employment. Counsel for the plaintiff relied very heavily on the principles laid down in *Bazley*. Drawing upon the key tenets of the decision it was argued that the disparity in rank between the plaintiff and the Sergeant Major led to a situation where the latter exercised great power over the plaintiff and could command unquestioning obedience from him. It was further submitted that another of the principles laid down in *Bazley* was met because an element of intimacy and camaraderie was encouraged in the Army in circumstances where employees worked in close quarters together. Finally, it was suggested that within a culture where complaining was discouraged and was largely fruitless, a person in the position of the plaintiff was particularly vulnerable to a wrongful exercise of power by a superior officer. The claim was rejected:

> While undoubtedly the first named defendant exercised a supervisory and disciplinary role where the plaintiff was concerned, he was not in the same position as a school teacher or boarding house warden in relation to a child. Nor was the nature of the employment one which would have encouraged close personal contact where some inherent risks might be said to exist as, for example, might arise if the first named defendant had been a swimming instructor in close physical contact with young recruits. There was no intimacy implicit in the relationship between the plaintiff and the first named defendant nor was there any quasi-parental role or responsibility for personal nurturing which was found to exist in the cases where vicarious liability was established.[37]

It is a matter of speculation whether the outcome of the case would have been the same had attention been focused on the risks generated by the enterprise rather than the individual. Much would have depended upon the evidence advanced as to army culture and ethos.

[36] [2009] IESC 22. [37] Ibid.

5

The enterprise

It is obviously extremely important to determine what constitutes the enterprise for the purposes of enterprise liability. In particular the complexities of corporate structures pose challenging questions.[1] A grouping of interconnected companies can allocate risk across the group in ways that have significant impact on third parties. The effect, in a tort case, can be hugely significant:

> English company law possesses some curious features, which may generate curious results. A parent company may spawn a number of subsidiary companies, all controlled directly or indirectly by the shareholders of the parent company. If one of the subsidiary companies, to change the metaphor, turns out to be the runt of the litter and declines into insolvency to the dismay of its creditors, the parent company and the other subsidiary companies may prosper to the joy of the shareholders without any liability for the debts of the insolvent subsidiary.[2]

The impact on tort litigation can be graphically illustrated in cases involving multiple claimants such as claims in respect of industrial diseases or environmental pollution. The number of plaintiffs may be great, as may the amounts claimed for. The potential liabilities of defendants in cases of this sort may be vast, though assessing the full extent of liability may also be problematic. The harm, for instance, in an industrial disease case may remain latent for a very long time. In cases of this sort a subsidiary may be forced into insolvency by the magnitude of the claims. The subsidiary, on the other hand, may well be unconcerned about meeting the liability arising out of a run-of-the-mill tort claim.[3] The benefits of limited liability and corporate structure for a defendant parent company can be huge as the US case of *Dept of Environmental*

[1] See M. Eroglu, *Multinational Enterprises and Tort Liabilities* (Cheltenham: Edward Elgar, 2008).

[2] *Re Southard* [1979] 1 WLR 1198, 1208 and quoted in B. Pettet, 'Limited Liability' (1995) 48 Current Legal Problems 125, 149.

[3] J. J. White, 'Corporate Judgment Proofing' (1997–8) 107 Yale L.J. 1363, 1365.

Protection v Ventron[4] demonstrates. For thirty years a company called Berk operated a mercury-processing plant and dumped untreated waste material, along with mercury-laden effluent, onto soil. Berk sold the concern to Wood Ridge who were a wholly owned subsidiary of Velsicol. Indeed Wood Ridge had been incorporated for the sole purpose of purchasing Berk's assets and operating the mercury-processing plant. The parent company's domination was such that the subsidiary was effectively a division within the company. The trial judge found that:

> All directors of Wood Ridge were officers of Velsicol, and the Wood Ridge board of directors met monthly in the Velsicol offices in Chicago. At the meetings, the board not only reviewed financial statements, products development and public relations, but also the details of the daily operations of Wood Ridge. For example, the Wood Ridge board considered in detail personnel practices, sales efforts, and production. Velsicol arranged for insurance coverage, accounting, and credit approvals for Wood Ridge. Without spelling out all the details, we find that the record amply supports the conclusion of the trial Court that 'Velsicol personnel, directors, and officers were constantly involved in the day-to-day operations of the business of [Wood Ridge]'.

Notwithstanding the control and domination exercised by the parent company the claimants, in the context of claims arising from damage caused by pollution, failed to persuade the court to lift the veil. The historical reasons for such a decision are very apparent: where the values of tort and corporate law come into conflict the latter is far more likely to win out; as a result tort's ability to achieve its goals of deterrence and compensation is diminished. The fact that a case such as *Ventron* may provoke moral outrage is neither here nor there. This is confirmed in the industrial disease context by the decision in *Adams v Cape Industries*.[5] The background to *Adams* was that the defendants (Cape) were a holding company who presided over a group of subsidiary companies engaged in the mining in South Africa, and marketing, of asbestos. A number of employees and ex-employees raised personal injuries actions in the US courts alleging that harm had been suffered as a result of exposure to asbestos dust. It was accepted by the Court of Appeal that the parent company had created subsidiaries because it wanted sales of asbestos to continue in the USA but intended, by any lawful means open to it, to reduce the appearance of its, or its subsidiaries', involvement there and to reduce the risk of its being held liable for US

[4] 468 A.2d 150. [5] [1990] Ch 433.

taxation or subject to the jurisdiction of the US courts. It was argued that the Court of Appeal should pierce the corporate veil because the purpose of the corporate structure was to allow the holding company to have the benefits of the group's asbestos trade in the USA without the risks of tortious liability. The argument was irrelevant in that the holding company was held to be perfectly entitled to organise the group's affairs in this way. The courts in the UK will not lift the veil merely because the corporate structure has been used so as to ensure that liability in respect of the activities of the group will fall on a subsidiary rather than a holding company. Such a motive is not seen as an abuse of corporate law. The courts adopt a different stance where a limited company is established with a view to avoiding the impact of an existing obligation (such as a restrictive covenant entered into a personal capacity). Such a case may lead to the lifting of the corporate veil on the basis that formation was a sham.[6] However, determining upon corporate structure with a view to avoiding future obligations which may arise is viewed altogether differently, as *Adams* shows. This would appear to be the case even if the prospect of incurring such obligations is very real and hence the motive behind the creation of the subsidiary. There are of course also a considerable number of non-contentious reasons for forming a subsidiary.[7]

The aggrieved third party will be anxious to attach liability to the parent company. It may attempt to persuade the courts to lift the corporate veil or to impose direct liability on the parent company. Neither route is likely to produce the desired outcome. Thus the decision in *Adams* was not particularly surprising given the approach in the UK over the years. Nor, as will be seen, would the outcome have been likely to be different in other jurisdictions. Admittedly the claimants were not without hope; the reasoning in *DHN Food Distributors v Tower Hamlets*[8] was extremely helpful to them. There the veil was lifted to the benefit of the company in a case for compensation under compulsory purchase legislation.[9] It was held that where the question at issue was the entitlement of the owner of a business to be compensated for its extinguishment

[6] *Gilford Motor Co. Ltd v Horne* [1933] Ch 935.

[7] Strasser points out that 'corporate structure in the modern corporate group is more often chosen for managerial, accounting, tax, personnel, or other strategic business considerations, including accommodation to local law and culture in multi-national enterprises'. (K. Strasser, 'Piercing the Veil in Corporate Groups' (2004–5) 37 Conn. L. Rev. 637, 660.)

[8] [1976] 3 All ER 462.

[9] *DHN Food Distributors v Tower Hamlets* [1976] 1 WLR 852. And see F. Rixon, 'Lifting the Veil Between Holding and Subsidiary Companies' (1986) 102 LQR 415.

and on the facts the trading company was in a position to control the subsidiary companies in every respect, the court could pierce the corporate veil and treat the group as a single economic entity for the purpose of awarding compensation for disturbance. The third edition of Gower's seminal work on company law was quoted to the effect that 'there is evidence of a general tendency to ignore the separate legal entities of various companies within a group, and to look instead at the economic entity of the whole group'.[10] The closely knit grouping of companies – characterised by the fact that the parent possessed total control – pointed towards the group being treated as a single entity in law. *DHN* it must be said represents something of an aberration and, in general, an 'economic realities' approach has not found favour with the courts in the UK. Shortly after the decision in *DHN* the House of Lords cast grave doubt on its validity.[11] However, the courts still do not speak with complete consistency on the matter. The Privy Council have accepted that, in principle, a covenant which seeks to protect the interests of associated companies as well as the employing organisation is enforceable.[12] In *Stenhouse Australia v Phillips* it was said that the:

> evidence is clear that the business of the *Stenhouse* group was controlled and co-ordinated by the appellant company, and all funds generated by each of the companies were received by the appellant. The subsidiary companies were merely agencies of instrumentalities through which the appellant company directed its integrated business. Not only did the appellant company have a real interest in protecting the businesses of the subsidiaries, but the real interest of so doing was that of the appellant company.[13]

The effect of the approach in *Stenhouse* is to give an associated company rights against the employee of another company. At the same time the employee gains no rights against the associated company. In the event, for example, of payment being owed for entering into the covenant the employee would not be able to go against the associated company should default arise on the part of his/her employer. Disquiet over the lack of

[10] L. C. B. Gower, *Modern Company Law*, 3rd edn (London: Sweet & Maxwell, 1969), p. 216.

[11] *Woolfson v Strathclyde RC* 1978 SC (HL) 90.

[12] *Stenhouse Australia v Phillips* [1974] AC 391.

[13] Ibid., 404. In a similar vein, in *Group 4 v Ferrier* 1985 SC 70 Lord Ross held that it was reasonable for the petitioners to protect the business interests not only of themselves but of their subsidiary or associated companies. Unfortunately, on appeal, the Inner House declined to express a concluded view on the matter.

reciprocity aside, the decision in *Stenhouse* goes against the principles of separate legal personality. Indeed the Court of Appeal in *Beckett Investment Management Group v Hall*[14] recently expressly acknowledged that the decision conflicted with 'a purist approach to corporate personality'. After all, the House of Lords emphasised in *The Albazero*[15] that 'each company in a group of companies (a relatively modern concept) is a separate legal entity possessed of separate legal rights and liabilities'. Where a business organisation has chosen, by way of incorporation, to structure its affairs in a particular way it seems wrong that it should be able to set this aside at its convenience. The claimants in *Adams* and *Ventron* might be forgiven for taking the view that the disparity of treatment was inequitable and unjustifiable. The Australian courts[16] display a similar degree of caution when it comes to lifting the veil, though in Canada the picture is a little different and it may be that the Supreme Court would be more sympathetic to the sort of approach seen in *DHN*.[17] In *Aluminium Co. of Canada v City of Toronto* the Supreme Court was willing to pierce the corporate veil where the subsidiary was a mere 'puppet' of the holding company: 'In such a case it is not accurate to describe the business as being carried on by the puppet for the benefit of the dominant company. The business is in fact that of the latter.'[18] The key question for the Supreme Court was 'whether or not the parent company is in fact in such an intimate and immediate domination of the motions of the subordinate company that it can be said that the latter has, in the true sense of the expression, no independent functioning of its own'.[19]

14 [2007] ICR 1539. 15 *The Albazero* [1977] AC 774.

16 R. P. Austin and I. M. Ramsay, *Ford's Principles of Corporations Law*, 12th edn (LexisNexis Butterworths, 2005), para. [4.250]. In *Tate v Freecorns Pty Ltd* [1972] WAR 204, 208 it was said that: 'No doubt the fact that Central Provision Stores Pty Ltd is a company controlled and wholly owned by the defendant company may throw some light upon that question but it cannot be decisive. One is still required to look at all the facts to see what the true relationship was and unless the facts show that relationship to be one of principal and agent one cannot, apart from estoppel and consistently with the authorities "ignore the separate legal entities of various companies within a group and … look instead at the economic entity of the whole group" – see proposition 4(1)(b) at pp. 1–6 of *Gower* (above) – so as to make the parent company either vicariously or directly liable for the tortious acts of its wholly owned subsidiary or for the tortious acts of the servant of the wholly owned subsidiary.'

17 A. Hargovan and J. Harris, 'Piercing the Veil in Canada: a Comparative Analysis' (2007) 28(2) Company Lawyer 58. But see N. C. Sargent, 'Corporate Groups and the Corporate Veil in Canada' 17 Man. L.J. 155.

18 [1944] SCR 267, 271. And see *City of Toronto v Famous Players' Canadian Corp. Ltd* [1936] SCR 141.

19 *Aluminium Co. of Canada*, ibid.

Where the parent company acts in a way that is at odds with the corporate structure, liability may ensue. Depending upon the manner of involvement in the affairs of the subsidiary, liability in tort may arise on the part of the parent company by virtue of an assumption of responsibility. In *Heinrich v Goodyear Tire*[20] the parent company had taken responsibility for health and safety issues for the group as a whole. It had adopted the practice of providing employees of a wholly owned subsidiary with health and safety information relating to chemicals used in the business. The information was of a nature that would normally be provided by the actual employer. An employee of the subsidiary contracted an occupational disease and raised an action for personal injuries against the parent. Given the assumption of responsibility such an action was found to be relevant and suitable for trial. *Boggs v Blue Diamond*[21] provides a further illustration. The parent company (Blue Diamond) described itself 'as a multi-unit enterprise consisting of a group of wholly owned subsidiaries under its control'. The evidence established that, as a matter of fact, Blue Diamond had assumed the primary responsibility for 'mine safety functions' at one of the subsidiaries. It was said that Blue Diamond provided management, engineering and safety services to a subsidiary, Scotia, including advice and assistance in mine ventilation. It was alleged that Blue Diamond's management had recognised that improvements in the ventilation of a mine operated by Scotia were needed in order to minimise the accumulation of methane gas, but negligently delayed construction of these improvements. It was also said that Blue Diamond authorised removal of existing ventilation and safety devices in order to open a new tunnel of the mine but concealed the changes from federal mine inspectors who would have taken immediate steps to correct the dangerous condition or to close the mine had they known of the changes. The ventilation changes were said to have increased the methane gas in the existing tunnel and caused an explosion. The widows of coal miners who were killed in the explosion brought wrongful death actions. The claimants maintained that Blue Diamond recklessly created a dangerous situation and put the miners' lives at risk in order to increase its profits in a rising market. The action was allowed to go to trial. The parent company would owe a duty of care to the employee of the subsidiary should the mooted assumption of responsibility in law be established. It was observed that 'the tort system should not deny recovery in an increasingly concentrated economy to an

[20] 532 F. Supp. 1348. [21] 590 F.2d 655.

injured employee due to the fortuitous circumstance that the tortfeasor is not a stranger but is controlled by the same business enterprise that controls his immediate employer'.[22]

The dominance of corporate law

As has been seen, where corporate law and tort law collide the former prevails. The capacity of claimants to overcome this through routes such as lifting the veil is decidedly limited. The impact on tort victims of this hierarchy of values has been a matter of controversy for a long time.[23] Separate legal personality allows parent companies to evade the policy imperatives of enterprise liability.[24] The basic notion of equity that the enterprise should bear the losses where the risks of one of its activities materialise is defeated. This is despite the fact that the control possessed by the parent company will have been exercised to set the activity in motion in the first place. Profits from the activity may also have been declared by way of dividend to the benefit of the parent. For example, in the *Ventron* case very substantial dividends had been declared and paid to the parent company. As a result the subsidiary's capacity to meet liabilities arising from tort actions was much diminished.[25] There is also an impact on the goal of deterrence in that the parent company is able to embark on risky activities at arm's length and will not be deterred by a finding (or the prospect thereof) of negligence against a subsidiary. The parent company lacks an incentive to provide resources to guard against the risk arising or to arrange for insurance cover. The structure of a corporate group allows externalisation of risk to take place and the social costs of the activity will be met by the victim in the event of the subsidiary defaulting. It is therefore in some ways surprising that it

[22] Ibid., para. 7.

[23] W. O. Douglas and C. M. Shanks, 'Insulation from Liability through Subsidiary Corporations' (1929–30) 39 Yale L.J. 193; A. A. Berle, 'The Theory of Enterprise Entity' (1947) 47 Colum. L.R. 343.

[24] It has been suggested that there is more in the way of 'moral hazard' where the parent-subsidiary relationship is concerned because subsidiaries have less incentive to insure: 'In publicly held corporations, the inability of managers to diversify their firm-specific investments in human capital creates incentives to insure. The same is not true for managers of subsidiaries if, as often will be the case, these people are also managers of the parent. Bankruptcy of the subsidiary will not cause them to lose their positions in the parent or suffer any other loss of form-specific human capital . . .' (F. H. Easterbrook and D. R. Fischel, 'Limited Liability and the Corporation' (1985) 52 U. Chi. L. Rev. 89, 111.)

[25] N. A. Mendelson, 'A Control-Based Approach to Shareholder Liability for Corporate Torts' (2002) 102 Colm. L. Rev. 1203, 1251.

may be more difficult (at least in the USA) to pierce the corporate veil in a tort case. One notable study suggests that involuntary creditors may find it more difficult to persuade a court to view a group of companies as a single legal entity than someone with a contractual claim.[26] The author would suggest that current enthusiasm for enterprise liability may provoke further interest in lifting the veil on the basis that, in economic terms if not in law, a single entity exists. Resort to the more traditional justifications for lifting the veil are unsatisfactory as they tend to be predicated upon the basis that incorporation was in some way improper and, therefore, one can only lift the veil where the corporate structure is found to be a 'sham' or a 'facade'. However, the imperatives of tort policy (in particular enterprise liability) may point to companies being treated as one in the absence of any claim of impropriety. The real question is whether the goals of the law of tort should continue to be trumped by those of corporate law. The answer may well depend upon whether the exposure to more extensive liability of an individual shareholder as opposed to a parent company is in issue.

Should an economic-entity approach become more in vogue the expectation would be for courts to focus more on the ways in which the entities concerned are managed and organised and not look for 'moral culpability or wrongful conduct involved in the case'.[27] The experience of several US states where an approach of the type seen in *DHN Food Distributors v Tower Hamlets* has been adopted suggests that the creation of criteria would not be beyond the courts. In *Paramount Petroleum v Taylor Rental Centre*[28] the Court of Appeals of Texas adopted an approach which sought to establish whether the resources of the entities involved were integrated in pursuit of a common business purpose. The following factors were regarded as relevant to this question: 'common employees; common offices; centralized accounting; payment of wages by one corporation to another corporation's employees; common business name; services rendered by the employees of one corporation on behalf of another corporation; undocumented transfers of funds between corporations; and unclear allocation of profits and losses between corporations'. Other states deploy somewhat different

[26] R. B. Thompson, 'Piercing the Corporate Veil: An Empirical Study' (1991) 76 Cornell Law Rev. 1058, 1068. On the other hand, Easterbrook and Fischel, n. 24 above, at 112 take the view that it is easier.

[27] K. A. Strasser, 'Piercing the Veil in Corporate Groups' 37 Conn. L. Rev. 637, 646.

[28] 712 S.W.2d 534.

tests to determine whether a single entity exists.[29] Assessing the respective merits of the various competing formulae is a matter for company lawyers, but it seems clear that the courts do not appear unduly troubled by the challenge of devising criteria to identify a single economic entity. It should be reiterated that the courts are not seeking to identify impropriety but instead organisations which, in substance, are singular; albeit that formally they are comprised of a number of separate legal entities.

It would be wrong not to acknowledge that there are powerful considerations underpinning limited liability, but should such considerations continue to outweigh the policies underpinning enterprise liability? Certainly where individual shareholders are concerned the current position in respect of tort liability is defended on a number of grounds. If potential investors were faced with the prospect of unlimited liability it is conceivable that they would be much less willing to invest and become shareholders. The spectre of losses on a scale which might consume all their assets would act as a huge deterrent. Limited liability reduces the risk to shareholders and makes more capital available to enterprises. Unlimited liability would also deter individual investors in that it would be financially riskier than at present to be a passive shareholder. Should shares be purchased the investor would be compelled to incur costs monitoring the management of the company:

> limited liability efficiently enables individuals with money, but with neither the skill nor the information needed for business management, to invest in the enterprise of others. Under unlimited liability, a small investor could conceivably lose an entire portfolio if any investment went truly sour. If the investor were to properly manage the risk, she would have to acquire detailed information on corporate questions, potential corporate liability, and her potential individual exposure in the event of such liability.[30]

Again any investor would be concerned by the financial standing of fellow shareholders, and the possibility of monitoring costs again arises in that regard. The strength of these arguments is very much contested and some would argue that a move to unlimited liability would not have negative consequences. For present purposes what matters is that treating a group of companies as a single entity does not give rise to such

[29] In *Green v Champion* 577 So.2d 249 some eighteen factors were put forward which included (as well as control): inadequate capitalisation; receiving no business other than that given to it by its affiliated corporations; common employees; excessive fragmentation of a single enterprise into separate corporations.

[30] Mendelson, n. 25 above, 1217.

concerns.[31] For example, the parent of a wholly owned subsidiary will have ready access to the information required for effective monitoring. Facilitating recovery in tort against a parent company will not have a negative impact upon investment. At most a parent company would be less likely to divert resources into setting up a subsidiary.

Conclusions

The issue of tort liability of corporations may well be of greater significance than in the past: 'Changes in technology, knowledge, liability rules, and procedures for mass tort litigation have for the first time raised the prospect of tort claims that exceed the net worth of even very large corporations. Environmental harms, such as oil spills or the release of toxic materials, are one potential source of massive liability; hazardous products and carcinogens in the workplace are others.'[32] Against that backdrop, it would be timely for the judiciary to reappraise their approach when tort and company law interact. There is nothing inevitable about the present position. When one turns to the interaction between company and competition law, judicial evaluation of the various policy considerations is much more likely to lead to a lifting of the corporate veil: 'Antitrust is concerned with maintaining competitive markets, and there is no realistic prospect that corporate entities within the same enterprise will actually compete with each other. Thus, when they act together, they are not combining separate bits of market power, so their acting together does not make a conspiracy that violates antitrust policy.'[33] In both the USA and the EU the demands of competition law have prompted the courts to treat a parent and subsidiary company as one. In the USA, in *Copperweld v Independence Tube*,[34] a parent company and its wholly owned subsidiary were sued on the basis that they had conspired to violate section 1 of the Sherman Act. It was held that a parent corporation and its wholly owned subsidiary were not legally capable of conspiring with each other.[35] A decision to the contrary would have led to an artificial distinction between the position of a subsidiary and a division of the parent company which had never been

[31] Strasser, n. 27 above, 660.

[32] H. Hansmann and R. Kraakman, 'Toward Unlimited Shareholder Liability for Corporate Torts' (1990–1) 100 Yale L.J. 1879, 1880.

[33] Strasser, n. 27 above, 662. [34] 467 US 752.

[35] The court made clear it was confining its ruling to the position of the wholly owned subsidiary.

incorporated. Where the latter was concerned there was no question of a conspiracy arising because the operations of a corporate enterprise organised into divisions must be judged as the conduct of a single actor. It was noted that a division pursues the interests of the corporate entity, rather than its own separate interests. A corporation 'establishes divisions to further its own interests in the most efficient manner'. In substance the position was no different where a wholly owned subsidiary was concerned: 'A parent and its wholly owned subsidiary have a complete unity of interest. Their objectives are common, not disparate; their general corporate actions are guided or determined not by two separate corporate consciousnesses, but one.' The Supreme Court concluded by observing that the impact of competition law should not depend on whether a unit of a corporation is organised as an unincorporated division or a wholly owned subsidiary. A corporation has complete power to maintain a wholly owned subsidiary in either form.

A similar approach has been adopted by the European Court of Justice in cases dealing with Article 105; *Viho Europe v Commission*[36] holding that the latter Article aimed at discrimination which was the result of an agreement, a decision or a concerted practice between separate and autonomous economic entities and not the result of unilateral conduct by a single undertaking. Where a parent company and its subsidiaries form a single economic unit within which the subsidiaries do not enjoy real autonomy in determining their course of action in the market, but carry out the instructions issued to them by the parent company which wholly controls them, it was correct to view the grouping as a single undertaking. Relations within an economic unit could not amount to an agreement or concerted practice between undertakings which restricts competition. Where competition law is concerned decisions on separate legal personality are much more likely to be 'reasoned with reference to the public policy goals and objectives of the statutory regime'.[37]

[36] Case C-73/95P. [37] Strasser, n. 27 above, 662.

6

The borrowed employee

The law of vicarious liability has had to address the issue of responsibility for the negligence of an employee who is lent by his/her employer to another organisation. There are two key features of the common law's response. First, where enterprises are genuinely distinct the traditional view has been that the employer has sole responsibility and joint responsibility would not arise. Such an atomised view might be thought to be at odds with the interdependence between enterprises that frequently exists. Second, the permanent employer and not the temporary employer will normally be held to bear that sole responsibility.

The leading UK case on the latter point is *Mersey Docks v Coggins.*[1] There a harbour authority (the permanent employer) let a mobile crane to a firm of stevedores for loading a ship, and provided a craneman. The general hiring conditions stipulated that the craneman was to be the employee of the hirers. In the course of the operation he injured a third person by negligently driving the crane. It emerged that the employer had engaged the craneman, paid his wages, prescribed the jobs he should undertake and alone had power to dismiss him. The firm of stevedores had the immediate direction and control of the operations to be executed by him with the crane, e.g. to pick up and move a piece of cargo from shed to ship, but had no power to direct how he should work the crane, the manipulation of the controls being a matter for him. The permanent employer was found to be vicariously liable; the key question being who possesses the right of control in the sense of who is entitled to give orders as to how the work should be done.[2] The House of Lords confirmed that the burden of proof rests on the general or permanent employer to shift the prima facie responsibility for the negligence to the hirer or temporary employer. The Lords were at pains to stress that 'this burden is a heavy one and can only be discharged in

[1] [1947] AC 1.

[2] J. G. Fleming, *The Law of Torts*, 9th edn (Sydney: Lawbook Co., 1998), p. 419.

quite exceptional circumstances'.[3] This approach to burden involved something of a departure from previous cases and has meant (at least in the UK) that the temporary employer is very unlikely to be held liable. The general employer was seen as best placed to deter negligence:

> Here the fault, if any, lay with the appellants who, though they were not present to dictate how directions given by another should be carried out, yet had vested in their servant a discretion in the manner of carrying out such directions. If an accident then occurred through his negligence that was because they had chosen him for the task, and they cannot escape liability by saying that they were careful in their choice.[4]

Given the approach adopted in *Mersey Docks* it has proved extremely difficult to show that the temporary employer has become vicariously liable for the acts of the borrowed employee.

A new approach?

In the UK the Court of Appeal in *Viasystems v Thermal Transfer*[5] adopted an innovative approach by holding that liability can be shared between the temporary and general employer. Under this regime of shared liability both employers are regarded as joint tortfeasors and, in line with general principles, the plaintiff can recover in full from either of them. It may be said that this judicial reform took place against the backdrop of a decidedly unexceptional set of facts. *Viasystems* paints a picture of an extremely commonplace situation where construction/engineering work is undertaken by a number of parties. *Viasystems* had employed the first defendants to install air conditioning. The latter had subcontracted part of the work (the installation of the air ducting) to the second defendants who, in turn, had borrowed employees of the third defendants to assist. The harm was caused by the negligence of an employee of the third defendants when he was working for the second defendants under their 'instruction or supervision'. It appears that the borrowed employees were given instruction by the second defendants about methods of working, including safety. It was also clear that an employee of the second defendants was responsible for site safety. Any summary of the facts would be incomplete without mentioning that two employees of the general employer had been lent: the negligent employee and his supervisor. This element was, in the eyes of the court, to assume considerable and, the author would suggest, undue significance.

[3] *Mersey Docks*, n. 1 above, 10. [4] Ibid., 18. [5] [2005] IRLR 983.

At first glance the decision in *Viasystems*, with the adoption of dual responsibility, appears to be a bold one. This is certainly true in so far as the treatment of the existing authorities was concerned. Previously the orthodox view was that 'it is doubtful whether such a solution is open to the courts except where both employers are engaged in a joint venture'.[6] That apart, the author would argue that the decision is actually a remarkably conservative one. This becomes apparent once it is appreciated that the ratio of the decision is that dual responsibility can only arise when the right of control is shared. Whilst the ratio seems clear, one of the two judges in the Court of Appeal (Rix LJ) appeared to be less than fully committed to this stance. May LJ emphasised: 'the crucial relationship being the employers' right (and theoretical obligation) to control the relevant activity of the employee'. Similarly, in line with the ratio, Rix LJ inclined to the view that 'it will only be where the right of control is shared that vicarious liability can be dual'. *Viasystems* regards *Mersey Docks* as authoritative (as it was bound to do) and concludes that allocation of responsibility can only arise (whether shared or not) on the basis of a right of control. As a consequence the decision constitutes a modest refinement of *Mersey Docks.* One might describe the approach as a labour law one because of the role traditionally allocated to the right of control in determining the existence of a contract of employment. Similarly *Mersey Docks* relies upon this factor to determine whether a temporary transfer of employment (purely for the purposes of vicarious liability) has taken place.

Viasystems would have given rise to greater interest if it had had regard to the practical aspects of control that fall short of direct legal rights. The lending of an employee's services gives rise to a triangular arrangement for the organisation of work, whereby the right of control is separated from its exercise, yet *Viasystems* fails to countenance a role for factual control. Nevertheless, it would be difficult to conceive of a situation where the temporary employer did not possess a measure of control; whether as a matter of right or not. It 'would be surprising if . . . the end-user did not have powers of control or direction over such a person in such a working environment. The end-user is the ultimate paymaster.'[7] *Viasystems* does not take full account of the ways in which work tends to be organised when a number of employers are involved in, say, a construction project. As a result, it fails to ensure that

[6] *Clerk and Lindsell on Torts*, 18th edn (London: Sweet & Maxwell, 2001), para. 5.22, n. 93.
[7] *Dacas v Brook Street Bureau (UK) Ltd* [2004] IRLR 358, 368.

responsibility goes hand in hand with the possession of actual control. Given this stance, it is perhaps not surprising that the court took the view that *Mersey Docks* itself was not a case of dual control: 'the employee is used, for a limited time, in his general employer's own sphere of operations, operating his general employer's crane, exercising his own discretion as a crane driver. Even if the right of control were to some extent shared, as in practice it is almost bound to be, one would hesitate to say that it is a case for dual vicarious liability.'[8] The focus on the rights formally possessed by the two employers precludes consideration of the realities of the worker's relationship with the temporary employer. In *Mersey Docks* though it was the temporary employer who, as a matter of fact, was directing operations at the time the accident occurred and, to that extent at least, control had been transferred.

An important consequence of the reasoning in *Viasystems* is that a holding of dual control will be an uncommon occurrence: 'in many, perhaps most, factual situations, a proper application of the *Mersey Docks* principles would not yield dual control, as it so plainly does in the present case'.[9] Given this, the outcome in *Viasytems* itself might be thought to be surprising since, in the author's opinion, the facts were utterly unremarkable. The intermingling of workers which occurred might be thought to be a common characteristic of a construction project carried out by several employers. More particularly, the way in which control was shared was typical of a temporary/general employer relationship in that the former was in charge of the workers on the site and supervised that work. Again, the temporary employer assumed responsibility for safe working on the site. The court, however, appear to have regarded it as significant that a supervisor was lent along with the negligent employee. The general employer's supervisor was seen as 'interposed' between the negligent worker and the temporary employer's supervisor, an arrangement that was seen as indicative of joint control. This seems to me to be a complete red herring. There is nothing surprising about a group of employees being lent and, where this occurs, they may have different levels of responsibility. The underlying question remains that of determining who exercised 'real' control in the workplace; here it was surely the temporary employer.

The position prior to *Viasystems* remains the law in Australia.[10] The Supreme Court of Canada considered those matters in

[8] *Viasystems*, n. 5 above, 994. [9] Ibid., 989.
[10] *Oceanic Crest Shipping Co. v Pilbara Harbour Services* (1986) CLR 826.

Blackwater v Plint,[11] which was a sexual abuse case. The defendants were the State and the United Church of Canada who had operated a residential school. Actions were commenced by former residents of the school claiming damages for sexual abuse and other harm. The trial judge held a dormitory supervisor, Plint, liable to six plaintiffs for sexual assault. He went on to hold that the State and the Church were jointly and vicariously liable for these wrongs. The fact that the latter was found to be vicariously liable is not surprising as it was running the school and might have been assumed to be the employer. The fact that the State was also vicariously liable offers more food for thought, as does the finding that more than one party could be held to be vicariously liable. The Supreme Court upheld this analysis. Atiyah was relied upon to justify holding two employers vicariously liable: '[t]here is, of course, no reason why two employers should not jointly employ a servant, and this would normally be the case with the employees of a partnership. Here the servant is the servant of each partner and of all jointly, and they are all jointly and severally liable for the servant's torts.'[12] The Supreme Court formed the view that joint vicarious liability was undoubtedly acceptable where there was a partnership: 'Indeed, if an employer with *de facto* control over an employee is not liable because of an arbitrary rule requiring only one employer for vicarious liability, this would undermine the principles of fair compensation and deterrence.'[13] In *Blackwater* itself the trial judge had viewed the relationship between the parties as akin to a partnership and the Supreme Court agreed with this. There was of course no partnership in law but the control exercised by both defendants was crucial. In situations where the State exercises statutory functions and delegates the operation of an institution to a voluntary association it will often have little or nothing to do with the day-to-day running. This was not the case in *Blackwater* where the State was found to be involved in managing the school and exercising a measure of control over the employees.

For instance, the State hired and paid all the teachers at the school and took the initiative for and funded training programmes for dormitory supervisors such as Plint. Management responsibility for operational matters was seen as being only partially in the hands of the Church. The references to partnership are somewhat misleading. The key factor

11 [2005] 3 SCR 3.
12 P. S. Atiyah, *Vicarious Liability in the Law of Torts* (London: Butterworths, 1967), p. 149.
13 *Blackwater*, n. 11 above, 20.

in finding that joint vicarious liability existed was the element of joint control. It is not though axiomatic that such a finding gives rise to joint responsibility and it remains unclear how influential *Blackwater* will be.

The role of enterprise liability

Viasystems and *Blackwater* indicate that the longstanding orthodoxy is under a degree of threat. Nevertheless, for the time being at least, temporary employers will normally continue to avoid the burden of responsibility, shared or otherwise. The author would suggest that, should regard be had to current trends in tort law, it is conceivable that in the future sole responsibility will be placed on the shoulders of the temporary employer. The key in cases such as *Mersey Docks* is to identify the enterprise responsible for the creation of the risk. Identification is contingent upon accurate determination of an enterprise's constituent parts. This question of composition is not straightforward and nor is it value free. In a *Mersey Docks* type of case one might reasonably conclude that, functionally, the borrowed employee was engaged in the conduct of the temporary employer's enterprise at the time the tort occurred. Such a worker is furthering the aims of the enterprise just as much as the core employees. For the duration of the loan period the worker could be said to be part of that enterprise. The temporary employer would be the primary beneficiary of the worker's endeavours, and concomitant (and sole) responsibility should attach. It may be objected that the general employer also benefits from the payment for the worker's services. Atiyah has argued that 'in virtually every case, the servant is manifestly engaged on both businesses at the relevant time'.[14] In the author's opinion, the argument that, since both the general and temporary employer benefit from the worker's services liability should be shared, is very much open to question. A number of parties may stand to gain from the fulfilment of a contract including, for example, other contractors and, not least of all, the client who commissioned the work. It would not be suggested that all such parties should share responsibility. As between the general and temporary employer it would seem likely

[14] P. S. Atiyah, n. 12 above, p. 163. In a similar vein Fleming has argued that where machinery is hired 'it is clear that the servant operator is participating both in the business of equipment renting and in the business for which the equipment is rented. Clearly both enterprises require the operator's services in order to accomplish their tasks and to make their profits.' (J. G. Fleming, 'Borrowed Servants and the Theory of Enterprise Liability' (1966–7) 76 Yale L.J. 807, 811.)

that the latter will have the greater opportunity for profit from the undertaking of the activity.

Ultimately, however, the fundamental objection to giving greater weight to factors such as the opportunity for gain is that, cumulatively or otherwise, they would still provide an insufficient basis for liability. The present judicial conceptualisation of enterprise liability founds its appeal to equity by being grounded in the nexus between risk creation and enterprise gain. It has already been noted that this policy consideration has been accorded the first importance and, in effect, it gives rise to an essential prerequisite which must be met before vicarious liability will arise. Consistency with this position requires the imposition of sole responsibility on the temporary employer. Enterprise liability requires that the enterprise be responsible for the risks generated by it. Where an employee (such as a crane operator) is lent it is easy to assume that the risks involved are simply the ones that arise in general from the use of a crane. However, the actual risk cannot be determined without regard to the use to which the employee is put by the temporary employer. The generic risk is mediated through the medium of the latter's enterprise. The risks associated with the work of a janitor may well differ depending upon whether he is working in a school or an office. This would also be in accord with that body of tort doctrine which advocates internalising costs to the risk-creating enterprise so that the appropriate social cost is exacted for the service offered.

Of course it would be possible to approach the matter from a reconfigured enterprise liability perspective, underpinned by a different weighting of policy factors, and allow for a holding of dual responsibility. Given that, as we saw in Chapter 1, a number of approaches to enterprise liability exist, the solution adopted in a particular context may vary depending upon which one is selected. Interestingly, in *Viasystems*, Rix LJ, who was less than wholly wedded to the approach to control adopted therein, may have displayed something of an inclination towards dual responsibility: 'I would hazard, however, the view that what one is looking for is a situation where the employee in question, at any rate for relevant purposes, is so much a part of the work, business or organisation of both employers that it is just to make both employers answer for his negligence.'[15] Attention might be drawn to the fact that the theory of enterprise liability adopted in *Bazley* also assumes that a secondary, but weighty, justification of vicarious liability is that it

[15] *Viasystems*, n. 5 above, 993.

promotes deterrence. Where both a temporary and general employer are involved, promotion of effective deterrence might be thought to point towards dual liability in that both have a responsibility in respect of recruitment and selection. However, a theory of enterprise liability informed much more centrally by general deterrence may favour placing liability on the shoulders of the general employer. Fleming contrasts the position of a crane-hire company with that of a building company who hires from it. In general the former is said to have:

> a better statistical background for estimating the likelihood of crane accidents, and thus can make more accurate insurance and pricing decisions. In contrast the building contractor will probably lump all the potential accident costs of his project together and use a broad insurance policy. He is unlikely to isolate the costs of accidents involving cranes, for the purpose either of demanding safer practices from the crane company or of considering safer and cheaper substitutes. There will be, in other words, too little pressure on the contractor for reduction of crane accident costs, or on the crane company for safer operation. Finally, even if the builder attempted to evaluate crane accident costs, the task would be more expensive for him than for the crane owner.[16]

The author would, however, argue that the party in the best position to ensure that the task in hand is carried out safely is the temporary employer. But the traditional approach enshrined in *Mersey Docks* means that the courts do not in fact look 'to see which employer could best have prevented the specific accident in question; they openly disregard the real influence of the employers in the job situation in favour of the abstract power over the employee in his whole course of duty'.[17] Again the placing of responsibility on the temporary employer will encourage it to deal with reputable lenders of labour.

Conclusions

It may be said that a move to joint liability would have a limited impact on claimants and defendants alike. As between the two employers this is because the matter will tend to be regulated by the contract between them. However, this does not wholly negate the merit in the creation of a default rule. There will inevitably be cases where the issue is not provided for. Notions of estoppel or personal bar may also enter the equation. The recent decision of the Court of Appeal in *Hawley v Luminar Leisure*[18]

[16] Fleming, n. 14 above, 817. [17] Fleming, n. 14 above, 811. [18] [2006] IRLR 817.

dealt with a company (Luminar) who ran nightclubs and who had contracted with ASE to provide bouncers. An employee of ASE assaulted a customer and the court had to consider whether Luminar (the temporary employer) were vicariously liable. The issue was decided with reference to *Mersey Docks* but much greater emphasis was placed upon factual control than traditionally would have been the case. It was found to be appropriate to render the temporary employer vicariously liable because, in practice, it 'sought to have, and did exercise detailed control not only over what the [workers] were to do in supplying services but how they were to do it'.[19] In addition, the outer manifestations of the relationship between the temporary employer and the worker suggested that the former was the actual employer. In *Hawley* third parties would have been unable to differentiate between borrowed workers and employees of Luminar: 'there can be no doubt that any customer, passer by or police officer seeing the doormen decked out in Luminar uniforms would have assumed they were Luminar staff. In effect this is what they were held out to be. The doormen were not recognisable physically as the employees of ASE.'[20] It does not seem unreasonable to suggest that the court may have viewed Luminar as estopped from denying that it was in an employment relationship. In the result, the presumption in *Mersey Docks* could be overcome.

[19] Ibid., 825. [20] Ibid., 826.

7

Independent contractors

In his seminal work on vicarious liability Atiyah questioned whether vicarious liability should extend to the actions of independent contractors. He noted that there was much to be said on both sides of the argument but observed that it had been argued that:

> When a person employs a contractor, it is his business which is being done, he is the party benefiting from the work, and in the long run he should pay his share of the costs . . . Further, the imposition of liability for independent contractors encourages employers to seek out and contract with financially responsible contractors who can meet any damages awarded against them (or indemnify the employer against liabilities imposed on him) and this is in the public interest.[1]

Atiyah's concerns seem all the more relevant given contemporary working practices where many businesses have become increasingly dependent on the contribution of workers, and other service providers, who are not employees. Such a phenomenon is not confined to one country but occurs globally. The construction industry provides a particularly good example here. A builder may well remain responsible to the client for the completion of the project but is unlikely to rely solely upon his own employees. Various elements of the work may well be subcontracted, some of which may be subject to further subcontracting. It is also noteworthy that there may be a great deal of variance between the resources possessed by the subcontractors involved. There are, broadly speaking, two options open to the courts should they wish to address these issues with a view to imposing liability on the employer for tortious behaviour. First, given the seemingly permanent opaqueness of the demarcation line between a contract of employment and one for services, the courts can without undue difficulty seek to allocate more relationships to the former category: 'yet the servant and the independent contractor are nearly indistinguishable in an economic sense; in both

[1] P. S. Atiyah, *Vicarious Liability in the Law of Torts* (London: Butterworths, 1967), p. 333.

cases the superior commands, finances and profits from the work done. Because of this similarity of function, courts have never been able to define clearly which employees are servants and which are contractors.'[2] The second and far more radical solution would be to abandon the existing position and hold that employers may be vicariously liable for independent contractors.

The demarcation line

In both Australia and the UK the judiciary have in fact taken account of the developments in working practices in distinguishing contracts of employment from other forms of contractual relationships.[3] Indeed, the desire to protect third parties has led to decisions in favour of the existence of an employment relationship which would probably not have been made in a different context. The best, or perhaps most explicit, example of this in the UK is the Court of Appeal decision in *Lane v Shire Roofing Company*.[4] There the plaintiff was a builder who traded as a one-man firm. He was taken on by the defendants to work on a roofing contract at a fixed daily rate. He then went on do another roofing job for them for an all-in fee but suffered an accident while doing this work. He had self-employed status for fiscal purposes. The nature of his business was described as follows: 'he solicited work through advertisements, and when engaged by clients would of course be responsible for estimating, buying in materials, and matters of that kind. But that work had dried up. His public liability insurance had lapsed. At the time he answered the respondent's advert he was usually working for others.'[5] This description is strongly suggestive of self-employment; albeit that this was proving to be financially unrewarding. Nevertheless, the plaintiff was held to be an employee in the context of a personal injuries claim. The court explicitly stated that they regarded it as correct to approach the determination of status 'in the context of who is responsible for the overall safety of the men doing the work in question'.[6] Moreover, 'when it comes to the question of safety at work, there is a real public interest in recognising the employer/employee relationship when it exists, because

[2] J. B. McHugh, 'Risk Administration in the Marketplace: A Reappraisal of the Independent Contractor Rule' (1972–3) 40 U. Chi. L. Rev. 661, 661.

[3] See E. McKendrick, 'Vicarious Liability and Independent Contractors: A Re-Examination' (1990) 53 MLR 770.

[4] [1995] IRLR 493. The approach in *Lane* was applied in *Jones v BBC* [2007] All ER (D) 283.

[5] *Lane*, ibid., 496. [6] Ibid.

of the responsibilities that the common law and statutes ... place on the employer'.[7] Such a context-specific approach has undoubted attractions (though it may be problematic in terms of the coherence of the law as a whole) and seems also to have appealed to the High Court in *Hollis v Vabu*.[8] The High Court acknowledged that the policy concerns underpinning vicarious liability may inform a decision as to the legal classification of a worker's contract. In *Vabu* the worker concerned was a bicycle courier and, at first instance, it had been held that the relationship was one of self-employment. Vabu provided radio equipment to the bicycle couriers and allocated delivery jobs to them by radio. The couriers were required to be available at a certain time every day and were not allowed to refuse the delivery jobs that were allocated to them. Vabu issued uniforms to the couriers and required them to wear the uniforms. It also directed the couriers to conduct their work in accordance with specific instructions concerning dress, appearance, language, delivery procedures and dealings with clients. The couriers had to provide their own motor vehicles or bicycles. They received no salaries or wages but were remunerated in accordance with the deliveries that they made. They were taxed as independent contractors. Vabu deducted a certain amount from the couriers' payments each week to contribute towards the cost of Vabu's insurance. This was partly because there had been a previous decision, on very similar facts, involving Vabu couriers which had held that for tax purposes the couriers were independent contractors.[9] Key evidence in that case included the fact that the couriers were required to provide their own bicycles and that two-thirds to three-quarters of them would have owned more than one bicycle; that the couriers had to bear the expense of providing and maintaining those vehicles; and that the couriers were required to provide their own equipment, other than a radio and uniform. However, in the later decision, in the context of a personal injuries action, a finding of employment was arrived at. Different aspects of the parties' relationship were highlighted, such as the fact that Vabu set the rates of remuneration and that there was no scope for negotiation of those rates, and that Vabu allocated the work, with no scope for bidding for individual jobs by the couriers. Again the couriers were required to wear Vabu's livery at all times, partly due to the employer's desire to advertise its services; and that requirements such as insurance and deductions from pay were

[7] Ibid., 495. [8] [2001] 207 CLR 21.
[9] *Vabu v Federal Commissioner of Taxation* (1996) 3 ATR 537.

therefore imposed by Vabu without opportunity for negotiation. In the court below, Davis J had viewed the workers as being integrated into the employer's organisation in that they functioned as part of it.[10]

Another route to imposition of liability is to look to the different tests which may be used to determine the existence of a contract of employment. The decision as to selection may influence the nature of the outcome. In *Stevenson, Jordan and Harrison v MacDonald*,[11] Lord Denning put forward the integration test (sometimes referred to as the organisation test): 'One feature which seems to run through the instances is that, under a contract of service, a man is employed as part of the business, and his work is done as an integral part of the business; whereas, under a contract for services, his work, although done for the business, is not integrated into it but is only accessory to it.' The applicability of this test has been accepted by the Supreme Court of Canada.[12] In *Sagaz* the trial judge had held that vicarious liability did not arise on the basis that the tortfeasor was an independent contractor, a conclusion ultimately endorsed by the Supreme Court by applying the 'business on your own account' test.[13] The Court of Appeal for Ontario had taken a different view on the basis of the organisation test: the staff in question were said to function as 'integrated elements' of the employing organisation.[14] By holding that a relationship of employment existed the broader question, of whether an employer should be vicariously liable for the activities of an independent contractor, did not need to be tackled directly. The invocation of the integration test may, in general, make a finding of employment more likely. The Supreme Court noted that 'if the question is whether the activity or worker is integral to the employer's business, this question can usually be answered affirmatively'.[15] Judges have a degree of latitude as to which test to utilise in determining whether a contract of employment exists. Wider application of the integration test may hold appeal for some as it would lead

[10] [1999] NSWCA 334. [11] [1952] 1 TLR 101.

[12] *Co-operators Insurance Association v Kearney* (1964) 48 DLR (2d) 1. In *Mayer v J Conrad Lavigne Ltd* (1979) 27 OR (2d) 129, 133 MacKinnon ACJO applied the organisation test in holding that a commission agent who sold advertising for a television station was in an employment relationship: 'the relationship satisfies the "organization" test. The respondent's work was a necessary and integral part of the appellant's business. It supplied the financial life-blood of the appellant, and his work was subject to the coordinational control of management. His work was clearly integrated into the business and not merely accessory to it.' The High Court of Australia has rejected the test: *Stevens v Brodribb Sawmilling* [1986] HCA 1.

[13] [2001] 2 SCR 183. [14] 183 DLR (4th) 488. [15] [2001] 2 SCR 183.

to more workers being classified as employees rather than independent contractors. The test can also be seen as an expression of enterprise liability: 'There are some similarities between the expression of this test ("part and parcel of the organisation") and other attempts to explain vicarious liability by reference to an analysis of "enterprise risk" (for example, as considered by the Supreme Court of Canada.'[16] The greater the degree of integration the easier it is to say that the enterprise should be responsible. The application of the integration test may allow a more accurate assessment of the composition of the enterprise to be arrived at.

The judicial response in *Lane* and *Vabu* offers a solution (the efficacy of which is unclear in that it cannot be determined how many classification decisions will be affected) on the basis that the underlying problem is one of 'disguised' employment. However, if the correct rationalisation of vicarious liability is indeed enterprise liability, a more radical approach is called for. One fundamental issue is to determine precisely what constitutes the employer's enterprise. The approach taken by modern health and safety law offers valuable guidance. In this regard, section 3 of the UK Health and Safety at Work Act 1974 is worthy of close attention. It deals with an employer's responsibility to those who are not its employees. More significantly, in the context of present discussion, it elaborates on what amounts to the employer's enterprise (or undertaking). Section 3(1) provides that it is the duty of every employer to conduct its undertaking in such a way as to ensure, so far as is reasonably practicable, that persons not in its employment who may be affected by such conduct are not thereby exposed to risks to their health and safety. A key element of the section is the concept of undertaking since its content determines the extent of the employer's responsibility. In the leading case of *R v Associated Octel*[17] the House of Lords held that, in an approach consistent with a broad application of enterprise liability, the duty was breached by the behaviour of an independent contractor. There the employer had engaged a specialist contractor (RGP) to effect repairs to plant. During the carrying out of the work one of RGP's employees was badly burnt. Counsel for the employer had argued that 'RGP were independent contractors and the cleaning of the tank was part of the conduct of their undertaking. Control was essential to liability under section 3(1) and Octel had no right to control the way in which its independent contractors did their work'.[18] This argument

[16] *Sweeney v Boylan* (2006) 226 CLR 161. [17] [1996] ICR 972. [18] Ibid., 976.

was rejected and the maintenance work performed by the contractor was regarded as part of the conduct of the employer's undertaking. This result was arrived at by taking a functional approach, rather than allowing enquiry to be restricted by the nature of the contractual relationships that the employer had entered into: 'It imposes a duty upon the employer himself. That duty is defined by reference to a certain kind of activity, namely, the conduct by the employer of his undertaking. It is indifferent to the nature of the contractual relationships by which the employer chooses to conduct it.'[19] This approach is in stark contrast to that traditionally taken by the law of vicarious liability. On a similar basis, the fact that there is an absence of control over the contractor will not avail the employer: 'If, therefore, the employer engages an independent contractor to do work which forms part of the conduct of the employer's undertaking, he must stipulate for whatever conditions are needed to avoid those risks and are reasonably practicable.'[20] Having introduced risks enterprise liability requires that they be managed. It is not open to the employer to contract-out by recourse to the kinds of private law devices that allow a denial of responsibility at common law.

Reforming the common law

Australia

It would not have been particularly surprising if the Australian courts had chosen to reform the common law in a radical way. The old case of *Colonial Mutual Life v Producers and Citizens Co-op Assurance*[21] could be seen as providing a platform for change. There the person, for whose statements the employer was sought to be made vicariously liable, had been hired to canvass for proposals for life insurance. The statements which it was alleged that he made, and which were slanderous of the claimant, had been uttered in the course of his attempting to induce persons to take out life insurance. It was accepted that he was not an employee but it was still held that the employer was vicariously liable for his statements because he made them in acting as the company's agent. Since the decision particular attention has been paid to the judgment of Dixon J, who accepted that a contract of employment did not exist but felt that employers could be vicariously liable for contractors where the

[19] Ibid., 977. [20] Ibid.

[21] (1931) 46 CLR 41. And see L. McCarthy, 'Vicarious Liability in the Agency Context' [2004] QUTLJJ 7.

function entrusted is that of representing the person who requests its performance in a transaction with others. He highlighted the fact that the very service to be performed consists in standing in his place and assuming to act in his right and not in an independent capacity. Where that representative function occurred, as in *Colonial Mutual Life* itself, vicarious liability would follow. There appears to be no good reason why this exception, rather than any other, should exist but, nevertheless, invoking notions of representation gives wide scope for expansion of an employer's responsibility. It could, almost invariably, be said that a contractor represents his employer in the sense that he acts for the employer's benefit. Indeed the decision in *Colonial Mutual Life* exercised a strong influence over McHugh J's judgment in *Vabu*, where the learned judge concurred as to the result but deployed very different reasoning to the rest of the majority. That judgment demonstrates that even where judges are unwilling to depart from a conventional analysis of a worker's status, the imperative of enterprise liability may lead to a holding of vicarious liability by another route. A majority of the court held that the worker was an employee, though McHugh J regarded him as an independent contractor. Nevertheless, the latter, by recourse to the reasoning employed in *Colonial Mutual Life*, was still able to render the employer vicariously liable. He took the view that a principal should be held responsible when the conduct occurs while the agent is carrying out a task for the benefit of the principal as his representative.[22] Enterprise liability pointed to such a conclusion:

> It is also *fair* to make Vabu compensate Mr Hollis for the negligence of its courier in the same way as it is fair to hold an employer liable for the negligence of its employees. This notion of fairness stems from Vabu's control of the couriers and the fact that the couriers were acting for the economic benefit of Vabu. It was Vabu who introduced into the community a business activity that carried with it the risk of injury to users of public thoroughfares. When the accident occurred, the courier was "on the business" of Vabu. He was also serving its economic interests in other respects. He was carrying out its core business activity – the delivery of documents.[23]

It was also difficult for the employer to object given that the workers were presented to the public, and to those using the employer's services, as emanations of the business. Indeed there was a requirement to wear company uniform.

[22] And see *Rogers v Night Riders* [1983] RTR 324, discussed by McKendrick, n. 3 above, 775.
[23] *Vabu*, n. 8 above, 56.

The issue of the proper extent of the employer's responsibility for those that work for it has troubled the Australian courts in a number of other recent cases. In *Northern Sandblasting v Harris* McHugh J referred to the arguments put forward by Atiyah[24] suggesting that responsibility should extend to the activities of independent contractors and took the view that they were, and are, convincing.[25] In the same decision Kirby J flagged up the following factors as pointing to the need for the question to be re-examined: 'the rationalisation of past classifications of liability, the growing catalogue of instances of suggested "non-delegable duty", the criticisms voiced about the lack of a coherent theory, the retreat from the control test as an adequate explanation of the differentiation between employees and independent contractors and changing social conditions by which tasks formerly performed by employees are increasingly performed by contractors'.[26] The view that the Australian courts might be inclined to indulge in radical reform gained support from *Scott v Davis*,[27] where the High Court justified why a principal is vicariously liable for an agent. Such a conclusion was said to promote deterrence in that the principal will have an incentive to provide training, for example. It was also thought that, as between the principal and the injured third party, equity dictated that any loss should fall upon the shoulders of the former. Such considerations were seen as having particularly strong contemporary relevance given that 'the contracting out of work – "outsourcing" – has become common place. Agents in such situations often operate in very competitive markets and work on small margins. Many of them are likely to be tempted to take risks and thereby avoid the inconvenience and expense of procedures that would avoid the occurrence of tortious conduct.'[28] Outsourcing involving contractors rather than agents is just as likely to present such difficulties and the case for imposition of liability is just as compelling.

The case of *Sweeney v Boylan*[29] presented the High Court with the opportunity to adopt Atiyah's analysis. There the claimant went to buy a carton of milk at a convenience store. When she opened the door of the refrigerator in which the milk was kept, the door came off and hit her on the head. She sued the store owners and the company which maintained

[24] Atiyah, n. 1 above, 333–336. [25] (1997) 188 CLR 313. [26] Ibid., 392.
[27] (2000) 74 AJLR 1410. [28] Ibid., 1427.
[29] Note 16 above. And see D. Rolph, 'A Carton of Milk, A Bump to the Head and One Legal Headache: Vicarious Liability in the High Court of Australia' (2006) 19 AJLL 294; and J. Burnett, 'Avoiding Difficult Questions: Vicarious Liability and Independent Contractors' [2007] Syd. L. Rev. 5.

the refrigerator (the respondent). At trial it was held that the respondent was vicariously liable for the negligence of a mechanic it had sent to service the refrigerator on the basis that he was an employee. Before the High Court, in support of the conclusion of the trial judge, the claimant invoked the seeming endorsement of enterprise liability contained in the joint reasons in *Vabu*: 'In general, under contemporary Australian conditions, the conduct by the defendant of an enterprise in which persons are identified as representing that enterprise should carry an obligation to third persons to bear the cost of injury or damage to them which may fairly be said to be characteristic of the conduct of that enterprise.'[30]

The High Court took the view that the mechanic was a contractor and was unwilling to opt for the radical outcome of a finding of vicarious liability. It did not suffice that one could say that the contractor was acting for the benefit of the employer:

> Yet it is clear that the bare fact that the second person's actions were intended to benefit the first or were undertaken to advance some purpose of the first person does not suffice to demonstrate that the first is vicariously liable for the conduct of the second. The whole of the law that has developed on the distinction between employees and independent contractors denies that benefit or advantage to the one will suffice to establish vicarious liability for the conduct of the second.[31]

No explanation is offered as to why this dichotomy exists. In an attempt to render the employer vicariously liable for the activities of the contractor *Colonial Mutual Life* was invoked. The majority viewed that decision in narrow terms and held that it merely established:

> that if an independent contractor is engaged to solicit the bringing about of legal relations between the principal who engages the contractor and third parties, the principal will be held liable for slanders uttered to persuade the third party to make an agreement with the principal. It is a conclusion that depends directly upon the identification of the independent contractor as the principal's agent (properly so called) and the recognition that the conduct of which complaint is made was conduct undertaken in the course of, and for the purpose of, executing that agency.[32]

As has been seen, *Colonial Mutual Life* could have formed the basis for a much more radical reappraisal of the law. It is difficult to see any basis for confining the decision to tortious statements but not acts. It did however inspire Kirby J in the minority. He, whilst holding that

[30] *Sweeney*, n. 16 above, 172. [31] Ibid., 167. [32] Ibid., 170.

the mechanic was not an employee, found that vicarious liability arose on the basis that the mechanic was the representative agent of the party sued, performing that party's functions and advancing its economic interests, effectively as part of its enterprise. Although an independent contractor, the wrongdoer carried out his activities 'representing the person who requests its performance in a transaction with others, so that the very service to be performed consists in standing in [its] place and assuming to act in [its] right and not in an independent capacity'.[33] Kirby J regarded *Colonial Mutual Life* as helpful given the changing patterns of employment and the increasingly extensive reliance by enterprises on contractors. The courts needed to take a wider view of the types of working relationships that could amount to an employment contract so that the doctrine of vicarious liability could function effectively in contemporary society. Kirby J also, as he had done in *Vabu*, took the view that representations by the respondent were material. He noted that the invoice stated that 'Our mechanic is authorised to collect the amount due'. This was regarded as a representation that the mechanic belonged to the employer's enterprise and the employer should not thereafter be allowed to deny responsibility. He may also have been influenced in his dissent by the organisation test (albeit this was not invoked by the claimant).[34] In this regard it should be noted that 'in the insurance claim form, Boylan's officer made it clear that, for the purpose of Boylan's activities, Mr Comninos was integrated into its enterprise. Thus, "We tightened the door screws", "we received a call", "our mechanic went to the Service Station" and the door fell on Mrs Sweeney "after we previously fixed it". There could scarcely have been a clearer contemporaneous indication of the mind and purpose of Boylan and the complete integration of Mr Comninos into its enterprise for this purpose.'[35] Such a conclusion of 'complete integration' seems reasonable when it is appreciated that the mechanic performed work for the respondent on a daily basis and performed the same work as the respondent's employees, carrying out the same activities on its behalf as the respondent's work requirements necessitated. Kirby J was careful to restrict the scope of his judgment:

[33] Ibid., 191.
[34] *Sweeney*, n. 16 above. For discussion of the organisation test in this context see above, p. 78.
[35] *Sweeney*, n. 16 above, 188.

> The result is that an independent contractor, with its own business, cannot generally look to the principal to assume vicarious liability for its wrongs. But if the contractor has been armed with the authority to act as the principal's representative, law and justice sustain the rule in CML that, if sued, the principal will be liable for its representative's wrongs to others acting within the scope of that authority. The mere fact that an independent contractor acted at the request of a principal for the latter's benefit, does not, without more, attract the exception.[36]

Some of the judgments in a number of recent High Court cases have shown a great deal of critical awareness of the difficulties caused by the present law of vicarious liability. In some ways, the High Court was also in a prime position to reform the law given the groundwork that had been done by *Colonial Mutual Life*. All that said, the law in Australia has remained fundamentally the same. Why should this be so? A difficult question to answer, but it seems that the existing law was regarded as too firmly entrenched to be changed other than by the legislature. Of late the High Court has said in *Leighton Contractors v Fox* that 'whatever the logical and doctrinal imperfections and difficulties in the origins of the law relating to vicarious liability, the concept of distinguishing between independent contractors and employees is one too deeply rooted to be pulled out'.[37] The High Court has shown a strong awareness of changes in working arrangements but, rather than prompting radical reform, this merely encouraged a purposive approach to the conventional tests on classification of working relationships to make a finding of employment more likely when vicarious liability was in issue.

Canada

In Canada the case of *Ontario Ltd v Sagaz Industries Canada*[38] gave the Supreme Court the opportunity to decide that the employer should be vicariously liable. A degree of willingness to depart from the orthodox position was displayed. It was said that the categories of relationship that attract vicarious liability were not closed but, on the fundamental issue before the court, a conservative stance was taken. The lack of control over a contractor was seen as significant:

> This basis for vicarious liability discloses a precise limitation on the scope of the doctrine. If the employer does not control the activities of the worker it is clear that vicarious liability should not be imposed, for then

[36] Ibid., 190–1. [37] [2009] HCA 35, para. 22. [38] [2001] 2 SCR 983.

> insulated risk-taking [by the employer] does not occur. Only the worker, authorized to complete a task, could have affected the probability of loss, for he alone had control in any respect. Thus, because there is no mischief where employer control is absent, no remedy is required.[39]

The assumption made is that, in the case of the employee, the control possessed by the employer allows negligent behaviour to be deterred. As a result one of the fundamental aims of the law of negligence is fulfilled. This view seems resonant of the old-fashioned assumptions about control that used to be made in common law cases on the classification of working relationships. There the limitations of a test based upon an employer's right or capacity to control have been well documented and make abundantly clear that employers frequently lack, at least in fact, control over their employees.[40] Cases involving skilled employees often demonstrate this: '... persons possessed of a high degree of professional skill and expertise ... may nevertheless be employed as servants under contracts of service, notwithstanding that their employers can, in the nature of things, exercise extremely little, if any, control over the way in which such skill is used'.[41] However, it is also important to stress that

[39] Ibid., 999.

[40] A seminal critique of the control test was put forward by Kahn-Freund over fifty years ago in the *Modern Law Review*: 'The traditional test [of a contract of service] was that a person working for another was regarded as a servant if he was "subject to the command of the master as to the manner in which he shall do his work" but if the so-called "master" was only in a position to determine the "what" and not the "how" of the services, the substance of the obligation but not the manner of its performance then the person doing the work was said to be not a servant but an independent contractor, and his contract one for work and labour and not of employment. This distinction was based upon the social conditions of an earlier age: it assumed that the employer of labour was able to direct and instruct the labourer as to the technical methods he should use in performing his work ... The technical and economic developments of all industrial societies have nullified these assumptions. The rule respondeat superior ... applies even though the work which the servant is employed to do is of a skilful or technical character, as to the method of performing which the employer himself is ignorant. To say of the captain of a ship, the pilot of an aeroplane, the driver of a railway engine ... that the "employer" controls the performance of his work is unrealistic and almost grotesque. But one need not think of situations in which the employee is physically removed from his employer's premises: a skilled engineer or a toolmaker, draftsman or accountant may as often as not have been engaged just because he possesses that technical knowledge which the employer lacks. If in such a case the employee relied on the employer's instructions "how to do his work" he would be breaking his contract ... No wonder that the Courts found it increasingly difficult to cope with the cases before them by using a legal rule which, as legal rules so often do, had survived the social conditions from which it had been an abstraction.' (O. Kahn-Freund, 'Servants and Independent Contractors' (1951) 14 MLR 504, 505.)

[41] *Whittaker v Minister of Pensions* [1966] 3 All ER 531, 537.

even where the right of control (or its existence as a matter of fact) is present that is perfectly consistent with the contract in question being one for services. The mirror image of control of the employee might be thought to be the freedom and discretion of the self-employed worker, but this can be heavily restricted without affecting the classification of the contract: 'there may be cases when one who engages another to do work may reserve to himself full control over how the work is to be done, but nevertheless the contract is not a contract of service'.[42] Control, as a means of distinguishing employment from self-employment, is doubly fallible. Its absence is consistent with the existence of a contract of employment and its presence with self-employment. Control would seem equally flawed as a means of justifying the current position on vicarious liability. One may well ask, for example, why the presence of control over a self-employed worker should not point to vicarious liability arising.

Surprisingly, in the wake of *Bazley*, limited reference is made to enterprise liability by the court in *Sagaz*. Admittedly it is said that: 'Vicarious liability is fair in principle because the hazards of the business should be borne by the business itself; thus, it does not make sense to anchor liability on an employer for acts of an independent contractor, someone who was in business on his or her own account.'[43] On this analysis enterprise liability does not point to vicarious liability because a contractor is not viewed as part of the enterprise. This is a major assumption to make and the reasoning is entirely circular. What of an enterprise which is heavily dependent on the performance of contractors? This question will be returned to later in the chapter. It also must be said that deterrence appears to be seen as the dominant policy concern. It is striking that, so shortly after *Bazley*, *Sagaz* engages in a re-ordering of the relevant policy concerns. More recently the Canadian Supreme Court has again denied, in *KLB v British Columbia*, that enterprise liability renders the employer vicariously liable for the acts of contractors: 'Compensation will not be fair where the organization fixed with responsibility for the tort is too remote from the tortfeasor for the latter to be acting on behalf of it: in such a case, the tort cannot reasonably be regarded as a materialization of the organization's own risks.'[44]

[42] *Market Investigations v Minister of Social Security* [1969] 2 QB 173, 183.

[43] *Sagaz*, n. 38 above.

[44] [2003] 2 SCR 403, 418. In *KLB* it was also said, at 418, that 'vicarious liability will have no deterrent effect where the tortfeasor is too independent for the organization to be able to take any measures to prevent such conduct'. Equally there will be numerous occasions where such independence is lacking.

The suggestion that such an extension would be inequitable is surprising. It appears to be based on the notion that the contractor's involvement is too 'remote'. The same, of course, could be said of employees on the occasions where their behaviour is not closely connected to their employment. Where, at the time the accident occurs, the contractor can be said to be engaged in the conduct of the enterprise, it is surely arguable that the requisite linkage exists and liability can be justified on the basis of enterprise liability. One cannot automatically deny responsibility for contractors on the basis of remoteness.[45]

In *Sagaz* it was noted that the categories of relationship which give rise to vicarious liability are not closed and, in the subsequent case of *KLB v British Columbia*, the Supreme Court considered the position of foster parents. *KLB* raised the issue of whether the government could be held liable when children are abused by their foster parents in the government-administered foster care system. Arbour J, in the minority, noted that the law sets out two requirements for the imposition of vicarious liability so as to ensure that such liability is imposed in order to further its policy objectives. First, the relationship between the tortfeasor and the principal must be sufficiently close that the tortfeasor's activities can properly be regarded as a part of the principal's enterprise. Second, the wrongful act must be sufficiently connected to the tortfeasor's assigned tasks that it can fairly be said that the principal is the one who created the risk of harm. It is said that each of these requirements helps ensure that people are only held liable for risks that they introduce into the community and that vicarious liability is imposed in circumstances where there is a real possibility for the defendant to take effective measures to deter harm. It is, of course, the first of those requirements that is most pertinent to the present discussion. In dealing with this Arbour J thought that the key question was whether the foster parents could be said to be acting on behalf of the government; as with determining whether a contract of employment existed the issue of control was said to be highly significant in deciding if this was the case. On the facts in *KLB* Arbour J took the view that the government had sufficient power of control over the foster parents' activities to justify a finding of vicarious liability. Such a conclusion could be said to promote deterrence. The majority took the view that the discharge of a foster parent's responsibilities took place in a highly

[45] Atiyah (n. 1 above, 333) has argued that the imposition of liability for independent contractors would encourage 'employers to seek out and contract with financially responsible contractors who can meet any damages awarded against them (or indemnify the employer against liabilities imposed on him) and this is in the public interest'.

independent manner, free from close government control and that the imposition of vicarious liability was inappropriate. A decision on the position of foster parents may seem very far removed from the concerns of the present work. Nevertheless the fact that the claim went all the way to the Supreme Court strongly confirms that, in Canada at least, the law on vicarious liability may evolve to encompass a broader range of relationships. In particular, the approach of the minority demonstrates the extent to which the driver of enterprise liability is challenging traditional assumptions over vicarious liability.[46] Asking the question whether the relationship between the tortfeasor and the principal is sufficiently close that the tortfeasor's activities can properly be regarded as a part of the defendant's enterprise might, were it not for longstanding tradition, point to vicarious liability for a contractor arising. The focus on control (by both the majority and minority) would also point to some employer/contractor relationships being caught.

Canadian willingness to stretch the boundaries might be thought to be further demonstrated by *Lewis v British Columbia*.[47] *Lewis* demonstrates that, depending upon the circumstances, the courts may impose liability on the employer without resorting to vicarious liability. The case concerned whether the defendant was responsible for the negligent behaviour of an independent contractor. The state was aware that a rockface bordering a highway required scaling to prevent rocks falling on the highway. The Ministry of Transportation and Highways engaged a contractor to perform the work. The work was done negligently and rocks which should have been scaled or removed remained on the rockface. Unfortunately one of those rocks fell and killed someone driving on the highway. The sole issue for the Supreme Court was whether by engaging an independent contractor to do the work, the

[46] The New Zealand decision in *S v AG* [2003] NZCA 149 is in a similar vein. The majority took the view that the State was vicariously liable for the behaviour of foster parents on the basis that they were agents of the State. Tipping J agreed with the outcome but regarded the relationship as sui generis: "I do not regard it as either necessary or desirable to seek to characterise the relationship in terms of existing categories where vicarious liability arises, such as that of principal and agent. When the law encounters a relationship which does not fall naturally into one of the traditional categories which attract vicarious liability (primarily agency and employment), the best course in my view is to determine, as a matter of policy and analogy, whether vicarious liability should be found to exist. If so, one party to the relationship becomes bound to compensate the person injured by the misconduct of the other party. If, as here, the relationship arises in a statutory setting, the relevant policies and purposes of the statute may well have an important bearing on the vicarious liability question."

[47] [1997] 3 SCR 1145.

respondent was absolved from liability. One of the situations in which a non-delegable duty will arise is where a party owes a strict statutory duty. The case turned on the interpretation to be given to the relevant statutory provisions. Section 33(1) of the Highway Act stated that the Ministry is vested with the 'control of the construction and maintenance of every arterial highway'. Section 48 of the Ministry of Transportation and Highways Act provided that the Minister '*shall* direct the construction, maintenance and repair' of all highways (emphasis added). Section 14 of the same Act provided that the Minister has the 'management, charge and direction of all matters relating to the acquisition, construction, repair, maintenance, alteration, improvement and operation' of highways. The view was taken that these provisions gave rise to an absolute duty: 'These sections clearly indicate that the Ministry has the management and direction of all matters relating to construction, repair and maintenance of the highways and must direct those operations.'[48] The author would doubt whether this conclusion could be justified, at least in so far as repair was concerned. Whilst the legislation clearly imposed obligations in respect of management and direction there is nothing in the wording of the provisions to suggest that those obligations cannot be fulfilled by the taking of reasonable care. In a minority opinion, concurring as to the result, McLachlin J observed that the wording of section 48 was 'also consistent with a basic direction that works be undertaken'.[49] A number of policy reasons were seen by the majority as supportive of the approach to statutory construction. The author would suggest that they may have been much more determinative. The degree of control appears to have been highly relevant: 'the Ministry specifically retained control over the direction of Cerka's scaling work. Excerpts from the tender document executed by Cerka and the Ministry show that the Ministry retained full control over the designation of the areas to be trimmed, the type of equipment to be used and the specifications of various technical aspects of the project.'[50] Control of this nature is by no means uncommon in employer/employee relationships. The conclusion was said to reflect the legitimate expectations of road users:

> it seems both logical and reasonable to assume that members of the travelling public would look to the respondent to take reasonable care in the construction and maintenance of the provincial highways. It can be reasonably assumed that those who travel provincial highways have a reasonable expectation that the province will be responsible for the

[48] Ibid., 1160. [49] Ibid., 1173. [50] Ibid., 1162.

> negligent acts of its employees or independent contractors which occur in the course of repairing and maintaining those highways.[51]

This, though, raises the question of whether it was legitimate to hold such an expectation. The author would suggest that the requirement of legitimacy is only met on the assumption that the contractor can be regarded as constituting part of the defender's undertaking.[52] It is otherwise difficult to see what distinguishes this situation from many that may arise in the private sector. Take the case of a major construction project being carried out by a large building company which delegates some of the work to independent contractors. The general public will (the specialism of the contractor notwithstanding) presumably rely upon the former, not the latter.

Conclusions

It may be argued that the present exclusion from the scope of vicarious liability is justified because 'it is the contractor itself which is best able to prevent the risks incidental to it and absorb such losses as they occur'.[53] As a result, tort's goals of deterrence and loss distribution are thereby promoted. Clearly this view represents a generalisation, the overall validity of which could only be tested empirically.[54] However, it is clear

51 Ibid., 1165.

52 Reliance on the public body was also said to be reasonable (*Lewis*, n. 47 above, 1165): 'the vast majority of highway travellers are in no position to assess the extent or nature of the construction and maintenance work which should be done, the competence of those undertaking the work or the financial responsibility of any independent contractor performing the work. Their lack of knowledge and very natural tendency to rely upon the Ministry in these matters indicate the potential vulnerability of highway travellers when maintenance work is done negligently. They should be entitled to rely upon and to look to the respondent as the entity responsible for taking reasonable care in carrying out the repairs and maintenance of the roads. The Ministry is in complete control of repair and maintenance and travellers are dependent upon the Ministry for the reasonable performance of the work. In those circumstances, I can see no reasons why the respondent should not be responsible for the negligent acts of independent contractors it engages.'

53 J. Fleming, *The Law of Torts*, 9th edn (North Ryde, NSW: LBC Information Services, 1998), p. 433.

54 It may be argued that this points to a regime of joint liability with the question of risk distribution delegated to the parties. McHugh, n. 2 above, states at 675 that: 'The party who can avoid the risk or insure against possible liability at the lowest cost would become the indemnitor and the other party the indemnitee. Since the relative abilities of the parties may differ according to the type of risk involved, the agreement could assign some liabilities to the employer while reserving some to the contractor . . . Because indemnification by private bargain would more regularly place liability on the better risk

that there will, without doubt, be occasions where it does not hold good: 'neither the independent contractor nor his employer is the inherently superior risk distributor, since either party usually can, with equal facility, contract with an insurance company, which is, of course, highly effective in distributing such risks'.[55] The organisation of work on construction sites would provide a fruitful source of examples illustrating the complexity of the situation. The principal contractor may rely on the services of a wide range of individuals and corporate entities. In the case of employees it is clear the employer will almost certainly be in a better position to absorb any losses. Where contractors are concerned their economic position relative to that of the employer will vary greatly.[56] It is generally assumed that it is cheaper for the employer to insure.[57] Such assumptions may be unwarranted:

> many independent contractors are in at least as good a position to meet a verdict for their own wrongs (and those of their employees) as the principal may be. Without convincing economic data, it would be difficult for this Court to draw any inferences as to the overall danger to plaintiffs of leaving liability to fall on the independent contractors engaged by roads authorities to perform road maintenance and repairs. In the typical case, as here, it would appear that both the roads authority and the contractor would normally be in an equal position to meet any verdict.[58]

This indicates that recourse to considerations of loss distribution (without the benefit of empirical evidence) is of limited assistance in formulating any general rule. The same might be said about deterrence.

administrator than any indemnification imposed by rule of law, joint liability supplemented by private agreement is preferable to a rule comparable to *respondeat superior*.'

55 McHugh, n. 2 above, 672.

56 Atiyah, n. 1 above, observed at 333 that 'this form of liability is only likely to be of real importance where the contractor is unable to meet the damages, or where the contractor cannot be traced, or where it is not clear which of several contractors may have been responsible'. It might be thought that, given the changes in working practices since the time he wrote, the issue has assumed considerably more importance.

57 G. Calabresi, 'The Decision for Accidents: An Approach to Nonfault Allocation of Costs' (1964–5) 78 Harv. L.R. 713, 742.

58 *Leichhardt Municipal Council v Montgomery* (2007) ALJR 686, 712. McHugh, n. 2 above, states at 673 that 'the independent contractor sometimes has a higher exposure to the risk against which insurance is procured, since he engages regularly in the procedure generating the risk. He may, therefore, be able to procure insurance at lower costs, since he would have to negotiate with the company only once to cover a multitude of transactions. But neither employers nor contractors are as a class preferred insurers. A large employer may engage in a risk engendering activity more often than a small contractor whom he hires to perform part of the work. Thus, while the cheap insurer is the preferable party to bear liability, no single rule of liability can identify this party in every case.'

It will often be the case that management and control of the venture will lie in the hands of the employer, irrespective of the status of those conducting the work. When regard is had to the ultimate rationale of *Bazley* it becomes apparent that contemporary judicial policy requires that responsibility should be borne, by the employer, for the risks inherent in the conduct of the enterprise. Logically this would extend to contractors as long as they could be said, at the material time, to constitute part of the enterprise.

The pursuit of any particular activity may require the services not just of an entity's own employees but also those who contract on a different basis. The various contractual arrangements for the provision of work are, of course, simply different elements of the employer's strategy for achieving its goals. Whatever those goals might be they could not be attained, and the enterprise could not realise its profit, without the services of all concerned. Viewed from a perspective of functional necessity the subcontractor, for example, is just as much a part of the enterprise as the employee. Indeed on occasion the subcontractor's role will contribute more than the employee's to the accomplishment of the employer's objectives. As has been seen, such a functional analysis has been adopted by the House of Lords for the purposes of section 3(1) of the Health and Safety at Work Act 1974.

If one accepts that a law of vicarious liability, rationalised on the basis of enterprise liability, entails as a matter of logic that an employer's liability extends to contractors, a number of issues arise. In his 1956 article, Glanville Williams defines an independent contractor as any person, other than an employee, who is employed to do work.[59] It is, of course, the case that services may also be provided to an employer by corporate bodies. I would suggest that this should not act as a barrier to a finding of vicarious liability. It is worth noting that, in *Octel*, the contractor was a limited company. Indeed, on occasion, the employer and contractor may be viewed as, in substance, constituting part of the same enterprise: 'a firm can operate through numerous corporate entities, corresponding perhaps to different aspects of production, establishing a group of companies managing an economically integrated enterprise'.[60] In any event, enterprise liability would dictate that the employer be rendered liable. It benefits from the activities in

[59] G. Williams, 'Liability for Independent Contractors' (1956) CLJ 180.

[60] H. Collins, 'Ascription of Legal Responsibility to Groups in Complex Patterns of Economic Integration' (1990) 53 MLR 731, 736.

the same way as it would if an individual had been engaged. Responsibility for risk management also remains.[61]

The employer is, of course, not vicariously liable for everything that the employee does but merely for acts performed in the course of employment. It is clear that any expansion of responsibility for the behaviour of contractors should be similarly restricted.[62] It is noteworthy that in *KLB*, in the context of a judgment advocating the expansion of liability, Arbour J said that the wrongful act must be sufficiently connected to the tortfeasor's assigned tasks that it can fairly be said that the defendant is the one who created the risk of harm. The House of Lords in *Octel* made clear, in the context of statutory liability, that not everything done for the employer will be regarded as falling within the conduct of its undertaking. Repair or maintenance work carried out elsewhere would be likely to fall outwith such conduct: 'If he has a repair shop as a part of his plant, that is an ancillary part of his undertaking. Likewise, as in this case, if he has independent contractors to do cleaning or repairs on his own premises, as an activity integrated with the general conduct of his business. But not in the case of activities carried on by another person entirely separately from his own.'[63] The question was said to be one of fact though the place where the activity takes place was regarded as being of particular importance.

[61] A consequence of holding that the employer may be vicariously liable for the behaviour of a corporate body may be to spawn litigation. At present an employer found vicariously liable is entitled to recover against the employee responsible but, in practice, is unlikely to do so. Matters would be different were the employer to be vicariously liable for independent contractors who would often be in a position to meet a claim.

[62] A further ground of exception should be the case of the domestic/consumer contract.

[63] *Octel*, n. 17 above, 978.

8

Transferring the burden: the employer's right of indemnity

The manner in which risk is allocated by the contract of employment will obviously vary depending upon the express terms in question. However, there is a conventional allocation sanctioned by the standardised implied terms of the employment contract. Unless the parties indicate to the contrary this default position will apply. In all of this a key implied obligation requires the employee to take reasonable care in the performance of his/her duties. At present if the employee breaks that obligation and the employer suffers loss as a result then the employee will be liable in damages. The third party who is injured may also bring an action directly against the employee. The most famous instance of this dimension of the employment relationship is the decision of the House of Lords in *Lister v Romford Ice and Cold Storage.*[1] There the defendant employee injured his father, a fellow employee, in the course of his employment. The father brought an action against the company and recovered damages in respect of the son's negligent act. The employer, in turn, brought an action against the employee claiming that it was entitled to indemnification by way of damages for breach of an implied term that he would use reasonable skill and care in driving. It was held that the driver was under a contractual obligation of care to his employers in the performance of his duty as a driver and that the company was entitled to recover damages. It was also held that there was no implied term that the driver was entitled to be indemnified by the employer, even if the company was in fact insured or was required by the road traffic legislation to be insured. The argument that there was an implied term in favour of the employee in respect of indemnification had appealed to some:

> Take this very case ... where the insurers issue a writ in the employer's name against the servant without consulting either the employer or the servant beforehand. When the servant receives the writ he will take it to his employer and say 'Why are you suing me? Surely you have got the

[1] [1957] AC 555.

> money from your insurance company. So you cannot sue me.' This natural comment between master and man throws a flood of light on the implied understanding of the parties.[2]

Lister was a very controversial decision. The UK insurance industry was swift to react and circumvent it:

> as long ago as 1953 certain members of the British Insurance Association engaged in the employers' liability market entered into a "gentleman's agreement" under which they undertook that claims would not be instituted against the employees of an insured employer in respect of damages paid to a fellow employee without the prior consent of the employer. The only exception made to this agreement is where it transpires that there has been collusion or *wilful* misconduct by an employee.[3]

A powerful critique was put forward by Denning LJ in the course of his dissent in the Court of Appeal; his analysis was in part based on an enterprise risk perspective: 'The risk should be borne by the undertaking as a whole rather than by the servant who happens to make a mistake, especially when he is working his master's machine. The master takes the profits from using the machine and should bear the responsibility for the damage it does, even though the damage would not happen without some human error.'[4] The tendentious nature of *Lister* notwithstanding, it was followed in Australia[5] and Canada[6] and, moreover, remains good law in both jurisdictions.

Judicial critique

Judicial criticism of *Lister* has persisted over the years, both in the UK and elsewhere. Canada and Australia have continued to adhere to *Lister* but, at the same time, it tends to be seen as embodying the values of a bygone age. In *A. R. Griffiths & Sons Pty Ltd v Richards*,[7] Fitzgerald

[2] *Lister v Romford Ice and Cold Storage* [1956] 2 QB 180, 192.

[3] Gardiner G., 'Lister v The Romford Ice and Cold Storage Company Ltd (Report of the Inter-Departmental Committee)' (1959) 22 MLR 652.

[4] [1956] 2 QB 180, 186. In *Morris v Ford Motor Co. Ltd* [1973] QB 792, 798 Lord Denning MR reiterated the point: 'The risks attendant on that work – including liability for negligence – should be borne by the master. The master takes the benefit and should bear the burden. The wages are fixed on that basis. If the servant is to bear the risk, his wages ought to be increased to cover it.'

[5] *McGrath v Fairfield Municipal Council* (1985) 156 CLR 672.

[6] *Overmyer v Wallace Transfer* [1976] 2 WWR 656; *Pinto v BMO Nesbit Burns* (2005) 40 CCEL (3d) 293.

[7] [1996] QCA 417.

P (dissenting) observed that '*Lister* should, in my opinion, now be considered in this State as a decision which related to a different setting, in terms of time, place, social attitudes and legislative context'. The prospect of an implied term benefiting the employee in respect of indemnification has continued to appeal. In *Rowell v Alexander Mackie College of Advanced Education*, Samuels JA was inclined to think that an implied term existed which required the employer to maintain in force an insurance policy covering the employee's liability for loss caused by negligent driving in the course of his employment.[8] The most compelling challenge to *Lister* comes, however, from the Canadian Supreme Court in *London Drugs v Kuehne*.[9] There the claimants had delivered a transformer to the defendants for storage. The contract of storage included the following limitation of liability clause: 'The warehouseman's liability on any one package is limited to $40 unless the holder has declared in writing a valuation in excess of $40 and paid the additional charge specified to cover warehouse liability.' Against this backdrop the claimant chose not to obtain additional insurance from the defendant and instead arranged for its own coverage. Whilst the transformer was in the hands of the defendant two of its employees attempted to move it by lifting it, contrary to safe practice, with two forklift vehicles. In the course of this manoeuvre the transformer toppled over and was damaged. The claimants brought an action against both the employer and the employees.

The careless behaviour that occurred in *London Drugs* is very much the sort of thing that crops up with depressing regularity in industrial life. In the Supreme Court both the majority and minority were anxious that the burden of liability should not be placed upon the shoulders of the employees. The policy reasons prompting this outcome were broadly similar and centred on risk allocation. The plaintiffs had entered into the contract in the knowledge that the defendants would perform their side of the bargain through the services of the employees. It was reasonable to assume that the plaintiffs had consented to limit the warehouseman's liability to $40 for anything that would happen during that performance. The parties would have acted on this allocation of risk and made insurance arrangements accordingly: 'It stretches commercial credulity to suggest that a customer, acting prudently, will not obtain insurance because he or she is looking to the employees for recovery when generally little or nothing is known about the financial capacity and

[8] (1988) 25 IR 87, 90. [9] [1992] 3 SCR 299.

professional skills of the employees involved.'[10] The question then becomes one of explaining why, in law, liability did not arise on the part of the employees even though they had failed to take reasonable care in the performance of their duties.

The majority readily assumed that a duty of care was owed to the claimants and discussion moved swiftly into the realms of contractual doctrine. An outcome favourable to the employees was achieved by forging an exception to the law on privity of contract. The key question was whether they could obtain the benefit of the limitation of liability clause contained in the contract of storage between their employer and the plaintiff. The majority took the view that the employees were protected as they were third-party beneficiaries to the clause and were protected thereby. Such an exception to the normal rules on privity could be made where two requirements were satisfied:

(1) the limitation of liability clause must, either expressly or impliedly, extend its benefit to the employees (or employee) seeking to rely on it; and
(2) the employees (or employee) seeking the benefit of the limitation of liability clause must have been acting in the course of their employment and must have been performing the very services provided for in the contract between their employer and the plaintiff (customer) when the loss occurred.

Given the wording of the contractual provisions, the majority in *London Drugs* were able to arrive at a solution by fashioning an exception to the law on privity. This approach is a narrow one which cannot protect the employee in the absence of such a clause. Much more fundamentally it fails to answer the question whether, as a matter of principle, the employee should be obliged to indemnify. In contrast, in a very powerful minority opinion concurring as to the result, La Forest J focused much more closely on the employee's obligations. He took the view that a duty of care was, in general, owed by employees to third parties where personal injury or property damage arose. Such a conclusion was unremarkable on the basis of *Donoghue v Stevenson*.[11] However, the existence of a duty of care could be denied in *London Drugs* once account was taken of the contractual framework; that framework served to negative the proximity that would otherwise arise between the parties. Where, as in *London Drugs*, the third party and the employer have

[10] Ibid., 445. [11] [1932] AC 562.

entered into a contract, the obligations which arise thereunder help determine the position in tort. La Forest J noted that a 'planned transaction' had arisen between the plaintiffs and employers: 'a transaction in which someone acquires or disposes of property of any kind or services of any kind'.[12] A claimant who had entered into such a transaction would have envisaged that the defendant's employees would carry out the services on the defendant's behalf. Should those services be performed carelessly it is appropriate that the court looks to the matrix of obligations contained in the contract providing for the performance of the services in considering the question of recovery. If this is not done the allocation of risk arrived at, voluntarily, by the parties may be disturbed. Such an approach makes sense as between the commercial parties. In *London Drugs* itself the claimants 'found it advantageous not to require KNI to insure performance. So long as there are no concerns about unconscionability and no overriding social interest protected by tort is involved, this ability of the parties to modify their possible tort and contract liability is an unquestionable advantage. The customer benefits from the ability of the future defendant to contract out of its tort liability.'[13] La Forest J focused on the obligations owed by the employee and the fairness of this position. However, as with the analysis of the majority, his judgment only offers a partial solution. Its capacity to protect the employee is again contingent upon the contractual position between the employer and third party.

La Forest J's judgment involves a detailed review of policy concerns. In his view they dictate that the employer should bear the risk rather than the employee. For him it was important to be clear as to the fundamental role of vicarious liability. It should not be viewed simply as a means of ensuring that an employee's liability to a third party was capable of being discharged. Instead the key was 'the broader function of transferring to the enterprise itself the risks created by the activity performed by its agents'.[14] Thus where third parties are concerned the enterprise should bear the risks arising from its activities; vicarious liability ensures that this occurs. It may be said that it does not automatically follow that risk be allocated between employer and employee in quite the same way. Nevertheless La Forest J argued that risk-shifting

12 J. Blom, 'Fictions and Frictions on the Interface Between Tort and Contract' in Paisley Conference on the Law of Negligence, *Donoghue v Stevenson and the Modern Law of Negligence* (Vancouver: Continuing Legal Education Society of British Columbia, 1991), p. 139 at p. 159.

13 *London Drugs*, n. 9 above, 351.

14 *London Drugs*, n. 9 above, 339.

to the employee is inappropriate, partly because as a matter of practical reality most employees are unlikely to be able to meet losses that may arise. Certain types of employment are particularly fraught with risk: 'in these days of increasingly complex technology, employees are required to handle ever more sophisticated machinery. Minor employee error can result in major equipment breakdown and, consequently significant damages.'[15] Were employees to be obliged to indemnify on a more regular basis they would be obliged to insure. This would be economically inefficient: 'The employer will almost always be insured against the risk of being held liable to third parties by reason of his vicarious liability: the cost of such liability is thus internalized to the profitable activity that gives rise to it. There is no requirement for double insurance, covering both the employee and his employer against the same risk.'[16] In *Lister* the view had been taken that an indemnity would go against a fundamental aim of the law of tort that careless behaviour be deterred.[17] Standard management tools such as discipline and dismissal were seen by La Forest J as being far more effective than the remote possibility of legal action by a third party. Indeed the introduction of even more sophisticated management techniques could be envisaged: 'the employer is free to establish contractual schemes of contribution from negligent employees as an element in the employer's campaign to reduce accidents. The amounts could be better calibrated on the extent of the employee's fault and the real deterrent effect would be greater.'[18]

The foregoing analysis is premised upon the belief that the enterprise whose activities give rise to the risk should bear responsibility. It is wholly understandable that an enterprise may wish to shift that risk through contractual provision such as a contract of indemnity. Such an

[15] *Douglas v Kinger* 2008 ONCA 452, para. 58. [16] *London Drugs*, n. 9 above, 341.

[17] In *Lister*, n. 2 above, 579 the following was stated: 'It was contended, too, that a term should not be implied by law of which the social consequences would be harmful. The common law demands that the servant should exercise his proper skill and care in the performance of his duty: the graver the consequences of any dereliction, the more important it is that the sanction which the law imposes should be maintained. That sanction is that he should be liable in damages to his master: other sanctions there may be, dismissal perhaps and loss of character and difficulty of getting fresh employment, but an action for damages, whether for tort or for breach of contract, has, even if rarely used, for centuries been available to the master, and now to grant the servant immunity from such an action would tend to create a feeling of irresponsibility in a class of persons from whom, perhaps more than any other, constant vigilance is owed to the community.'

[18] *London Drugs*, n. 9 above, 341.

aim is perfectly compatible with enterprise liability and indeed may (the contract of insurance comes to mind at this juncture) be a means of ensuring that the enterprise can meet its responsibilities. However, in the context of this book, the pertinent question is whether the contract of employment is a vehicle which should be used for risk-shifting. It has been judicially observed that the reasons for imposing vicarious liability involve the relationship between a business and an injured third party; they do not address the relationship between the business and its negligent employee.[19] Recovery against the employee is often regarded as inappropriate on policy grounds. First, it is said to be a matter of sound resource allocation that the burden remain with the employer. Certainly the employee will, far more often than not, be unable to meet the cost of an award of damages. Secondly, it is said that a right of indemnity may result in double insurance being taken out.[20] Clearly this would be economically inefficient. It may also be the case that it is cheaper for the employer to take out insurance.[21] There is much merit in this position though a word of caution is called for. The policy arguments advanced may not be universally applicable and, in any event, can ultimately only be validated empirically. In *London Drugs* La Forest J also suggests that recovery against the employee is inconsistent with the equitable demands of enterprise liability. Why would it be unfair for the employer to go against the errant employee? The policy arguments derived from the law on vicarious liability are focused on how relations between the employer and the injured third party ought to be regulated. When the position between employer and employee is in issue it cannot be assumed that those arguments are equally relevant. The author would suggest that it cannot be determined whether the employee's obligation is inappropriate without having regard to the content of the contract as a whole. If we wish to maintain that a right of indemnity is inequitable we must look more closely at the bargain struck by employer and employee. When this is done it becomes apparent that the imposition of an obligation of indemnity on the part of the employee is at odds with the nature of the employment contract. The author would suggest that if it were truly inherent in an employment contract that a right of

[19] *Douglas*, n. 15 above.

[20] In *London Drugs*, n. 9 above, La Forest J added that removal of the right of recovery would ensure that loss distribution occurs through the conduit of the employer's enterprise by means of liability insurance or higher prices.

[21] N. Siebrasse, 'Third-Party Beneficiaries in the Supreme Court: Categorisation and the Interpretation of Ambiguous Contracts' (1995) 45 UTLJ 47, 65.

indemnity existed one would expect that the provisions in the contract which deal with reward would be formulated much more on the basis of a sharing of gross profits (thereby allowing for the sharing of losses). There would be a much closer resemblance to a contract of partnership. However, the employment contract is not structured in this way, wages being given in return for work done (or possibly being available for work).[22] The common law assumes that the employee's reward is a fixed sum and is determined neither by the amount of gains nor losses.[23] Of course, by virtue of the express terms, the remuneration package may include an element of profit-sharing, but implied terms in law are formulated on the basis of what is seen as inherent in a relationship of a particular type. Where the employment contract is concerned there is no expectation of such an element being present. A relationship which is not predicated upon the sharing of profits is unlikely to assume that the burden of loss should be treated differently. It would seem surprising if a position to the contrary was contemplated by the parties. After all, given the infrequency with which employers seek recovery against employees, it cannot be said that wages are set to allow for the possibility that a deduction will be made.

The way in which the various implied obligations interact is also highly relevant. At the time of *Lister* the importance of the duty of co-operation to the law of the employment contract was not fully appreciated. However, it is now clear that the employer should not place the employee in a position where they cannot, in practical terms, meet their obligations.[24] Such an outcome would be inevitable should liability to indemnify arise in the absence of insurance cover. When account is taken of the duty of co-operation the continued existence of a right of indemnity seems particularly incongruous. After all, it is highly unlikely that employees will hold insurance cover. It is conceivable that a term might be implied to require the employee to do so but the author would suggest that both sides to the employment relationship would be greatly surprised at any such suggestion. It would be unconscionable (at least in

[22] See D. Brodie, *The Employment Contract: Legal Principles, Drafting, and Interpretation* (Oxford University Press, 2005), Ch. 6; and C. Sappideen, P. O'Grady and G. Warburton, *Macken's Law of Employment*, 6th edn (Sydney: Lawbook Co., 2009), Ch. 5.

[23] It is pointed out by P. S. Atiyah, *Vicarious Liability in the Law of Torts* (London: Butterworths, 1967), p. 18, many years ago, that 'if a company makes very large profits in any one year ... the company may indeed be faced with demands for increased wages in the following year, but the fact remains that the surplus profit earned by the company during that year goes to the ordinary shareholders'.

[24] B. A. Hepple, *Employment Law*, 4th edn (London: Sweet & Maxwell, 1981), pp. 134–5.

the absence of provisions as to profit-sharing) to take advantage of the inequality of bargaining power inherent in employment relations and transfer the burden of the cost of insurance to the employee.

Consideration of the structure of the employment contract confirms La Forest J's view that it is inequitable that a right of indemnity arises. It is also the case that there is a further problem where the loss suffered is purely economic and the employee continues to be under an obligation to take reasonable care to protect the employer's interest. In stark contrast the employer is not under a duty to protect the employee from suffering such loss. This appears to be the case in the UK, Canada and Australia. The position is well illustrated by *Reid v Rush and Tompkins*[25] where the plaintiff suffered injury abroad whilst in the course of his employment. The plaintiff was employed by the defendant as a quarry foreman in Ethiopia, a territory in which there was neither compulsory third-party motor insurance nor any scheme for compensating persons injured in accidents caused by the negligence of uninsured or untraced drivers. Whilst driving in Ethiopia in the course of his employment the plaintiff suffered severe injuries in a collision caused solely by the negligence of the driver of the other vehicle, whose identity was not known. Having been unable to recover any compensation for his injuries, the plaintiff brought an action against the defendant for damages in respect of the economic loss which he had suffered in being unable to recover such compensation. He alleged that his employers were in breach of their duty of care in failing either to insure him or to advise him to obtain such insurance cover for himself. It was held that there was no breach of duty on the employer's part. The case for implication was surely strong. In so far as the obligation was one to provide advice the employer was surely in a far better position to obtain accurate information:

> A company which recruits a man in this country to work upon a large project in Ethiopia should, it was argued, be treated as assuming responsibility to use proper care in telling such a man what he needs to know about conditions in that country in order to make a properly informed decision whether to take the job and, if he decides to take it, whether there are many steps which he needs to take for his own protection. A man who takes that employment, and who goes out to do the work in Ethiopia, should, in the absence of evidence to the contrary, be treated as impliedly relying upon the employer for having told him what he needed to know.[26]

[25] [1989] IRLR 265. [26] *Reid*, n. 25 above, 269.

The employee's case would seem particularly strong where, as was presumably the case here, the employer possessed information that the employee could not reasonably be expected to be aware of and where release of that information would protect the employee's interests. The position in respect of provision of insurance cover is less straightforward. The employer's position in *Reid* may be defended on the basis that there is no general obligation in the UK that the employer provide insurance cover for risks not caused by the fault of the employer or fellow employees. The broader question becomes one of deciding whether that is just. The answer is arguably no. The risk is run for the benefit of the employer and the employer should pay. In situations where the taking of reasonable care fails to protect the employee because the accident is caused by a third party, what then? The absence of accident cover will be devastating for the economic wellbeing of the employee but, at least in the UK, the statutory framework may act as a barrier to further common law development:

> The legislation has not in general extended even the duty of compulsory employer's liability insurance in respect of employment out of this country. It has not been suggested that the master is required to provide personal accident insurance in those cases where in this country his servant is exposed to the risk of suffering injury in the course of his employment through the fault of a third party who cannot pay. The common law cannot in my judgment devise such a duty which the legislature has not thought fit to impose and it could not be just or reasonable for the court to impose it.[27]

As has been seen, the employer is not under a duty of care to protect the employee from suffering pure economic loss – even where that loss is a consequence of physical injury arising in the course of employment (as was the case in *Reid*). By way of contrast the careless employee will undoubtedly be liable in damages for economic losses caused through incompetent performance. In *Janata Bank v Ahmed*,[28] for example, a manager of a bank was found liable in damages as a result of not taking reasonable care over the granting of credit. *Malik v BCCI*[29] also strongly suggests that where the employee's loss arises through the employer's incompetent running of the business then recovery will still not take place. The decision of the Lords permitted the plaintiffs to proceed in trying to show that the corrupt running of the business had stigmatised them and caused them loss.[30] However, had the allegations been that incompetent

[27] Ibid., 273. [28] [1981] IRLR 429. [29] [1998] AC 20.
[30] Subsequently they failed in this: *BCCI v Ali (No. 3)* [1999] IRLR 508.

running of the business had led to the workers being stigmatised then they would have been regarded as irrelevant. By running a business badly an employer does not breach the obligation of mutual trust and confidence:[31]

> there are many circumstances in which an employee's reputation may suffer from his having been associated with an unsuccessful business, or an unsuccessful department within a business. In the ordinary way this will not found a claim of the nature made in the present case, even if the business or department was run with gross incompetence. A key feature in the present case is the assumed fact that the business was dishonest or corrupt.[32]

In *Malik* recoverable reputation damages are based on the premise that employees take the risk of being associated with a badly run business but not with a corrupt one. Should the employer be in breach of the employment contract by running the business incompetently? If the answer is no then the employee should not be liable if a failure to take reasonable care leads to purely economic loss.

Solutions

As has been seen *Lister*, and the employer's right of indemnity, remain good law. One solution, on occasion, is for the employee to take advantage of the protection devices offered by the common law. Where negligent misrepresentation is concerned, Lord Reid, in the seminal case of *Hedley Byrne v Heller*, stated the following:

> A reasonable man, knowing that he was being trusted or that his skill and judgment were being relied on, would, I think, have three courses open to him. He could keep silent or decline to give the information or advice sought; or he could give an answer with a clear qualification that he accepted no responsibility for it or that it was given without that reflection or inquiry which a careful answer would require; or he could simply answer without any such qualification. If he chooses to adopt the last course he must, I think, be held to have accepted some responsibility for his answer being given carefully, or to have accepted a relationship with the inquirer which requires him to exercise such care as the circumstances require.[33]

In *Northwestern Mutual Insurance v O'Bryan* the British Columbia Court of Appeal took the view that the employee concerned (who had

[31] It would presumably not avail a plaintiff employee to plead, in the alternative, that the employer had breached its obligation to take reasonable care.

[32] *Malik*, n. 29 above, 42, per Lord Nicholls. [33] [1964] AC 465, 486.

provided incorrect information concerning the plaintiff's insurance position) could have taken advantage of this advice and, for example, kept silent and declined to provide the information.[34] However, this suggestion is utterly impractical in the case of the employee who is hired to give advice and therefore runs the risk of making a negligent misstatement to a third party: 'one imagines a rather short career for an employee hired to serve the public who kept silent and declined to give information for fear of engaging personal liability in tort'.[35] Indeed where an employee is hired to provide advice but declines to do so a breach of contract will arise.

Judicial disquiet over the existence of the right of indemnity has prompted the emergence of a number of approaches aimed specifically at protecting employees. McNair J distinguished *Lister* in *Harvey v R. G. O'Dell Ltd*[36] and modified the obligation owed to the employer. In *Harvey* the defendant's employee was employed as a storekeeper. On occasion, as a favour to the employer, he used his own motorcycle on its business and was so using it at the time of the accident. The court declined to hold that, by doing so, he should be held in law to have impliedly agreed to indemnify his employer if he committed an act of negligence. McNair J was of the view that *Lister* should be restricted to cases in which the employee is hired to do a particular skilled job and the loss flows from a failure in the doing of that very job. The approach in *Harvey* has been influential elsewhere. In *Overmyer v Wallace Transfer*[37] a majority of the court held that a general manager had failed to exercise his duties with reasonable care and skill and as a consequence he was liable for the loss suffered by his employer. Seaton JA dissenting was content to follow the approach in *Harvey* and was untroubled by the fact that the obligation owed to the employer might be less onerous than that owed to the third party:

> in the event of injury to a stranger it is reasonable that the person who caused that injury ought to bear the loss even if his error be only slight. But the same reasoning is not applicable to the employer-employee situation. If by the slightest error an employee causes loss, that is one of the risks of the enterprise that the employer accepts. No employee is infallible and the employer allows for that. He takes it into account when he insures and when he supervises that employee and when he estimates his costs. Losses due to employee error are one of the expenses of the business.[38]

[34] (1974) 51 DLR (3d) 693. [35] *London Drugs*, n. 9 above, 352.
[36] [1958] 2 QB 78. [37] (1975) 65 DLR (3d) 717. [38] Ibid., 721.

The exception created by *Harvey* is decidedly limited in scope. It only acts to the employee's benefit where injury is caused by the employee acting in a manner which does not relate to the skills for which he/she was hired. It also does not ameliorate the position where a third party brings the action. A more radical way of ensuring that issues of indemnity do not arise is to prevent a duty of care arising in the first place. So far the orthodox view remains as stated by La Forest J in *London Drugs*, namely that the employee owes a duty of care to a third party whose person or property is injured by his/her actions. However, where the giving of advice is concerned, the concepts of assumption of responsibility and reasonable reliance may mean that the employee is not liable personally. The position is illustrated by the decision of the Supreme Court of Canada in *Edgeworth Construction v NDL*[39] where a firm of engineers was held to owe a duty of care in respect of a misrepresentation. The position of the individual engineers was said to be different. The basis upon which they were sued was the fact that each of them had affixed his seal to the design documents. It was held that this did not give rise to a duty of care: 'The seal attests that a qualified engineer prepared the drawing. It is not a guarantee of accuracy. The affixation of a seal, without more, is insufficient to found liability for negligent misrepresentation.'[40] The approach of the majority in *Edgeworth* is a narrow one which offers little in the way of assurance for employees in future cases. A policy decision to utilise the concept of reliance to avoid employees being held personally liable has the potential to provide that assurance. In *Edgeworth* La Forest J justified his decision on the basis of reliance. He was of the view that the claimants relied upon the company and not the employees immediately involved:

> The situation of the individual engineers is quite different. While they may, in one sense, have expected that persons in the position of the appellant would rely on their work, they would expect that the appellant would place reliance on their firm's pocketbook and not theirs for indemnification; see *London Drugs, supra*, at pp. 386–87. Looked at the other way, the appellant could not reasonably rely for indemnification on the individual engineers. It would have to show that it was relying on the particular expertise of an individual engineer without regard to the corporate character of the engineering firm. It would seem quite unrealistic, as my colleague observes, to hold that the mere presence of an individual engineer's seal was sufficient indication of personal reliance (or for that matter voluntary assumption of risk).[41]

[39] [1993] 3 SCR 206. [40] Ibid., 222. [41] Ibid., 212.

The concept of reasonable reliance offers the prospect of a generalised solution in the case of employees providing advice or performing services for a client of their employer. It is not reasonable to rely upon the individual worker to provide indemnification should things go wrong. After all, the client will know that the worker was not party to any discussion over the basis upon which the risk was allocated:

> The employer is being paid to assume the risk of damage to the transformer, but except in the most theoretical sense the employees are not. They are selling their labour, not a form of insurance. The risk of doing \$40,000 worth of damage is imposed on them, but as employees (and here their position would be different from independent contractors) they are badly placed to arrange things financially to cope with that risk. They can get their employer to include them as insureds under its liability policy, but then suing them is indistinguishable from suing the employer; it is the same insurance.[42]

Moreover, it will again be known that the worker is unlikely to be in a position to meet any liability that may arise. An approach based upon reliance will reduce but not eliminate situations where a duty of care is owed by employees. Commentators have argued that, in cases of personal injury, the mere fact of contracting with a corporation will not be taken as an acceptance that only the corporation can be sued. Nevertheless, where relevant its impact would be considerable in cases of, for instance, negligent advice or services. In *Williams v Natural Life*[43] La Forest J's approach was regarded as representing the law in England.

Matters become more complicated where the behaviour of key personnel such as directors is in issue. In *Williams v Natural Life* the principal question for the House of Lords was whether a director of a franchisor company was personally liable to franchisees for loss which they suffered as a result of negligent advice given to them by the franchisor company. The decision turned on whether the director could be said to have assumed responsibility on the basis of the 'extended' *Hedley Byrne* principle. The claim failed. The House of Lords held that there had been no exchanges or conduct which could have conveyed to the claimants that the director had assumed responsibility. Where directors are concerned

[42] Blom, n. 12 above, 161.

[43] [1997] 1 BCLC 131. And see S. Griffin, 'Company Director's Personal Liability in Tort' (1999) 115 LQR 36 and S. Todd, 'Assuming Responsibility for Torts' (2003) 119 LQR 199. *Williams* may not represent the law in Australia: N. Foster, 'Personal Civil Liability of Company Officers for Company Workplace Torts' (2008) 16 TLJ 20.

some would argue that there is a particular need for caution lest the principle of separate legal personality be undermined:

> The law does, however, recognise a category of case in which a director of the representor will be fixed with personal liability for the negligent misstatement. It is a rare category, and a severely restricted one. If that were not so, representees could set at naught the protection which limited liability is designed to confer on those who incorporate their business activities. The mesh is kept fine by the stringency of the question which the law requires to be asked: do the circumstances, when viewed as a whole, involve an assumption by the director of personal responsibility for the impugned statement?[44]

This concern becomes even more acute where the one-person company is concerned. However, the fact that the person incorporating will almost inevitably be the one possessed of the key qualities essential to the functioning of the company does not, of itself, convey that the managing director is willing to be personally answerable to the customers of the company.

The decision in *Williams* suggests that those wishing to find key personnel, such as managing directors, personally liable for negligent advice will face a considerable challenge – a view confirmed by the New Zealand Court of Appeal decision in *Trevor Ivory v Anderson*[45] where Cooke P said that: 'It is not to be doubted that, in relation to an obligation to give careful and skilful advice, the owner of a one-man company may assume personal responsibility ... But it seems to me that something special is required to justify putting a case in that class.' In that case the plaintiffs hired as consultant the first defendant, a one-person company carrying on a business as an agricultural supplier and advisory service. The first defendants, through the second defendant, Mr Ivory (managing director of a one-person company), advised the plaintiffs to use a particular herbicide. This they did with unfortunate consequences. The court acknowledged that a client will often desire the active and extensive involvement of particular staff, but it made clear that it does not follow that this leads to a conclusion of a personal assumption of responsibility. The normal assumption is that the acts of the director are to be treated as the acts of the company and that clear evidence is needed before a conclusion to the contrary is arrived at. In the alternative the adoption of corporate structure can be seen as

44 *Williams*, n. 43 above, 154.

45 [1992] 2 NZLR 517. For critical discussion, see P. Watts, 'The Company's Alter Ego: An Imposter in Private Law' (2000) 116 LQR 525.

performing the same function as an exclusion clause. The question of whether a director has assumed responsibility turns, in the last resort, on the facts of the situation at issue.

In advice/services cases the courts are inclined to approach matters on the basis that reliance is placed on the entity rather than the individual and, in consequence, it is the former that should be liable. It is respectfully submitted that this approach is correct. Reliance on an ordinary employee will rarely if ever be reasonable. The position would be different if there was an express or implied undertaking of responsibility by the employee to the plaintiff. Mere performance of the contract by the employee, without more, is not evidence of the existence of such an undertaking since such performance is required under the terms of the employee's contract with the employer. However, the judicial approach in such cases cannot be regarded as altogether settled. In particular, where directors are concerned the extent of the protection offered by *Williams* is not entirely clear and certainly not without controversy.[46] Moreover, *Williams* notwithstanding, a surveyor who was an employee was found personally liable by the Court of Appeal in *Merrett v Babb*[47] where, his firm having been instructed, he had provided a valuation which he had signed. The firm became insolvent and the claimants looked to the employee to recover the loss suffered. It was argued that his duty was to his employer and that the purchasers should be taken to have relied on the employer, not on him personally. This line of defence was rejected: the defendant was viewed as signing the report in a personal capacity and thereby assumed personal responsibility for it.[48] The court was aware that the employee was uninsured but was not concerned, as this sort of claim would normally be covered by the employer's indemnity insurance. *Babb* is unsatisfactory as it seems clear that the statement was made on behalf of his employer and not in a personal capacity.[49] The decision seems out of line with *Williams*. The case also suggests that the concept of reasonable reliance will only offer employees significant protection if regard is had to policy. If the matter is approached on a purely factual basis the conclusion might well be reached that reliance was placed upon the employee:

[46] S. H. C. Lo, 'Liability of Directors as Joint Tortfeasors' (2009) JBL 109.

[47] [2001] 3 WLR 1. [48] Ibid., 19.

[49] For detailed discussion see J. Edelman and E. McKendrick, 'Employee's Liability for Statements' (2002) 118 LQR 4.

> Were we to have asked Miss Merrett and Mrs Scheppel, when their pens were poised above the contract, upon whom they were relying in their decision to pay £47,500 for the property, their answer would surely have been 'Upon whichever valuer wrote that report'. Had we then explained to them that the professional surveyor and valuer who inspected the property and wrote the report did so as an employee of another professional surveyor with whom the building society had contracted for the supply of the report, I cannot think that the ladies would have wished to amend their answer in any way, other than perhaps to add 'So what?' What reasonably mattered to them, as to Mr and Mrs Harris, was the professional expertise of the man on the ground.[50]

Conclusions

Denning LJ pointed out in *Lister* that losses are inevitable in the conduct of an enterprise and the employer should bear them as well as gain from the profits: 'The risk should be borne by the undertaking as a whole rather than by the servant who happens to make a mistake.'[51] In advocating this position the celebrated judge was very much ahead of his time. In all jurisdictions under discussion *Lister* remains good law but much maligned. In some jurisdictions it has been the subject of legislative intervention. Section 66 of the Insurance Contracts Act 1984 (Australia) provides that where:

> (a) the rights of an insured under a contract of general insurance in respect of a loss are exercisable against a person who is the insured's employee; and
> (b) the conduct of the employee that gave rise to the loss occurred in the course of or arose out of the employment and was not serious or wilful misconduct;
> the insurer does not have the right to be subrogated to the rights of the insured against the employee.

Whilst this approach limits the insurer's right of subrogation it does not prevent the employer suing. However, legislation in New South Wales, South Australia and the Northern Territory has abrogated the right of an employer to claim an indemnity from an employee and has provided to the employee a statutory right of indemnity from the employer.[52]

[50] Ibid., 23.
[51] *Romford Ice and Cold Storage v Lister* [1956] 2 QB 183 (CA), 186, per Denning LJ.
[52] Employees Liability Act 1991 (NSW), s. 3; Wrongs Act 1936 (SA), s. 27C; Law Reform (Miscellaneous Provisions) Act 1956 (NT), s. 22A.

By giving an employee a right to indemnity from the employer, the employee's exposure to liability is removed (except where the employer is insolvent). The employer's liability is not increased as he/she is already vicariously liable for the employee and liability arising from the indemnity would be covered by existing insurance policies for vicarious liability. Again there are limits on the statutory protection. The legislative scheme does not apply to a tort committed by an employee if the conduct constituting the tort: (1) was serious and wilful misconduct; or (2) did not occur in the course of, and did not arise out of, the employment of the employee.

Similar measures may well have emerged in the UK had the need for legislative intervention not been pre-empted by the voluntary action taken by the insurance industry. However where the legislature has failed to intervene, what should the common law do? Judicial disquiet has led to a measure of amelioration where *Lister* is concerned. The most significant example of this is the use of the concept of assumption of responsibility to deny a duty on the part of the employee in advice/information cases. Where the harm arises as a result of an accident involving the employee and a third party who is not dealing with the employer the position is more difficult, the classic example being the lorry driver who, in the course of his employment, injures another road-user. Enterprise liability suggests that a duty of care should not be owed by the employee who is acting within the scope of employment. Proximity can be regarded as negatived by the contractual framework within which the employee operates. How then to protect the third party? In arriving at a solution one should consider whether someone acting in the course of his/her employment should owe a duty of care to a third party at all. If they do not then it is clear that, even in exceptional situations such as the employer becoming insolvent, the employee would not be liable. This would ensure that the liability was always that of the enterprise. The third party's prospects of recovery against the enterprise would not be diminished if the master's tort theory was adopted: 'According to this view the law attributes the *act* rather than the *tort* of the servant to the master. The master is not vicariously liable for the servant's tort, but is to be treated as having committed a tort through his servant.'[53] Such a solution is not beyond the bounds of judicial creativity. The Canadian courts have held that even though an action cannot

[53] Atiyah, n. 23 above, 6. For recent discussion see R. Stevens, 'A Servant of Two Masters' (2006) 122 LQR 201.

proceed against the employee because a defence is available to him/her the employer may still be liable.[54] In the UK Denning LJ had been of the view in *Broom v Morgan*[55] that the employer remains responsible for negligence even though the employee may for some reason be immune. The doctrine was rejected by the House of Lords in *Staveley v Jones*. An alternative approach would be to overrule *Lister* and imply a right of indemnity into the employment contract. A position, as was pointed out in *London Drugs*, that has been adopted by the German courts.[56]

[54] *Co-Operators Insurance Association v Kearney* [1965] SCR 106.

[55] [1953] 1 QB 597.

[56] 'Following the decision of the Great Senate of the *Bundesarbeitsgericht* of 25 September 1957 (BAG 5, 1, 18) this Senate now holds that in a case where the employee's fault is "less than grave", his liability is excluded by the employer's business risk concept, applying § 254 BGB by analogy. For this purpose normal or medium carelessness, as well as slight fault, should count as "less than grave", as the words suggest. *In view of the increased liability brought about by technological developments*, to attribute business risk on a case-by-case basis as the *Bundesarbeitsgericht* has hitherto done is not an appropriate way of dealing with its liability in cases where the employee has been guilty of normal fault. Thus, *damage done by an employee without intention or gross negligence while engaged on a dangerous job is one of the employer's business risks and must be borne by him alone*. To allot damage done by the employee to the risks of the business, in the absence of gross negligence, is justified by the fact that *it is the division of labour within the business which exposes the employee to the risks specific to his work. Division of labour and organizational structure are matters for the employer whose ownership and power of management enable him to determine how the work of the business is to be organized*. The employee, on the other hand, given his subordinate position, has little or no influence on these factors which are relevant to the damage caused. Since *the employer is better able to deploy technical and organizational measures to reduce the special risks of the business and to take out any necessary insurance, it is right to treat damage as a risk of the business to be borne by him alone unless it is due to the intentional or grossly negligent conduct of the employee*.'

9

Risk and the employment relationship

As discussed in Chapter 3, recourse to enterprise liability has had a major impact on the allocation of risk between enterprises and third parties. The question then arises whether that is also true in respect of internal relations within the employing organisation where, in contrast to the position between the enterprise and the third party, the relationship between employer and employee is governed by the law of contract. Historically, recourse to the policies underpinning the workmen's compensation legislation would have prompted a positive answer.[1] Where the common law is concerned the picture is very different; whilst the contract of employment serves to allocate risk it does so in a way which appears to be uninfluenced by enterprise liability. The author would suggest that were account taken of the doctrine, risk might be allocated in a quite different way. This chapter will explore one dimension of this issue by focusing on the position in respect of psychiatric harm, which is very much a contemporary issue in a number of jurisdictions.

In truth the ways in which the conduct of the employer's business might impact on the employee's mental health are boundless. Reported cases often reveal complaints of stress stemming from excessive workload but claims will also flow from less commonplace events. Take the Australian case of *Vaughan v Patrick Stevedores*[2] where the plaintiff sued to recover damages for quite severe psychiatric injuries which he claimed to have sustained when crossing a picket line to enter the port where he was employed by the defendant. In the course of those journeys he was subjected to extremely hostile behaviour on the part of the pickets. The trade dispute had arisen because in 1998 the employer decided to take steps to break the longstanding monopoly of the Maritime Union of Australia (MUA) in providing waterside workers for the loading and unloading of vessels. The Court of Appeal of New South Wales found

[1] See Chapter 1.. [2] [2002] NSWCA 275.

that this gave rise to a risk of harm for those workers, such as the plaintiff, who were asked to carry on working and cross picket lines: 'It was also inevitable that if Patricks sought to bring workers onto the site, those workers would be at risk of physical or psychological harm. If Patricks had had due regard to the safety of its employees, it would never have sent them by bus through the angry milling crowd of unionists and union supporters.'[3] It was held that a breach of duty had arisen. This risk was not one which was merely incidental to the employment but was created by the employer when it decided, for its own economic benefit, to take steps to break the monopoly of the trade union. The result in the case was entirely consistent with an enterprise liability analysis. After all, where the risk of psychiatric harm arising is created or enhanced by the enterprise then the employer should be liable. However, when we turn to the approach currently adopted in the UK and Australia, matters appear less straightforward. The position in Canada will not be addressed since the Canadian courts have not explored the question of liability in tort for psychiatric injury arising from the employment relationship. Handford attributes this to the fact that tort actions for work-related injuries are excluded by workmen's compensation legislation.[4]

The principles of negligence and recovery for psychiatric harm

Employees frequently complain that their work situation has given rise to psychiatric harm rather than mere emotional distress. The underlying cause will often be said to lie in the excessive stresses and pressures of the job. Cases of this sort have become increasingly common in recent years and have proved troublesome for the courts, irrespective of the jurisdiction in which the question has been raised. Sometimes this has been because difficult issues of causation and remoteness have arisen.[5] In adjudicating, judges must confront limitations in the understanding of the medical profession:

> there remains a considerable difficulty in identifying how and why particular psychiatric consequences come about. That is not to say that experts cannot say that a particular event did, or did not, play *a part* in bringing on the observed psychiatric illness, but what role did other

[3] Ibid., para. 22.

[4] P. Handford, *Mullany & Handford's Tort Liability for Psychiatric Damage*, 2nd edn (Sydney: Lawbook Co., 2006), p. 537.

[5] *Tame v New South Wales* (2002) 211 CLR 317, para. 210.

> events play in that onset? Were those other events just as important as the event which came about because of the defendant's negligence?[6]

There is, however, a more fundamental problem from a legal perspective in that the courts are not always convinced that harm of this nature should be treated in the same way as physical harm. At first glance this is surprising as the employer's duty of care in respect of physical harm could not be more firmly entrenched at common law and one might assume a 'straight' application of negligence principles would take place where psychiatric harm is concerned. The decision of the New Zealand Court of Appeal in *AG v Gilbert* would suggest that this assumption is well-founded.[7] The case concerned a claim by a probation officer for breach of the employment contract. The contract included express terms that the Probation Department would comply with the provisions of the State Sector Act 1988 and the Health and Safety in Employment Act 1992. Compliance with that legislation before 1 April 1993 required the Department to be a good employer, to provide good and safe working conditions, and to take all reasonable precautions for the safety and health of workers. From 1 April 1993 the legislation required the Department to provide a safe working environment, to have in place effective methods for identifying hazards to employees, and to take all practicable steps to eliminate, isolate or minimise significant hazards. There were also said to be implied terms to the effect that the employer would take all reasonable care to avoid exposing the employee to unnecessary risk of injury or further injury to his/her physical or psychological health.

The work situation in *Gilbert* presented some of the classic features of a stress at work claim. The claimant was expected to carry out an 'excessive' workload 'without the support, resources, and supervision he needed in order to do so safely'.[8] Staffing levels were inadequate due to budgetary pressures. The employer also failed to put in place the conventional safety measures for a job of this nature:

> The Department failed to provide peer review and support from 1993 for Mr Gilbert (as opposed to managerial supervision), despite such peer review being accepted safe practice for occupations such as probation officers ... The absence of an appropriate system for psychological assistance was in breach of recognised safe practice in occupations comparable to the probation service.[9]

[6] Ibid., 259.

[7] [2002] 2 NZLR 342. Such a claim would also be possible in New Zealand were it to be framed in tort: *Urbani v Gillions* [2004] NZCA 45. In *Urbani* the claim failed on the facts.

[8] *Gilbert*, Ibid., 349. [9] Ibid.

In addition the employer failed to react to indications (such as high levels of sick leave) that staff as a whole were likely to be suffering from stress. The findings of the trial judge that the employer was in breach of the duties owed were upheld on appeal. The employer sought to argue that such an outcome would place an unreasonable burden on employers. This was rejected on the basis that the 'reasonable man' test offered sufficient protection and that the employer was only required to take such steps which were proportionate to known and avoidable risks: 'What is "reasonably practicable" requires a balance. Severity of harm, the current state of knowledge about its likelihood, knowledge of the means to counter the risk, and the cost and availability of those means, all have to be assessed.'[10]

Up until recently the Australian courts had also appeared wedded to a position of parity of treatment where psychiatric and physical harm are concerned. In *Tame v New South Wales* the High Court acknowledged that the employer's duty is governed by the same rules, and has the same content, irrespective of the kind of injury or damage that can reasonably be foreseen: 'Exactly the same considerations of the control that an employer has over the place and system of work which require finding that an employer owes a duty of care with respect to physical injury support a conclusion that a duty is owed to take reasonable care about the place and system of work so as to avoid psychiatric injury'.[11] This was borne out by a number of subsequent decisions. The decision in *Sinnott v FJ Trousers*[12] was a somewhat routine stress at work case. The claimant alleged, amongst other things, that in the course of his employment the defendant required or permitted him to work under excessive stress and pressure and excessively long hours, failed to heed numerous requests made by him for assistance and technical support in the performance of his work, and failed to heed numerous complaints made by him in respect of his excessive workload. Factual allegations of this sort are commonplace in cases of this type. The Supreme Court of Victoria found such a claim utterly unproblematic in principle given that a decision to the contrary would mean that 'although an employer cannot break the body of his employee during the course of his employment, nevertheless he is permitted to break the mind at will irrespective of the circumstances'.[13] The following observations were also made:

> an employer requires an employee to work in an extremely stressful and demanding job which ultimately causes patent anxiety problems and results in a mental breakdown. The employee takes sick leave and returns

[10] Ibid., 360. [11] *Tame*, n. 5 above, 281. [12] [2000] VSC 124. [13] Ibid., para. 39.

> to be confronted with exactly the same situation. He is required to continue in the same employment carrying out the same duties even though there would be steps available to the employer to avoid or minimise the risk. It affronts common sense and justice to suggest that when the employee suffers a further breakdown resulting in his total incapacity that the employer can then turn around and say, that he is not entitled to recover damages because they are of a purely psychiatric nature despite his gross negligence perpetrated with full knowledge of the stresses and strains placed in the employment and the susceptibility of the employee to mental illness.[14]

The foregoing approach dictated that the risks of psychiatric harm arising were as much the responsibility of the employer as those in respect of physical harm. The approach by the House of Lords in *White v Chief Constable*[15] (discussed below) was seen by the Australian courts as being unattractive. As will become apparent, the courts in Australia no longer wholly adhere to the position in *Tame*. This means that, in both the UK and Australia, the employee who maintains that the stresses of his employment have caused psychiatric harm is likely to find that recovery against the employer is much less straightforward than that of a colleague who claims to have been physically injured. Risks of the former type will often be borne by the worker rather than the enterprise. This chapter now turns to the control devices that have been deployed to achieve this allocation and then seeks to understand what has promoted their use.

Control devices

The practical propositions

In *Hatton v Sutherland*[16] in the Court of Appeal Hale LJ (as she then was), giving the judgment of the court, set out a number of 'practical propositions' to assist the courts in determining whether a breach of duty has taken place (these are set out in full in the Appendix to this chapter). For instance, in determining whether harm was reasonably foreseeable it is said that because of the nature of mental disorder, it is harder to foresee than physical injury, but may be easier to foresee in a known individual than in the population at large. This guidance was

[14] Ibid., para. 129. [15] [1999] 2 AC 455. [16] [2002] ICR 613.

approved by the House of Lords in *Barber v Somerset CC*,[17] though it was emphasised that Hale LJ's speech provided 'useful practical guidance, but it must be read as that, and not as having anything like statutory force'. It needs to be appreciated that the formulation of the 'practical propositions' owes much to policy considerations. The application of the conventional calculus of risk in the law of negligence, in determining whether there has been a breach of duty, is not a mechanical process and this is particularly true where psychological harm is in issue. The application is driven by policy concerns and is moderated in workload cases in the UK so that the requisite standard of care is 'not set too high'.[18] If it were, the judiciary perceive that there might be unfortunate consequences for the employment market: for instance, 'employers may be even more reluctant than they already are to take on people with a significant psychiatric history or an acknowledged vulnerability to stress-related disorders'.[19] Against this backdrop, the practical propositions emerge as an embodiment of common law policy on employer responsibility for occupational stress. In the author's view they make it less likely that the employee will be able to recover, a view recently endorsed by the Court of Appeal in *Veakins v Kier Islington*.[20] The value judgement is made that 'some things are no one's fault'.[21] The judiciary strive to achieve an acceptable balance between safeguarding the wellbeing of employees and not burdening employers with some of the risks which are inherent in working life. It is regarded as fair that some such risks are borne by employees since 'There is no such thing as a pressure free job. Every job brings its own set of tasks, responsibilities and day-to-day problems, and the pressures and demands these place on us are an unavoidable part of working life. We are, after all, paid to work and to work hard, and to accept the reasonable pressures which go with that.'[22] Given that the practical propositions are underpinned by contemporary policy concerns it must be assumed that they are susceptible to revision, or indeed outright rejection, should those concerns change. A likely catalyst for change would be an advance in medical understanding of the relationship between occupational pressure and stress and risk to health. It should be noted that *Hatton* indicated that a decision to allocate risk in a way which would be more burdensome to employers is seen as such a weighty one as to be a matter for Parliament: 'If knowledge advances to such an extent as to justify the imposition of

[17] [2004] IRLR 475. [18] *Hatton*, n. 16 above, 621. [19] *Hatton*, n. 16 above.
[20] [2009] EWCA Civ 1288. [21] *Hatton*, n. 16 above, 622. [22] *Hatton*, n. 16 above.

obligations upon some or all employers to take particular steps to protect their employees from stress-related harm, this is better done by way of regulations imposing specific statutory duties.'[23] It may be doubted whether all courts would be content with this rather passive stance.

The practical propositions offer guidance in determining whether a breach of duty has taken place. They tell us that the employer is usually entitled to assume that the employee can cope with the normal pressures of the job. The employer, at common law, does not come under any general monitoring duty.[24] Indeed 'most employees are sufficiently robust to withstand the stress of a heavy work load'.[25] Moreover, the employer is generally entitled to take what he/she is told by or on behalf of the employee at face value.[26] In terms of the risk of harm arising the notion that some forms of employment are more dangerous than others is rejected: 'it is not the job but the interaction between the individual and the job which causes the harm'.[27] *Hatton* indicates that the claimant may find it difficult to establish that harm was foreseeable: 'in view of the many difficulties of knowing when and why a particular person will go over the edge from pressure to stress and from stress to injury to health, the indications must be plain enough for any reasonable employer to realise he should do something about it'.[28] In *Koehler v Cerebos*[29] the High Court appears to accept that the 'practical propositions' are relevant to Australian litigation. To the extent that it does, it thereby adopts the same approach to risk allocation that the House of Lords did in *Barber.*

The employee's complaint against his/her employer might concern not only the pressures of workload but, in addition, problems caused by behaviour such as disparate treatment, bullying or harassment. In such a case the approach approved in *Barber v Sutherland* is of limited benefit since one has moved away from the pure workload scenario.[30] This is because the practical propositions do not address situations where the

[23] *Hatton,* n. 16 above, 622. [24] *Chapman v Lord Advocate* 2006 SLT 186.

[25] *Bonser v RJB Mining (UK) Ltd* [2004] IRLR 164, 167. [26] *Hatton,* n. 16 above, 626.

[27] *Hatton,* n. 16 above, 625. In *Hartman v South Essex Mental Health and Community Care NHS Trust* [2005] ICR 782 it was held that there was no basis for concluding that caring for children with serious learning difficulties is a high-risk occupation imposing a higher than normal standard of alertness on employees in respect of the risk that employees will sustain psychiatric injury.

[28] *Hatton,* n. 16 above, 627. [29] (2005) 222 CLR 44.

[30] For a view to the contrary, see the decision of the Court of Appeal in *Foumeny v University of Leeds* [2003] EWCA Civ 557.

employee's complaint is, at least in part, about bullying or harassment in the workplace or other such behaviour. At a practical level this is important because the existence of such behaviour must be highly relevant to both what is foreseeable and what might reasonably be done. More fundamentally, the practical propositions are premised on the belief that, prima facie, the normal pressures of employment may legitimately be placed upon the shoulders of the employee. As we have seen, the view is taken that some things are no one's fault. However, the language of fault is utterly apposite where bullying and harassment are concerned. Such behaviour is simply not acceptable in the modern workplace and it would be surprising if the judiciary were not more critical in such circumstances. It is noteworthy that, in the composite appeals in *Hatton*, the only plaintiff who was successful before the Court of Appeal was Jones. The case was one like *Waters v Metropolitan Police Commr*[31] in that 'the employer knew that the employee was being badly treated by another employee and could have done something to prevent it'.

Primary and secondary victims

The House of Lords decision in *White v Chief Constable*[32] established a further significant limitation on the scope of the employer's duty. It was held that the law does not recognise a duty to guard employees against psychiatric harm suffered as a result of witnessing injury to others, Lord Steyn noting that 'the pragmatic rules governing recovery of damages for pure psychiatric harm do not at present include police officers who sustain such injuries while on duty. If such a category were to be created by judicial decision, the new principle would be available in many different situations, e.g. doctors and hospital workers who are exposed to the sight of grievous injuries and suffering.'[33] The driver for this being a judicial desire not to place employees in a position more favourable than members of the public. The fact that friends and relatives had litigated without success in *Alcock v Chief Constable*[34] – an action which had arisen out of the same tragedy – weighed heavily on judicial minds. The result is that in a case such as *White*, in a situation where the employee is not in physical danger, he/she will only be able to recover should the rules applicable to secondary victims be satisfied. Such an outcome would not arise, in practice, unless one was presented with the

[31] [2000] 1 WLR 1607. [32] [1999] 2 AC 455. [33] Ibid., 498. [34] [1992] 1 AC 310.

highly unusual instance of the person harmed physically being a close relative of the employee.

The approach in *White* is not without difficulties. On the one hand, the employer who exposes the employee to a stressful working environment may be liable provided the 'practical propositions' can be overcome. On the other, the employer who, by failing to provide an adequate system of work puts the employee in a position where he/she witnesses appalling human suffering of the sort encountered in *White*, will not. The adverse consequences of an inadequate system of work in a case such as *White* may be all too foreseeable:

> It is well known that negligent crowd control at football matches can produce catastrophic results, and self-evident that the police on duty would be bound to be there before, during and for some hours after the horror, and that both the American and international classifications for PTSD make the point that events properly classified as such stressors can cause 'marked or pervasive distress' to almost anyone.[35]

Viewed purely from the perspective of the contract of employment such a distinction seems arbitrary.[36] The policeman whose health breaks down because of working excessive hours may be able to recover whereas a colleague carelessly exposed to the sight of horrific suffering on the part of others cannot. One might take the view that it is the employee in the latter position who most attracts our concern. After all, the scenes encountered in *White* itself have been described as follows: 'It was truly gruesome. The victims were blue, cyanotic, incontinent; their mouths open, vomiting; their eyes staring. A pile of dead bodies lay and grew outside gate three. Extending further and further onto the pitch, the injured were laid down and attempts made to revive them ... The scene was emotive and chaotic as well as gruesome.'[37] Against this backdrop, the Court of Appeal in *White* had mirrored the approach adopted in *Tame* and accepted that the employment relationship in itself gave rise to a duty of care:

> Once it is accepted that there is no justification for regarding physical and psychiatric injuries as different kinds of injury, when an employer negligently causes physical injury to one employee, it seems to me to be

[35] *Frost v Chief Constable* [1998] QB 254, 280.

[36] A point alluded to in the Scottish case of *Keen v Tayside Contracts* 2003 SLT 500 where Lady Paton felt unable to exclude the possibility that in certain circumstances, an employee might be entitled to recover damages in respect of injury to mental health caused by one single episode of acute stress at work, resulting in, for example, PTSD.

[37] *Frost*, n. 35 above, quoting from Taylor LJ's report: 'Interim Report on the Hillsborough Stadium Disaster' (1989) (Cm. 765), 15.

> impossible to contend that he is not equally liable to a fellow employee of normal fortitude working on the same task who sustains psychiatric injury, whether through fear for himself or through witnessing what happens to his fellow workman.[38]

Such considerations prompted the Supreme Court of New South Wales in *New South Wales v Seedsman*[39] to elect not to follow *White.* This divergence is far from surprising when it is recalled that the Australian High Court, in *Mount Isa Mines v Pusey,*[40] had previously allowed an employee to recover for psychiatric harm against the employer after witnessing an accident to a fellow employee. In *Mount Isa Mines* two of the employer's electricians carried out a test on a switchboard in the powerhouse using a multi-meter. Because of their mishandling of this instrument a short circuit of high-tension current occurred with the result that the two electricians were severely burned by an intense electric arc. The short circuit also caused a loud noise which was heard by the claimant – a fellow employee – as an explosion from where he was working on the floor below. The claimant hastened to the scene and found one of the electricians, with whom he was unacquainted, naked and very badly burnt. He went to his aid, supporting and assisting him down through the building to ground level where he was placed in an ambulance. The claimant would, on the basis of *White,* have failed to recover as he would not have been classified as a primary victim.[41] The High Court viewed matters very differently:

> I cannot doubt that it could properly be held that as an employer such an owner-operator could and ought to foresee that misuse of such an instrument in connexion with a high tension current of electricity might, through an intense electric arc, cause an employee in proximity to the conductors carrying such current to be severely burnt. I think it could be held that such an employer could and ought to foresee that the sight of a burning or recently burnt human might mentally disturb an employee whose proximity to the injured fellow employee ought to be foreseen.[42]

As psychiatric harm to the claimant was reasonably foreseeable there was no doubt that the employer's duty of care to employees was engaged and, on the facts, breached. The nature of the harm suffered did not give rise to any special considerations: 'Foreseeable harm caused by a master to the mind of his servant is just as much a breach of his duty of care to

[38] *Frost,* n. 35 above, 266. [39] [2000] NSWCA 119. [40] (1970) 125 CLR 383.

[41] And see *Robertson v Forth Road Bridge* 1995 SCLR 466.

[42] *Mount Isa Mines,* n. 40 above, 389.

him as harm to his body would be.' In subsequent decisions the Australian courts were content to recognise that the employer's duty extended to stress at work cases.[43]

The much more recent decision in *Seedsman* had concerned a claim brought by a police officer whose role was to investigate crimes against children. She had encountered victims with all manner of injuries, ranging from burns and bruising to many cases of 'shaken baby syndrome' – children who had been shaken until they suffered retinal detachment and haemorrhaging resulting in brain damage or death. It was noted that there were a number of particularly disturbing features of her employment:

> First, it involves a significant number of occasions of quite exceptional human depravity. Second, it involves a significant number of occasions of death and intense suffering of young children. Third, it involves frequent direct observation of dead or mutilated bodies of children. Fourth, it involves a very young police officer with no relevant training and provided with no relevant preparation.[44]

The appellate court upheld the trial judge's finding that the employer had failed in its duty to provide a safe system of work. The employer had neglected to take steps such as providing training that would have enabled the claimant to cope with the stresses of the job. The trial judge had also held that if there had been advice and counselling available to the claimant, it was more probable than not that PTSD could have been avoided or its severity reduced. This finding was again upheld by the Court of Appeal. Had this reasoning been applied in *White*, the claimants would have recovered because the chief constable had failed to take reasonable care in deploying the officers engaged in crowd control.

It must be said that the Australian courts, in determining the extent of an employer's responsibilities, have been far more willing than their UK counterparts to take account of the wide range of employment situations that give rise to harm. For instance, the exclusion from legal protection of a single episode of acute stress – as in *White* – leads to invidious distinctions between employees. It might also be said that the Australian courts have displayed far greater realism in appraising the nature and extent of the risks which are liable to be encountered by employees. In *New South Wales v Fahy* the High Court had this to say with reference to the police:

43 E.g. *Arnold v Midwest Radio* (1998) Aust. Tort. Rep. 81, para. 65.

44 *Seedsman*, n. 39 above, para. 37.

> The duties of police officers commonly expose them to danger, sometimes from people who deliberately seek to cause them harm. Individual responses to stressful situations vary greatly, and police officers are sometimes called upon to deal with situations that many ordinary citizens would find unbearably stressful. Police service is not unique in this respect. Many callings expose people to forms of stress with which outsiders would be unable to cope ... The duties of police officers sometimes present them with circumstances of violence, horror, death, anger and destruction. In such circumstances, the risk of PTSD as a consequence of employment duties is far from far-fetched or fanciful. It is actual and real.[45]

As a result the employer's obligations with regard to the provision of a safe system of work have tended to be more onerous than in the UK and may involve more by way of precautionary and supportive measures.

The contractual matrix

The interface between tort and contract can give rise to difficult issues and, as will be seen, that interface is central to the High Court's approach to stress at work cases. The ideology of freedom of contract continues to exert a, perhaps surprisingly, strong influence in negligence cases. Whilst *volenti* as such no longer has a role to play, the common law remains intuitively sympathetic to contracting-out. Take the UK case of *Johnstone v Bloomsbury*[46] which addressed the relationship between the implied term of reasonable care and the express terms of the contract. The plaintiff doctor was employed by the defendant health authority as a senior house officer under a contract which by clause 4(b) stipulated that his hours of duty should consist of a standard working week of forty hours and an additional availability on call up to an average of forty-eight hours a week over a specified period. The plaintiff, in compliance with the contract, worked some weeks in excess of eighty-eight hours and, as a result of working those hours with inadequate sleep, he became ill. He brought an action against the defendants, seeking, inter alia, a declaration that he should not be required to work in excess of seventy-two hours a week and damages for personal injuries and loss allegedly suffered as a result of breach by the defendants of their duty to take reasonable care for his safety. The judges did not speak with one voice in addressing the relationship between express and implied terms. Stuart-Smith LJ was of the view that the express term as to working hours 'had

[45] [2007] 81 ALJR 1021, 1025. [46] [1992] QB 333.

to be exercised in the light of the other contractual terms and in particular their duty to take care for his safety',[47] the latter being an implied term in law. Leggatt LJ spoke the language of contractual orthodoxy and arrived at the diametrically opposite conclusion: 'In the light of the provisions of ... [the clause as to working hours], which are simple and clear, no implied provision can, as a matter of construction, have the effect directly or indirectly of reducing the number of hours per week which the plaintiff is required to be available.'[48] Browne-Wilkinson VC agreed with this but also put forward the proposition that the situation was different where the express obligation involved a discretion. The Vice Chancellor noted that the express obligation could be divided into two constituent parts: 'an absolute duty on the plaintiff to work for 40 hours and in addition an obligation "to be available" for a further 48 hours per week on average, the defendants have a discretion as to the number of hours they call on the plaintiff to work "overtime"'.[49] On this basis the latter part of the express obligation was subject to the implied term in law of reasonable care.[50] This approach is entirely unconvincing given that all express powers are in a sense discretionary. After all, the employer in *Johnstone* could choose to waive the requirement that the doctor work all of the basic forty-hour working week any time it wished. In the eyes of Stuart-Smith LJ the overall effect of the express clause was to give the 'defendants the power to require the plaintiff to work up to 88 hours per week on average'. It must be noted that *Johnston* predates much of the modern development of the jurisprudence of the employment contract and, most pertinently, the evolution of the implied obligation of mutual trust and confidence and its role in policing the exercise of discretion. When account is taken of this, Stuart-Smith LJ's judgment would appear to be the most compelling, but he was, of course, in the minority on this point. Ultimately *Johnston* adopts a very traditional approach to the relationship between express and implied terms. It says in effect that in requiring the employee to

[47] Ibid., 344. On the other hand, the learned judge was also of the view that it would be possible to frame an express term to limit or exclude the implied duty of reasonable care. Such a clause would, however, be subject to the Unfair Contract Terms Act 1977.

[48] *Johnstone*, ibid., 347. [49] Ibid., 350.

[50] Browne-Wilkinson VC found some support for this in the Privy Council decision in *Ottoman Bank v Chakarin* [1930] AC 277 which was said to be authority for the proposition that the employer is bound to exercise optional rights conferred upon him by the contract subject to his obligation to safeguard the health of his staff. However, *Ottoman Bank* does not appear to distinguish between 'optional rights' and other express terms.

discharge the duties set out by the contract the employer is not constrained by the implied obligation of reasonable care. *Johnston* also allows the employer to avoid the parallel obligation in tort and, thereby, would appear to amount to a form of *volenti*. By consenting to the risks of the job (as revealed by the terms of the contract) the employee absolves the employer of legal responsibility. This would not be acceptable if physical risks were in issue. It should be made clear that the Court of Appeal refused to strike out the part of the claim founded on the Unfair Contract Terms Act 1977.

Contractual questions of a similar nature were to come to the fore in the leading Australian case of *Koehler v Cerebos*.[51] There the claimant was employed three days a week by the employer as a merchandising representative. She found that she could not perform the duties expected of her to her satisfaction and repeatedly told management that changes had to be made. She said that the work expected of her had to be changed, or she should have more time in which to do it, or she should have help to do it. No changes were made. Five months after starting this work she fell ill. At first a physical disorder was suspected but it became clear that she was suffering from a psychiatric illness. In the District Court of Western Australia it was found that the claimant's workload was excessive, that the employer needed no particular expertise to foresee that there was a risk of injury of the kind that ensued and that, by not increasing the claimant's hours of work or giving her assistance, the employer failed in its duty to ensure that all reasonable steps were taken to provide the claimant with a safe system of work. The High Court had regard to the interface between contract and tort and rejected the claim. It was stressed that the scope of the duty to take reasonable care to avoid psychiatric injury which an employer owes an employee cannot be considered without taking account of the obligations which the parties owe one another under the contract of employment.

As has been seen the Australian courts had rejected *White*, but in *Koehler* they have opted for retrenchment in cases where the underlying problem has been stress at work. This can be seen in the endorsement of *Hatton* but, much more significantly, by the way in which *Koehler* has placed the focus on the contractual matrix. General principles tell us that

[51] See n. 29 above. On which see C. Sappideen, P. O'Grady and G. Warburton, *Macken's Law of Employment*, 6th edn (Sydney: Lawbook Co., 2009), para. 5.275. See also L. G. Chan, 'Work Stress and Negligently Inflicted Psychiatric Illness' (2005) 28 UNSWLJ 821; and D. Butler, 'Psychiatric Injury in the Workplace: Directions for Cases Involving Stress or Bullying' (2006) 14 TLJ 124.

the matrix may impact upon the obligations owed by virtue of the law of negligence and result in their restriction.[52] By entering into the employment contract the High Court holds that the employee warrants (in the same way that they warrant that they possess the requisite skills) that they are mentally fit for the job:

> her agreement to undertake the work runs contrary to the contention that the employer ought reasonably to have appreciated that the performance of those tasks posed a risk to the appellant's psychiatric health. It runs contrary to that contention because agreement to undertake the work not only evinced a willingness to try but also was not consistent with harbouring, let alone expressing, a fear of danger to health.[53]

This, though, is to disregard the fact that the employee will often have no choice but to enter into the contract, irrespective of whether or not they believe it will be prejudicial to their health. Economic realities will often mean that the employee has to accept the offer of employment. This will remain the case even where it is clear at the outset that the demands of the job are unreasonable and carry a real risk of harm. *Koehler* might be thought to be explicable on the basis (as in *Hatton*) that an employer could not be expected to foresee that the normal pressures of a job voluntarily entered into would give rise to a risk of harm. However, the underlying rationale appears to be based more on the acceptability of contracting-out: 'notions of "overwork", "excessive work", or the like, have meaning only if they appeal to some external standard . . . Yet the parties have made a contract of employment that, by hypothesis, departs from that standard. Insistence upon performance of a contract cannot be in breach of a duty of care.'[54]

In decisions since *Koehler*, it must be said, the Australian courts have been reluctant to hold that contracting-out has taken place. For example, in *NSW v Burton*[55] the claimant was employed as a marksman in a specialist unit in the police force. During the course of his duties, the claimant was fired upon, but not hit, during a siege at a farm. He developed PTSD as a result of the incident. At trial it was held that the employer was negligent in failing to provide the claimant with proper psychiatric and psychological treatment and counselling given his exposure to stress at the siege. This finding was upheld on appeal and it was noted that there was ample evidence to support the conclusion that the employer itself had identified the risk of psychological or

[52] See W. Njoya, 'Employment, Implicit Contracts and the Duty of Care' (2005) LQR 33.

[53] *Koehler*, n. 29 above, 55–6. [54] Ibid., 56. [55] [2006] NSWCA 12.

psychiatric harm to an officer who had been involved in an incident where shots were fired at him. One might have taken the view that a stressful event of this sort was part and parcel of the job and that the employee consented to run these risks by joining the police force and agreeing to perform the duties of an officer. The same judicial reticence in applying the approach in *Koehler* was displayed in *New South Wales v Mannall*[56] where it was held that the employee, by taking on a managerial role, did not exclude the employer's duty of care, which also did not exempt the employer from having any responsibility for the mental wellbeing of the employee as the pressures (expected and unexpected) of the job began to take their toll. The reference to 'expected pressures' is of particular interest given the decision in *Koehler*. The court went on to emphasise that entry into a contract of employment does not in itself absolve the employer from the tortious duty to exercise reasonable care to prevent injury.

Commonality: restriction and disparity

Whilst the techniques used are somewhat different, the courts in both Australia and the UK have adopted a restrictive approach to the recovery of damages by employees for psychiatric harm. Both jurisdictions assume that, simply by entering into employment, the employee has consented to run certain occupational risks. *Hatton* and *Koehler* operate on the premise that the employee accepts that they cannot complain should they be adversely affected by the normal pressures and stresses of the job. It appears that the employer is benefiting from a defence along the lines of *volenti non fit injuria*. If this analysis is correct the position arrived at seems very odd, as *volenti* has played an almost invisible role in the workplace since the nineteenth-century case of *Smith v Baker*.[57] A key element of that decision was Lord Watson's realisation that the crux of the matter was whether the employee could be regarded as having consented to running the risk at his own expense. Over a hundred years later a finding to that effect would be an exceedingly rare occurrence. Lord Hodson observed in the 1960s case of *ICI v Shatwell*[58] that 'economic pressures are usually present which make it unjust to allow an employer where a servant has been injured to say in defence that the servant ran the risk with his eyes open, being fully aware of the danger he incurred'. In a case where an employee was physically injured

[56] [2005] NSWCA 367. [57] [1891] AC 325. [58] [1965] AC 656, 681.

it would be inconceivable that, truly exceptional circumstances aside, *volenti* would make an appearance nowadays.[59] It is seen to be as anachronistic as the old defence of common employment. On what basis might the re-emergence of a consent-based defence be justified where psychiatric harm is concerned? The recognition that the employee can give consent may be seen as being to their benefit as their autonomy is protected. Indeed more generally there are indications that the courts are placing more importance on this factor.[60] In a discursive judgment in *Barber*, Lord Rodger discusses the hypothetical example of the university researcher who risks illness by working excessive hours 'in the hope of making a breakthrough in deciphering an ancient language or unravelling some secret in genetics'.[61] Professional workers who often have considerable autonomy in respect of their working lives might be thought to be in an analogous position. Lord Rodger took the view that the employing university's obligation does not extend beyond warning of the dangers. There is said to be no obligation to be more interventionist and, for instance, instruct the employee to work fewer hours. Indeed Lord Rodger suggests that such a worker 'is entitled to continue working at high pressure'.[62] The author is not convinced that the employer's powers are quite as restricted as Lord Rodger suggests, nor that the employee possesses a right of this nature. Where a contract of employment did not have fixed hours of work (as might well be the case where an academic in a traditional university was concerned) one could argue that the employer's obligation of reasonable care required that the employee be instructed to work less hard. Certainly it would surely be the case that it would fall within the employer's capacity to issue a lawful and reasonable order to require this. Somewhat oddly, Lord Rodger refers to the employee's right 'to carry out his duty of research under his contract'. The right, which corresponds to this duty, is surely possessed by the employer who, of course, may waive it should they so choose. It should also be recalled that it is exceptional for employees to have the right to be given actual work to do. Lord Rodger's approach places respect for the employee's autonomy considerably above respect for his/her bodily security, a prospect that would be inconceivable at common law where physical injury is concerned since 'preservation of the physical integrity of the individual has long been of central

[59] The idea that it would be possible to 'buy off' a personal injuries claim would be unacceptable in the case of physical injury.

[60] *Chester v Afshar* [2005] 1 AC 134. [61] *Barber*, n. 17 above, 480. [62] Ibid.

concern'.[63] Lord Rodger's judgment might also be thought to display considerable naivety in that it allows employers to organise work in such a way that the employer's expectations can only be met if employees, notwithstanding the absence of fixed hours of work, choose to work excessive hours. An employer that expects its staff to work in this way can make its wishes clear in a variety of ways which do not involve imposing an express contractual obligation. On Lord Rodger's analysis, the employer is not responsible in law should the employee's health collapse because the decision to engage in 'long-hours culture' was that of the employee. The employee is held responsible for the adverse consequences of that decision. It would not be unduly cynical to hazard that the predominant motive, in setting up working arrangements in this way, might be to facilitate exploitation rather than promote autonomy.[64]

Justifying disparate treatment

The promotion of autonomy apart, are there reasons which would explain treating psychiatric harm differently? One possible explanation might be that illness of this nature continues to attract prejudice. Historically the 'common law has long feared dealing with assaults upon mental integrity, for fear of being unable to distinguish between the real and the feigned consequences of such an assault'.[65] Such fears may continue to hold sway. Another possible explanation is the perceived scale of the problem; courts in Australia and the UK have drawn attention to this factor. In England, in *Garrett v Camden London BC*,[66] it was noted that 'Many, alas, suffer breakdowns and depressive illnesses and a significant proportion could doubtless ascribe some at least of their problems to the strains and stresses of their work situation: be it simply overworking, the tensions of difficult relationships, career prospect worries, fears or feelings of discrimination or harassment, to take just some examples.' Even if the foregoing description is accurate, should

[63] *Tame*, n. 5 above, para. 259.

[64] The issue of autonomy influences judicial thinking in a variety of ways. For instance, whilst control of the physical environment is obviously the employer's responsibility, the employer is seen as being 'much less in control of the way in which many of his employees, especially professionals or those who are expected to prioritise their own tasks, choose to do their work and balance the demands of their work and life outside the workplace' (*Hatton*, n. 16 above, 11). This differentiation leads to the view that the employer's legal responsibilities should not be on a par with those pertaining to physical harm.

[65] *Tame*, n. 5 above, para. 259.

[66] [2001] EWCA Civ 395.

it lead to the normal common law rules being modified? Calls for modification would be understandable if the resulting burden on employers would be too great. However, if a 'straight' application of standard of care occurs employees will still find it difficult to recover. Often, for instance, psychiatric harm will have been caused by a number of factors and it may not be possible to establish a causal link between the harm and the work environment. A floodgates-type argument does not appear to offer an adequate justification (or even explanation) for the present stance.

The courts are also of the view that the occurrence of harm may be due as much, if not more, to the particular characteristics of the claimant than to the way in which the employer conducts the enterprise. This has implications when it comes to determining the obligations that it would be equitable to impose on the employer. In *Barber* Lord Rodger observed that:

> the judge was not satisfied that this pressure of work 'in itself' placed him at a materially higher risk of mental illness than another teacher working in a comparable position with a heavy workload. In other words, the demands placed on Mr Barber were not excessive in themselves, but only excessive in the case of Mr Barber because of some factor in his own personality or some condition that made him more vulnerable to developing a mental illness as a result of the stress involved in his work. There is therefore no question of the Council having reduced staffing to such a level as to put all their teachers at risk of developing a mental illness. Such a case would raise very different issues.[67]

The suggestion being, where the risk of physical injury is concerned, that it is reasonable to assume that employees are equally vulnerable but that this is far less likely to be true where psychiatric harm is concerned. All employees who, for example, work with unguarded machinery would be viewed as facing the same degree of risk, whereas those working in an employment with a 'long-hours culture' would not. It is true to say that individual susceptibility is likely to play a significant part in determining whether psychiatric harm is incurred, and it may also be thought significant that while stress is prevalent in working life the risk of any individual becoming ill is statistically low. Stress is only likely to lead to health issues when combined with particular individual characteristics. This, however, all goes to whether a breach of duty has arisen and, most of all, whether the employer could have foreseen that harm would occur.

[67] *Barber*, n. 17 above, 479.

It does not constitute an argument for treating psychiatric harm less favourably. The risk posed by the interaction between individual attributes and working environment would not have occurred but for employment by the enterprise and is as much a risk of the employment as risks of physical harm.

The perceived burden on the employer may also play a part in that the cost of taking precautions may be seen as excessive. There appear to be two strands to this line of thinking. Whilst the avoidance of physical harm also involves the employer in expense (e.g. improved safety devices on machinery) there appears to be a fear that the burden may be greater where psychiatric harm is concerned:

> We are not here concerned with such comparatively simple things as gloves, goggles, earmuffs or non-slip flooring. Many steps might be suggested: giving the employee a sabbatical; transferring him to other work; redistributing the work; giving him some extra help for a while; arranging treatment or counselling; providing buddying or mentoring schemes to encourage confidence; and much more.[68]

Such a claim could only be tested empirically but an element of scepticism would not seem unwarranted; the costs of avoiding physical harm will surely often be considerable. Complying with the highly detailed requirements of modern health and safety regulations will often be very costly. Those requirements will, in turn, impact on what is expected at common law. In any event, even if the fears are well founded, the common law has the capacity to accommodate them given that the calculus of risk only requires that the employer does what is reasonable having had regard to the cost and burden of precautions. The second strand of this is that, in effect, the operation of the obligation of reasonable care may serve to compel a variation of the contractual terms and impose a more expensive bargain on the employer. This emerges as a strong theme in *Koehler* and also in Lord Rodger's judgment in *Barber*.[69] It is claimed that it would place an unreasonable burden on the employer

[68] *Hatton*, n. 16 above, 627. Moreover, 'in all of these suggestions it will be necessary to consider how reasonable it is to expect the employer to do this, either in general or in particular: the size and scope of its operation will be relevant to this, as will its resources, whether in the public or private sector, and the other demands placed upon it'.

[69] In *Barber*, n. 17 above, 480 it was said that 'it is rather a different thing to say that the Council's duty of reasonable care to an employee requires them to provide him with assistance for an indefinite period even to the extent of employing a supply teacher so that he can do the amount of work he can cope with, but less than the amount for which he is being paid in terms of his contract'.

if they were forced to modify the employee's obligations whilst their own remained unadjusted. Despite the fact that the change results from the operation of an implied term (concurrently with the tortious duty) it seems to be viewed as if it were in some sense non-consensual. In *Koehler* the question was posed whether: 'If a contract of employment stipulates the work which an employee is to be paid to do, may the employee's pay be reduced if the employee's work is reduced in order to avoid the risk of psychiatric injury?'[70] At one level this is again an argument about cost since discharge of its common law duty will often involve added expense to the employer and less return on the wages paid to the employee. However, all that is equally true if the employee developed some physical ailment that required additional precautions.[71] It is doubtful whether there is a true dichotomy when the position of psychiatric harm is considered. Should the employee lose an eye in an accident outside the workplace additional safety precautions may be required which are not necessary for the workforce as a whole. Once the employer is aware of vulnerability on the part of the employee its obligations may become more onerous. The stress at work case of *Walker v Northumberland CC*[72] is a good example here. The plaintiff was employed by the defendant council as an area social services officer, responsible for four teams of field workers in an area in which during the 1980s child abuse references were particularly prevalent. During that period the volume of work rose considerably without any increase in staff. In November 1986 the plaintiff suffered a nervous breakdown, resulting from the impact of his work on his personality. He returned to work in March 1987 on the understanding that he would receive certain assistance with his duties for as long as was needed, having received medical advice that he should not go back to the same level of work responsibility. Within a month that support was withdrawn. Meanwhile the number of childcare cases continued to increase and staff numbers remained the same, and by September 1987 the plaintiff was once again suffering from a stress-related anxiety. In February 1988, following a further breakdown, he was dismissed on the ground of permanent ill health. The employer was held not to be in breach of duty with regard to the first nervous breakdown but, after the employee returned to work, what was required of the employer changed. The employer failed to discharge this obligation, though the only course of action which would have enabled the Council to discharge its duty and which 'would have had a reasonable probability

[70] *Koehler*, n. 29 above, 54. [71] *Paris v Stepney* [1951] AC 367. [72] [1995] IRLR 35.

of preventing another mental breakdown was the provision of continuous or at least substantial back-up'.[73]

Concerns in respect of 'unilateral variation' have prompted the courts to consider the interaction between the obligation to take reasonable care and general contractual principles (particularly those pertaining to variation). The author would suggest that judicial disquiet is caused in part by the inflexibility of the law of contract. Two scenarios might usefully be considered. First, the employee is able to discharge safely the full range of duties once support mechanisms have been put into place (to address the risk of psychiatric harm materialising). Secondly, the employee is only able to perform some of the duties but the partial performance which ensues is not sufficiently extensive to lead to frustration of contract. In both scenarios the employee's services are of a lower economic value to the employer than they were at the point when the level of wage was set. In the first scenario the employee would appear entitled to full pay. In the second he/she may be depending upon the terms of the work-wage bargain. In such scenarios the judicial concern is that the obligation of reasonable care requires that the work-wage bargain be rewritten so that the employee retains the same wage whilst the employee's work is worth less to the employer. In *Barber* Lord Rodger questioned whether an employer could be obliged to provide a teacher 'with assistance for an indefinite period even to the extent of employing a supply teacher so that he can do the amount of work he can cope with, but less than the amount for which he is being paid in terms of his contract'.[74] However, the underlying issue remains one of cost; albeit matters are compounded by the fact that the concerns in question are not going to be relieved by recourse to the law of contract given the common law's inflexibility. There is, for example, no concept of partial frustration that would lead to the variation of an existing bargain in the event of an unexpected change in circumstances. Nor is there likely to be an implied right of variation.

It also seems reasonable to conclude that adjudicating in stress at work cases is seen by the judges as particularly difficult. This is partly because predicting when stress is likely to be harmful is hugely problematic. Recovery will only take place where it is reasonably foreseeable that the stresses of the workplace give rise to a risk to health and the answer to this question will 'depend upon the inter-relationship between the particular characteristics of the employee concerned and the particular

[73] Ibid., 45. [74] *Barber*, n. 17 above, 480.

demands which the employer casts upon him'.[75] However, what judges may well be able to foresee is that the behaviour of the employer may lead to the employee being dissatisfied, anxious, embarrassed or upset, but the occurrence of such emotions does not constitute actionable damage. Instead it must be foreseeable that they are liable to be suffered to such a pathological degree as to constitute a psychiatric disorder.[76]

Conclusions

The risk of suffering from stress (as opposed to psychiatric harm) is viewed as different in nature to risks of physical harm, partly because it is seen by the judiciary as both inherent and unavoidable in working life. There is a consequent reticence about allocating that risk to the employer. It is one thing to blame employers for risks associated with their particular enterprise, but quite another to do so where risks of employment in general are concerned. The view is also taken that the risks of physical and psychiatric harm materialising cannot be equiparated, as the underlying trigger for the latter (stress) need not be harmful: 'Some pressures can, in fact, be a good thing. It is often the tasks and challenges we face at work that provide the structure to our working days, keep us motivated and are the key to a sense of achievement and job satisfaction.'[77] Again 'some people thrive on pressure and are so confident of their abilities to cope that they rarely if ever experience stress even in jobs which many would find extremely stressful'.[78] However, none of the explanations discussed in the preceding paragraphs offers a convincing justification as to why psychiatric harm should be treated differently. The policy decision appears to be that the risk of occurrence should be placed upon the shoulders of the employee to a greater extent than would be the case where physical harm is concerned. This seems wrong. Where the risk of psychiatric harm arising is created or enhanced by the enterprise then, on an enterprise liability analysis, the employer should be liable.

[75] *Hatton*, n. 16 above, 625. In *Sayers v Cambridgeshire CC* [2007] IRLR 29 it was said that different people have different capacities for the amount of work they take on and the number of hours they work.

[76] *Rorrison v West Lothian Council* 2000 SCLR 245.

[77] *Hatton*, n. 16 above, 621. [78] Ibid.

Appendix – The 'practical propositions'

In *Hatton* (n. 16 above), 631 the following summary was provided:

(1) There are no special control mechanisms applying to claims for psychiatric (or physical) illness or injury arising from the stress of doing the work the employee is required to do ... The ordinary principles of employer's liability apply ...
(2) The threshold question is whether this kind of harm to this particular employee was reasonably foreseeable ... this has two components (a) an injury to health (as distinct from occupational stress) which (b) is attributable to stress at work (as distinct from other factors) ...
(3) Foreseeability depends upon what the employer knows (or ought reasonably to know) about the individual employee. Because of the nature of mental disorder, it is harder to foresee than physical injury, but may be easier to foresee in a known individual than in the population at large ... An employer is usually entitled to assume that the employee can withstand the normal pressures of the job unless he knows of some particular problem or vulnerability ...
(4) The test is the same whatever the employment: there are no occupations which should be regarded as intrinsically dangerous to mental health ...
(5) Factors likely to be relevant in answering the threshold question include: (a) the nature and extent of the work done by the employee ... Is the workload much more than is normal for the particular job? Is the work particularly intellectually or emotionally demanding for this employee? Are demands being made of this employee unreasonable when compared with the demands made of others in the same or comparable jobs? Or are there signs that others doing this job are suffering harmful levels of stress? Is there an abnormal level of sickness or absenteeism in the same job or the same department? (b) Signs from the employee of impending harm to health ... Has he a particular problem or vulnerability? Has he already suffered from illness attributable to stress at work? Have there recently been frequent or prolonged absences which are uncharacteristic of him? Is there reason to think that these are attributable to stress at work, for example because of complaints or warnings from him or others?
(6) The employer is generally entitled to take what he is told by his employee at face value, unless he has good reason to think to the

contrary. He does not generally have to make searching inquiries of the employee or seek permission to make further inquiries of his medical advisers ...

(7) To trigger a duty to take steps, the indications of impending harm to health arising from stress at work must be plain enough for any reasonable employer to realise that he should do something about it ...

(8) The employer is only in breach of duty if he has failed to take the steps which are reasonable in the circumstances, bearing in mind the magnitude of the risk of harm occurring, the gravity of the harm which may occur, the costs and practicability of preventing it, and the justifications for running the risk ...

(9) The size and scope of the employer's operation, its resources and the demands it faces are relevant in deciding what is reasonable; these include the interests of other employees and the need to treat them fairly, for example, in any redistribution of duties ...

(10) An employer can only reasonably be expected to take steps which are likely to do some good: the court is likely to need expert evidence on this ...

(11) An employer who offers a confidential advice service, with referral to appropriate counselling or treatment services, is unlikely to be found in breach of duty ...

(12) If the only reasonable and effective step would have been to dismiss or demote the employee, the employer will not be in breach of duty in allowing a willing employee to continue in the job ...

(13) In all cases, therefore, it is necessary to identify the steps which the employer both could and should have taken before finding him in breach of his duty of care ...

(14) The claimant must show that that breach of duty has caused or materially contributed to the harm suffered. It is not enough to show that occupational stress has caused the harm ...

(15) Where the harm suffered has more than one cause, the employer should only pay for that proportion of the harm suffered which is attributable to his wrongdoing, unless the harm is truly indivisible. It is for the defendant to raise the question of apportionment ...

(16) The assessment of damages will take account of any pre-existing disorder or vulnerability and of the chance that the claimant would have succumbed to a stress related disorder in any event ...'

10

Enforcement of the employment contract

Enforcement of the employment contract raises a number of interesting issues. Traditionally – stemming from the hugely influential decision in *Addis v Gramophone*[1] – contracting parties in a variety of jurisdictions have been unable to recover damages for injury to feelings. In the field of commercial law this approach to recovery for mental distress remains uncontroversial. The courts assume that the parties take the risk of injury to feelings arising in the event of breach by the other side. Such an allocation of risk in employment relations is much more questionable. This is particularly so if it is accepted that the employment contract can no longer be characterised as commercial in nature. In my view any such characterisation is outmoded: the employment contract 'is not a simple commercial exchange in the marketplace of goods or services. A contract of employment is typically of a longer term and more personal in nature than most contracts, and involves greater mutual dependence and trust, with a correspondingly greater opportunity for harm or abuse.'[2] Given the nature of the employment relationship it cannot be assumed that an employee accepts the sorts of risks that commercial parties do. Indeed it may be said that nowadays employees do not expect to be treated in a humiliating or degrading fashion by their employer. Similarly flawed would be any attempt to defend *Addis* on the basis of remoteness. Having had regard to the contemporary view of employment relations the High Court of New Zealand has stated, in *Vivian v Coca-Cola Export*: 'No one would contend that it would not be in the reasonable contemplation of the parties to a contract of employment that an employee summarily dismissed in breach of contract will thereby suffer a blow not only to his self esteem but also to his standing and reputation.'[3]

1 [1909] AC 488.

2 *Wallace v United Grain Growers* (1997) 152 DLR (4th) 1, 46.

3 [1984] 2 NZLR 289, 292.

The position on damages is a matter of some consequence for this book. The present position, Canada and New Zealand apart, means that employees are denied full compensation should the employer break the employment contract. Despite the fact that there is a real risk that, should the employer breach certain terms, stress and anxiety will arise, the courts will not award damages. An award of damages for breach of contract looks to put the innocent party in the position he/she would have been in had the contract not been breached. Restricting the operation of the law of damages to deny recovery for injury to feelings serves to transfer risk between the parties. The employee must run the risk at his/her own expense despite the fact that it was one created by the enterprise. The more equitable position would surely be that the enterprise pays. The position might be thought to be particularly problematic where dismissal is concerned. The stance taken in Canada in this regard is to be commended. In *Honda v Keays*[4] the Supreme Court made clear that damages resulting from the manner of dismissal will be available where the employer engaged in conduct during the course of dismissal that is 'unfair or is in bad faith by being, for example, untruthful, misleading or unduly insensitive'. The impact of such a dismissal should not be underestimated: 'mental distress and injury to feelings are very real losses which may be suffered when the circumstances associated with dismissal aggravate the fact of dismissal itself'.[5] Moreover, the risk of managers dismissing unfairly or in bad faith can readily be attributed to the enterprise.

Australia

The Australian courts still adhere to *Addis*; the leading case is *Baltic Shipping Co. v Dillon.*[6] The contract was one for a pleasure cruise and the contract was therefore held to be one where the object was to provide for enjoyment and relaxation. As a result one of the well-recognised exceptions to *Addis* applied and the claimant was entitled to an award of damages for disappointment and distress. The judgments handed down

[4] (2008) 294 DLR (4th) 577. In the UK the House of Lords has held that the manner of dismissal does not give rise to a breach of mutual trust and confidence: *Johnson v Unisys* [2003] 1 AC 518. The Australian courts take the same view: *New South Wales v Paige* (2002) 115 IR 283.

[5] New Zealand Law Commission Report No. 18, 'Aspects of Damages: Employment Contracts and the Rule in *Addis v Gramophone*', p. 51.

[6] (1993) 176 CLR 344.

in the High Court make reference to a number of the justifications for the general rule. One concern was that a departure from *Addis* would lead to inflated awards; difficulties in quantification were also alluded to. The law on remoteness of damage was also invoked; mental distress arising from breach of contract is not ordinarily within the contemplation of the parties. This argument was seen as particularly relevant in the commercial context. It was also suggested that allowing for this head of claim would render transacting more difficult:

> no approximate estimate of liability could be formed if the subjective mental reaction of an innocent party to a breach and resultant damage were added on as further damage without proof of pecuniary loss by the innocent party. If the mental reaction to breach and resulting damage were itself a head of damage, the liability of a party in breach would be at large and liable to fluctuation according to the personal situation of the innocent party. If a promisor were exposed to such an indefinite liability in the event of breach, the making of commercial contracts would be inhibited.[7]

The Australian courts continue to follow *Dillon* in the employment context, a position recently confirmed by the New South Wales Court of Appeal in *Russell v The Trustees of the Roman Catholic Church*.[8] Nevertheless, in *Nikolich v Goldman Sachs*[9] the Federal Court of Australia held, obiter, that it is strongly arguable that the claim for injury to feelings fell within one of the exceptions to *Addis*. This conclusion was rendered permissible because of the express terms of the employment contract in issue. The purpose of the relevant provision 'was to provide assurance to existing and prospective ... employees concerning the manner in which they would be treated in their workplace and, in particular, about the support they would be offered by their employer'. This meant that one of the objects of the contract was to provide peace of mind. Should that clause be broken any resulting mental distress would be within the contemplation of the parties.

The UK

Despite the general rule of contract law set out in *Addis*, excluding claims for injury to feelings, the case law has, for some time, contained a considerable number of exceptions.[10] Indeed that list continues to

[7] Ibid., 369. [8] [2008] NSWCA 217. [9] [2006] FCA 784.
[10] *Jarvis v Swan Tours* [1973] 1 QB 233.

lengthen, the most notable recent instance being the decision of the House of Lords in *Farley v Skinner*[11] which allowed recovery where a major or important part of the contract, rather than the sole object, was to provide pleasure, relaxation, or peace of mind. Several judges, in contract of employment cases, have sought to distinguish *Addis* and extend the list of exceptions. One example is *Bliss v South East Thames RHA* where the view was taken that 'damages are recoverable where the parties contemplate that frustration, annoyance and disappointment may be suffered as a result of the breach'.[12] On the facts in *Bliss*, it was held at first instance that it was '... reasonably foreseeable by the parties that the plaintiff, on being required to undergo a psychiatric examination and being suspended on his refusal, would suffer ... distress and humiliation'. This approach was disapproved by the Court of Appeal.[13] The current position in the UK seems particularly incongruous given the emergence of the implied obligation of mutual trust and confidence; an obligation which has become central to the employment relationship. It should be emphasised that breach of the term, even where material, may not lead to pecuniary loss. Various forms of unreasonable behaviour by an employer may nonetheless cause much distress. Where the employer has broken the obligation of mutual trust and confidence it will surely be a real possibility that hurt to feelings will have arisen. If loss of this nature is not recoverable the term will lose much of its bite. The failure to allow a claim of this nature means that, in some circumstances, key obligations such as mutual trust and confidence are, in practical terms, incapable of enforcement. In New South Wales, in *Russell v Trustees of the Roman Catholic Church*,[14] the claimant's employment was terminated by the Church following its investigation into a complaint that he had been involved in the sexual abuse of children. He had made a successful claim of unfair dismissal under the statutory scheme and had been reinstated. This allowed him to make good his pecuniary losses. He then brought a claim in contract alleging that his employers had breached the implied term of mutual trust and confidence by the manner of their investigation of his conduct. He sought to recover damages under several heads including damages for distress,

[11] [2002] 2 AC 732.

[12] *Times*, 13 December 1983. A similar approach had previously been taken in *Cox v Philips Industries Ltd* [1976] 3 All ER 161.

[13] [1987] ICR 700. The Court of Appeal also took the opportunity to disapprove *Cox*, n. 12 above.

[14] See n. 8 above.

humiliation, and injury to feelings. The Court of Appeal (on the assumption that the contract contained an implied obligation of trust and confidence) held that the manner of investigation did not give rise to any breach. In any event, even if it had, a claim for injury to feelings was not competent.[15] This is disappointing; irrespective of how distressing and inappropriate the manner of investigation may have been, the employer would not be liable to pay compensation. A further glaring example of the need for effective remedies is furnished by the decision of the English Court of Appeal in *Gogay v Hertfordshire County Council.*[16] There the specific issue was whether the defendant local authority had acted reasonably in suspending the claimant from her post in a residential home while it investigated the circumstances surrounding a child living in that home. The letter of suspension informed the plaintiff that 'the issue to be investigated is an allegation of sexual abuse made by a young person in our care'. Ultimately the investigation concluded that there was no case to answer, but the claimant suffered psychiatric illness and loss of earnings as a result of her suspension. Before the Court of Appeal the question was whether the employer's decision to suspend amounted to a breach of mutual trust and confidence. It was held that the employers were in breach of the implied term because they had no reasonable grounds for suspending the plaintiff and had failed to carry out a proper investigation of the circumstances before suspending her. The devastating impact of such actions on employees was noted: 'Sexual abuse is a very serious matter, doing untold damage to those who suffer it. To be accused of it is also a serious matter. To be told by one's employer that one has been so accused is clearly calculated seriously to damage the relationship between employer and employee.'[17] Should a claim for injury to feelings be incompetent the only remedy left open to the employee is constructive dismissal. This is unfortunate. Employees should not be forced to choose between vindicating their right to dignity in the workplace and preserving their job security. The position in the UK looks even less satisfactory when it is recalled that compensation for injury to feelings is available where certain employment protection rights have been infringed. Discrimination statutes may allow for this expressly.[18] In such cases injury must still be proved, but: '[I]t will often be easy to prove, in the sense that no Tribunal will take much

[15] And see J. Riley, 'The Boundaries of Mutual Trust and Good Faith' (2009) 22 (1) AJLL 73.

[16] [2000] IRLR 703. [17] Ibid., 710.

[18] E.g. Sex Discrimination Act 1975, s. 65 (1)(b).

persuasion that the anger, distress and affront caused by the acts of discrimination has injured the applicant's feelings'.[19]

Canada and New Zealand

Traditionally the Canadian courts had also adhered to *Addis*,[20] but the Supreme Court's decision in *Wallace v United Grain Growers*[21] constituted a significant departure. In *Wallace* the court dealt with the remedies available where an employment contract was terminated in bad faith. The majority declined to find that the contract contained an implied obligation of good faith in respect of dismissal but, somewhat inconsistently, went on to hold that the manner of dismissal might impact upon the damages awarded in respect of the notice period. By assessing damages on this basis the Supreme Court accepted, rather circuitously, that the employer is indeed under a common law duty with respect to the way in which termination of employment is addressed. As a result an employee summarily dismissed on the basis of, for example, wrongful allegations could expect to receive compensation for injury to feelings. The nature of the employment relationship, and in particular the impact of termination on the more vulnerable party, necessitated a modification of the law:

> the loss of one's job is always a traumatic event. However, when termination is accompanied by acts of bad faith in the manner of discharge, the results can be especially devastating. In my opinion, to ensure that employees receive adequate protection, employers ought to be held to an obligation of good faith and fair dealing in the manner of dismissal, the breach of which will be compensated for by adding to the length of the notice period.[22]

Wallace might appear to represent a significant improvement on the position in *Addis* but the approach was still somewhat problematic. *Wallace* did not permit a claim for injury to feelings to be made in its own right; any element of damages for such loss had to be parasitic on another head of claim. This gave rise to several difficulties.

The Supreme Court returned to this aspect of the law of damages in *Fidler v Sun Life Assurance*.[23] There the claimant was an employee of a bank who developed chronic fatigue syndrome. The claimant, along with

[19] *Ministry of Defence v Cannock* [1994] IRLR 509, 524.

[20] *Peso Silver Mines v Cropper* [1966] SCR 673; *Vorvis v Insurance Corp. of British Columbia* [1989] 1 SCR 1085.

[21] [1997] 3 SCR 701. [22] Ibid., 742. [23] [2006] 2 SCR 3.

her fellow employees, was covered by a group policy provided by the defendant insurer, which included long-term disability benefits. Initially benefits were paid under the policy but payment ceased following an investigation (involving surveillance by private investigators) which led the insurer to conclude that the claimant's activities were inconsistent with the disability which she maintained that she suffered from. At the time of termination the insurer had no medical evidence to support this. The court in *Fidler* held that the failure to make payment was in breach of contract and went on to consider whether damages in respect of mental distress arose. The court rejected the orthodoxy of *Addis* which was seen as being contrary to first principles. The Supreme Court concluded that existing cases allowing for recovery for mental distress should be seen as an expression of the general principle of compensatory damages, rather than as an exception to that principle. Damages for injury to feelings should be recoverable provided it was within the contemplation of the parties and therefore not too remote. Freed from the shackles of *Addis*, claims of this sort return to the mainstream. *Fidler* was a case which arose out of the employment relationship but was not an action brought against the employer, though it quite easily could have been, had the employer agreed to provide disability benefits directly, given that the claim concerned the remuneration package. The wrongful withholding of any element of the package would be likely to be of immense concern to the employee. In 2008 the Supreme Court in *Honda Canada v Keays*[24] applied the reasoning in *Fidler* directly to the employment contract. This allowed the unorthodoxy of *Wallace* to be departed from whilst preserving entitlement to damages for mental distress. Keays had sued for wrongful dismissal and the trial judge had found that he was entitled to a notice period of fifteen months. Given the manner of dismissal this period was increased to twenty-four months. The Supreme Court upheld this award but reformed the law on '*Wallace*' damages. In future, in any particular case, it must be asked what would have been within the contemplation of the parties. The mere fact of wrongful dismissal will not give rise to a claim for injury to feelings; the claimant must have suffered the sort of treatment condemned by *Wallace*. The court endorsed contemporary thinking that there is an expectation by both parties to an employment contract that employers will act in good faith in the manner of dismissing an employee. *Honda*'s application of *Fidler* to the employment context means that the law as stated in

[24] (2008) 294 DLR (4th) 577.

Wallace is refined and brought within the main body of contract law. Damages in respect of injury to feelings become a head of claim in their own right and can be determined on a more principled basis, i.e. by reference to the extent of the distress caused. The amount given in respect of the notice period is no longer to be artificially adjusted.

The courts in New Zealand have been pioneers in this area and arrived at the current position in Canada some time ago. In *Whelan v Waitaki Meats* the plaintiff recovered damages for injury to feelings because the manner of dismissal was such as to cause him undue mental distress, anxiety, humiliation and loss of dignity.[25] The question boils down to what was in the reasonable contemplation of the parties.[26] The Court of Appeal has also pleaded for moderation in awards.[27]

Conclusions

The decision of the Supreme Court in *Honda* demonstrates that recognition of a claim for injury to feelings need not present any issue of principle. *Addis* can be seen as representing an aberration from the general principles of contractual damages and constituting a barrier to contract fulfilling its normal compensatory function. In a similar vein in *Farley v Skinner* Lord Scott had stated that the issue can and should be resolved by applying the well-known principles laid down in *Hadley v Baxendale*.[28] Traditional policy reasons have continued to dictate that the Australian and UK courts assume that the parties to a contract take the risk of upset should a breach arise. It was pointed out in *Johnson v Unisys* that, by the very fact of contracting, the contracting parties take the risk of the 'ordinary feelings of anxiety, frustration and disappointment caused by any breach of contract'.[29] However, the modern employee no longer accepts the sorts of risks that commercial parties do. It is, of course, the case that the rules on remoteness require that recoverable harm was within the contemplation of the parties at the time the contract was entered into. It must surely be the case that the parties would anticipate that should termination take place in a humiliating manner, harm might well arise. It is equally foreseeable that a breach of mutual trust also gives rise to a risk of injury to feelings. It is worthy of note that *Fidler* accepted that mental distress of the kind experienced by

[25] [1991] 2 NZLR 74; *Stuart v Armourguard Security* [1996] 1 NZLR 484.
[26] *Mouat v Clark Boyce* [1992] NZLR 559. [27] Ibid.
[28] (1854) 9 Exch. 341. [29] *Johnson*, n. 4 above, 547.

the claimant was reasonably within the contemplation of the parties when they entered into the contract of disability insurance.

What objections might there be to reforming the common law so that injury to feelings was compensated? It might be said that the courts would find it impossible to determine the amount due. This has not proved an insuperable difficulty in breach of contract cases where recovery in respect of upset or injury to feelings has been allowed.[30] Similarly where an award has been made under the auspices of employment protection law the courts and tribunals have dealt with the matter in a perfectly satisfactory way. The Court of Appeal, in *Vento v Chief Constable*, felt able to give general guidance on the approach to awards for injury to feelings.[31] The views of the New Zealand Law Commission are also worth noting:

> There may be residual concerns about the lack of predictability in quantification of damages for mental distress, injury to feelings and humiliation, and a reluctance to leave the matter to those tribunals and

[30] Again in *Vento v Chief Constable* [2003] IRLR 102, 110 it was said that: 'Employment Tribunals and those who practise in them might find it helpful if this Court were to identify three broad bands of compensation for injury to feelings, as distinct from compensation for psychiatric or similar personal injury. (i) The top band should normally be between £15,000 and £25,000. Sums in this range should be awarded in the most serious cases, such as where there has been a lengthy campaign of discriminatory harassment on the ground of sex or race. This case falls within that band. Only in the most exceptional case should an award of compensation for injury to feelings exceed £25,000. (ii) The middle band of between £5,000 and £15,000 should be used for serious cases, which do not merit an award in the highest band. (iii) Awards of between £500 and £5,000 are appropriate for less serious cases, such as where the act of discrimination is an isolated or one off occurrence. In general, awards of less than £500 are to be avoided altogether, as they risk being regarded as so low as not to be a proper recognition of injury to feelings.'

[31] In *Vento*, ibid., 109 it was said that '(i) Awards for injury to feelings are compensatory. They should be just to both parties. They should compensate fully without punishing the tortfeasor. Feelings of indignation at the tortfeasor's conduct should not be allowed to inflate the award. (ii) Awards should not be too low, as that would diminish respect for the policy of the anti-discrimination legislation. Society has condemned discrimination and awards must ensure that it is seen to be wrong. On the other hand, awards should be restrained, as excessive awards could, to use the phrase of Sir Thomas Bingham MR, be seen as the way to "untaxed riches". (iii) Awards should bear some broad general similarity to the range of awards in personal injury cases. We do not think that this should be done by reference to any particular type of personal injury award, rather to the whole range of such awards. (iv) In exercising that discretion in assessing a sum, tribunals should remind themselves of the value in everyday life of the sum they have in mind. This may be done by reference to purchasing power or by reference to earnings. (v) Finally, tribunals should bear in mind Sir Thomas Bingham's reference for the need for public respect for the level of awards made.'

> courts empowered to award compensation. If so, it would be possible for legislation to contain a ceiling. That might be prescribed in terms of a specific monetary limit or of a period of a particular employee's recent earnings.[32]

It may also be objected that: '[A]ny breach of contract that results in pecuniary loss to the injured party will inevitably cause some mental distress – rage and frustration at least.'[33] However, tribunals and the courts would almost certainly take the view that it would be unlikely to be in the reasonable contemplation of the parties that insignificant breaches would give rise to hurt to feelings. Such an application of the rules on remoteness would then tend to restrict the numbers of claims made. Policy reasons, including an enterprise liability approach to risk allocation, dictate that full recovery of losses sustained should take place in the employment context.

32 New Zealand Law Commission Report No. 18, n. 5 above, 57.

33 *Brown v Waterloo Regional Board* (1983) 150 DLR (3d) 729, 733.

11

Enterprise liability and non-delegable duties

Within the law of tort non-delegable duties have long given rise to controversy and strong criticism. Fleming noted 'the apparent absence of any coherent theory to explain when, and why, a particular duty should be so classified; and it has been questioned whether the resulting uncertainty and complexity of the law is matched by any corresponding advantages'.[1] Irrespective of whether the criticism is justified the concept is unusual within the common law of tort in that it is a form of strict liability. It also is at odds with the law's general approach to delegation which is to facilitate it. For example, the law does not tend to place barriers in the path of hiring an independent contractor. Employers frequently need to engage the services of a third party where performance of a task calls for some skill or experience which the employer does not possess. The courts are cognisant of the fact that economic activity is hugely interdependent. The law is normally willing to rest content on the basis that reasonable care over selection has taken place. The High Court of Australia has pointed out that, on occasion, it may be difficult to see how the obligation of reasonable care could be discharged in the absence of delegation: 'In many cases (although not in this) the independent contractor will have been engaged by the roads authority precisely because it enjoys technical expertise or a special capacity which would make the interference of the roads authority completely inappropriate – at least as a general rule.'[2]

Of late the law on non-delegable duties has attracted a good deal of attention, both academic and judicial. For instance, in cases such as *New South Wales v Lepore*[3] and *Lister v Hesley Hall*,[4] the courts may have to choose between a vicarious liability solution and the imposition of a non-delegable duty. In the UK, in *Lister*, the former approach was

[1] J. Fleming, *The Law of Torts*, 9th edn (Sydney: Law Book Co., 1998), p. 434.
[2] *Leichhardt Municipal Council v Montgomery* [2007] 81 ALJR 686, 714.
[3] (2003) 212 CLR 511. [4] [2002] 1 AC 215.

adopted though Lord Hobhouse appeared somewhat inclined to the latter.[5] The resolution of individual cases apart, both the judiciary and academics have sought to identify an overarching rationalisation of the various situations where a non-delegable duty has been imposed. Such endeavours look to the establishment of a general principle that will be determinative of future cases. For instance, Murphy has emphasised the importance of the concept of assumption of responsibility. He argues that 'the fact that X assumes a responsibility is a good reason both to describe the duty as personal, and to continue to hold X responsible for its fulfilment notwithstanding any attempt to delegate it to a third party, however carefully chosen'.[6] This synthesis of precedent was seen as 'a platform for the principled expansion of non-delegable categories'.[7] In the High Court of Australia, in an influential judgment in *Kondis v State Transport Authority*, Mason J hypothesised that a non-delegable duty is owed for one of two reasons: 'because the person on whom it is imposed has undertaken the care, supervision or control of the person or property of another or is so placed in relation to that person or his property as to assume a particular responsibility for his or its safety, in circumstances where the person affected might reasonably expect that due care will be exercised'.[8] The undertaking of any such rationalisation is predicated on the assumption that non-delegable duties can be viewed as a homogeneous class. In the author's opinion this assumption is precarious. The creation of non-delegable duties is driven (admittedly not always explicitly) by policy concerns which are often particular to specific contexts. Thus the Australian High Court has justified the existence of such a duty in the teacher/pupil relationship on the basis that it 'is the immaturity and inexperience of the children and their propensity for mischief that lie at the basis of the special responsibility which the law imposes on a school authority to take care for their safety'.[9] Such reasoning cannot be extended to a number of other contexts (such as employment) where a non-delegable duty has also been held to exist. Given this lack of underlying unity of purpose it is

[5] The High Court of Australia decision in *Lepore*, n. 3 above, displays similar tensions.

[6] J. Murphy, 'Juridical Foundations of Common Law Non-Delegable Duties' in J. W. Neyers, E. Chamberlain and S. G. A. Pitel (eds), *Emerging Issues in Tort Law* (Oxford: Hart Publishing, 2007), p. 390.

[7] Ibid., 391.

[8] (1984) 154 CLR 672, 687. Further elaboration of the thinking of the High Court is to be found in *Leichhardt*, n. 2 above, where it was said at 714 that 'the duties owed to them are personal because of their particularly high degree of dependence and vulnerability'.

[9] *Introvigne v Commonwealth* (1980) 150 CLR 258, 271.

difficult to see that one can extract a rationalisation which will not only encompass existing case law but also, critically, prescribe how the doctrine will operate in settings that have yet to come before the courts. In a similar vein, in *Scott v Davis* Gummow J accepted that the criteria identified in *Kondis* may explain at least some cases where a non-delegable duty has been held to exist, and thus be 'historically descriptive', but went on to doubt whether such criteria have the capacity to be 'normatively predictive'.[10] Stevens adds that the 'key to understanding non-delegable duties is that there are several situations where the law imposes strict liability with disparate underlying rationales.'[11] The task of rationalisation is further complicated by the fact that a significant number of the landmark cases were decided a long time ago. It is by no means certain that the underpinning policy considerations continue to pertain. If they do not the validity of some non-delegable duties may be in doubt and the task of induction more arduous still.

The employment relationship

The number of non-delegable duties is limited but it is trite law that the employer's duty to take reasonable care for the safety of employees cannot be delegated.[12] One might assume from this that it is one of the core rules governing an enterprise's responsibility for its staff. The operation of the law on non-delegable duties can result in the employer being liable, in the absence of fault, for the behaviour of an independent contractor. The duty owed to employees in respect of a safe system of work provides one such example. The fact that the employer has taken reasonable care in selecting an independent contractor who is to devise such a safe system is neither here nor there. It remains the employer's responsibility to manage it: 'In the case of the employer there is no unfairness in imposing on him a non-delegable duty; it is reasonable that he should bear liability for the negligence of his independent contractors in devising a safe system of work. If he requires his employee to work according to an unsafe system he should bear the consequences.'[13] The underlying notion is that the employer's duty towards its employees

[10] *Scott v Davis* (2000) 74 ALJR 1410, 1456.

[11] R. Stevens, 'Non-Delegable Duties and Vicarious Liability' in Neyers, Chamberlain and Pitel, n. 6 above, 331.

[12] For detailed exposition see B. Cotter and D. Bennett, *Munkman On Employer's Liability*, 15th edn (London: LexisNexis, 2009).

[13] *Kondis*, n. 8 above, 688.

is a fundamental responsibility of the enterprise which cannot be avoided; non-compliance results in the enterprise being liable.

The original policy reasons for the imposition of the duty in the employment context are easy to find. It is clear that the House of Lords in the seminal case of *Wilson and Clyde Coal Co. v English*[14] were concerned to circumvent the impact of the doctrine of common employment. In the words of Lord MacMillan: 'in this appeal your Lordships have to consider and accommodate the spheres of operation, in the law of master and servant of two competing doctrines, the doctrine of vicarious liability and the doctrine of common employment'.[15] The latter doctrine has long ceased to be a concern. There is, though, nothing in *Wilson* to suggest why a non-delegable duty should be imposed where the law of vicarious liability is not constrained by common employment.[16] The catalyst behind the imposition of a duty was the need to meet the gap, in the defendant's responsibilities, left by the law of vicarious liability, a gap that has long since vanished. Does this mean that the employer's non-delegable duty can no longer be justified? Should *Wilson* be overruled? It is arguable that the answer to these questions is yes, but such a conclusion is not inevitable. It is perfectly conceivable that factors particular to the employment context have emerged which can provide a satisfactory rationale for the continued existence of the duty.

The UK courts have yet to proffer a contemporary justification, though the High Court of Australia has. As we have seen, in *Kondis*, Mason J explained that non-delegable duties are established for one of two reasons: either because the defendant has undertaken the care, supervision or control of another or because he has assumed responsibility for that other person.[17] It seems incontrovertible that the employer

[14] [1937] 3 All ER 628. Recently, in *Farraj v Kings Healthcare NHS Trust* [2009] EWCA Civ 1203, Dyson LJ said at para. 72 that: 'Although the House of Lords did not articulate the reason for deciding that this duty was non-delegable, it would seem that it was based on the fact that (i) by reason of the doctrine of common employment, the employer was not vicariously liable for the negligence of the employee who was entrusted with the task and (ii) it was undesirable to leave an employee to pursue his claim for compensation against a fellow employee, a remedy of doubtful value.'

[15] Ibid., 637.

[16] Neither is there in the much more recent decision of the House of Lords in *McDermid v Nash Dredging* [1987] AC 966. This was despite the fact, as McKendrick has pointed out, that the case extended the scope of the employer's duty by including the operation as distinct from the provision of the system. See E. McKendrick, 'Vicarious Liability and Independent Contractors: A Re-Examination' (1990) 53 MLR 770, 773.

[17] *Kondis*, n. 8 above.

has undertaken the 'care, supervision and control' of employees but, at the same time, the presence of any or all of those elements does not allow one to differentiate between situations where the employer's liability is strict and those where it is not. The employer (vicarious liability aside), for example, is not liable in the absence of personal fault where an employee is harassed by a colleague in the workplace.[18] Mason J also suggests that the concept of assumption of responsibility may provide a rationalisation for the imposition of a non-delegable duty. This view has attracted academic support.[19] It is of course the case that the employer may come under tortious obligations by assuming responsibility towards an employee. Interaction between the parties over a specific issue can give rise to such an obligation. An instance of this is *Lennon v Metropolitan Police Commissioner*[20] where a claim was made against the employer over failure to give advice to the plaintiff about the preservation of entitlement to allowances upon the transfer to another force. The employer was found to have assumed responsibility because a member of the employer's staff had led the plaintiff to believe that he could leave it to the employer to make all the arrangements for the transfer. The employer was held to have breached this duty by failing to advise how leave might be taken in such a way as would not break continuity of service and thereby prejudice entitlement to an allowance. *Lennon* founded a duty on the basis of the interchange between the parties and the ensuing specific reliance. Where the notion of assumption of responsibility is invoked in the context of non-delegable duties it cannot be claimed that it arises in the same way. Instead it might be said that, simply by virtue of the employer's role in the employment relationship rather than anything that he has done in particular, 'general reliance' is placed upon him. However, irrespective of whether an assumption of responsibility is founded on the basis of specific or general reliance it need not require that more than reasonable care be exercised. Thus Mason J's second reason is no more convincing than the first and, in fact, suffers from the same deficiency. It may or may not offer a perfectly good rationale of why an employer owes a duty in negligence to employees but does not explain why that duty is strict and why reasonable care over delegation is not enough. Mason J addresses this by saying that 'there is no unfairness in imposing on him a non-delegable duty; it is reasonable that he should bear liability for the negligence of his

[18] *Waters v Commr of Police* [2000] 1 WLR 1607.
[19] See Murphy, n. 6 above. [20] [2004] IRLR 385.

independent contractors in devising a safe system of work. If he requires his employee to work according to an unsafe system he should bear the consequences.'[21] This simply offers no explanation at all. The question why it is reasonable is left unanswered. Echoing Denning LJ in the old medical negligence case of *Cassidy v Ministry of Health*,[22] Mason J also suggested that the fact that the employee is dependent on the employer's judgement in matters of safety points towards a duty being owed:

> The employer has the exclusive responsibility for the safety of the appliances, the premises and the system of work to which he subjects his employee and the employee has no choice but to accept and rely on the employer's provision and judgment in relation to these matters. The consequence is that in these relevant respects the employee's safety is in the hands of the employer; it is his responsibility. The employee can reasonably expect therefore that care and skill will be taken.[23]

Again the general assumption in the law of negligence is that dependence on the activities of others leads to nothing more than fault-based liability. A prime example is motoring, where road users are hugely dependent upon the behaviour of their fellows. Present-day concerns over the 'slaughter on the roads' notwithstanding, dependency does not trigger strict liability.

The role assigned by Mason J to assumption of responsibility gains support from the academic writings of Murphy.[24] However, the latter accepts that the concept also functions to 'ground an "ordinary" duty of care in negligence cases'.[25] In acknowledgement of the consequent problem of over-inclusion he suggests that 'some further criterion must be found to be working in tandem with an assumption of responsibility to ground' a non-delegable duty.[26] It is argued that the answer is to be found in the essential characteristics of non-delegable duties; they are presented as being affirmative in nature. Judicial support for this analysis is said to be contained in the judgment of Lord Wright in *Wilson*, where the learned judge said that 'the employer's personal duty is fulfilled by the exercise of due care and skill. But it is not fulfilled by entrusting its fulfilment to employees, even though selected with due care and skill.'[27] With respect this dictum does no more than confirm that the employer's duty is non-delegable; it does not say that it is affirmative. Murphy also

[21] *Kondis*, n. 8 above, 688.

[22] [1951] 2 KB 343. Lord Denning also regarded a patient's lack of control over the selection of those who treat him/her as significant.

[23] *Kondis*, n. 8 above, 687. [24] Murphy, n. 6 above. [25] Ibid., 387.

[26] Ibid. [27] *Wilson*, n. 14 above, 640.

cites the duty owed by a hospital to a patient, but again this duty is not affirmative in nature. In truth the relationships mentioned are simply ones in the course of which an affirmative duty in tort may arise. On any conventional analysis they cannot be characterised as affirmative.[28] In any event, even if some existing non-delegable duties could be so viewed, we would be no further forward in the search for a criterion which could be used in future cases to determine whether a non-delegable duty was owed; to say that a duty is affirmative is merely to describe its content. It is, therefore, submitted that Murphy's refinement of Mason J's approach does not cure the underlying deficiencies inherent in resort to assumption of responsibility.

Both of the rationalisations set out in *Kondis* may be defended on the basis that they provide accurate and comprehensive descriptions of situations where non-delegable duties have been imposed. However, this is achieved at the expense of their being expressed in such general terms that they are over-inclusive in that they are equally capable of describing fault-based liabilities. There is a further deficiency in that they fail to articulate the role of policy in the establishment of non-delegable duties and that the relevant policy concerns vary depending upon the context. The approach in *Kondis* may be contrasted with that taken by the courts where the law of vicarious liability has been concerned. There it has long been acknowledged that the law is firmly grounded in policy concerns. At the same time it would have been fair to say that there was much scope for debate as to which policy factors were relevant and how they inter-related. It is the contention of this book that *Bazley v Curry* has led to 'enterprise liability' becoming the primary justification for the imposition of vicarious liability.[29]

Enterprise liability and the employer's non-delegable duty

It is submitted that enterprise liability also offers a contemporary justification for non-delegable duties in the employment context. The possibility of defects in the system of work – and consequent imperilment of employees – are clearly risks run by the enterprise. Moreover, it is inevitable that failures in the system will arise from time to time. The employer will be liable if it has not taken reasonable care with regard

[28] It is, of course, the case that an obligation to take reasonable care will often contain a positive element.

[29] An approach heavily criticised by J. W. Neyers, 'A Theory of Vicarious Liability', (2005) (43) Alberta Law Review 287.

to the provision of a safe system. However, if the task of establishment or operation of the system is delegated, the law still regards that task as being undertaken as part of the conduct of the enterprise and, as an inevitable corollary, the risk remains one of the risks of the enterprise. As a result the enterprise should remain liable even if delegation was undertaken with reasonable care. The enterprise has created certain risks and the concept of non-delegable duties prevents legal responsibility being attributed elsewhere. It would not be surprising if enterprise liability played the same justificatory function in relation to non-delegable duties as it does in respect of vicarious liability. The business of an enterprise cannot be conducted unless the carrying out of its activities is delegated to the employees. Both legal concepts perform the same essential function of ensuring that delegation does not come at the price of the avoidance of legal responsibility by an enterprise for risks generated by it. In the case of vicarious liability this is ensured by stipulating that taking reasonable care in the hiring of staff does not absolve the enterprise of responsibility. If say a lorry driver is careless, responsibility is still to be attributed to the employer. Driving was required in pursuing the aims of the enterprise and careless driving is one of the risks inherent in that activity. Enterprise liability dictates that the enterprise should pay – the enterprise has created the risk and must, in all fairness, bear the consequences should it materialise. In contrast to the law of vicarious liability, cases involving non-delegable duties have been reticent about articulating the relevant policy factors.

Nevertheless such articulation as there has been is entirely compatible with according enterprise liability the same status of primary justification that it enjoys where vicarious liability is concerned. The policy factors that have been aired in non-delegable duty cases resemble the secondary justifications identified by the court in *Bazley*. Imposing a non-delegable duty on the employer has been said to promote deterrence. In *Lepore* Gummow and Hayne JJ quoted Pollock to the effect that to impose a duty upon the person who undertakes the venture may, in at least some cases, induce more careful conduct of that or similar ventures.[30] The compensatory function of the law of tort is also furthered in that the employer is more likely to be able to pay: 'Contractors may not, in fact, be insured or adequately insured. Recognition of a non-delegable duty of care would have the merit of enhancing

[30] *Lepore*, n. 3 above, para. 260.

the likelihood that an innocent victim of someone's carelessness (such as the respondent) could recover from a solvent defendant.'[31]

One benefit from invoking enterprise liability as a means of justification is that inconsistencies in the law can be addressed. At present, even within the employment context, the law on non-delegable duties contains an element of incoherence. The common law position on the provision of defective equipment provides one example. An attempt to expand the scope of the decision in *Wilson* was made in the 1950s in *Davie v New Merton Board Mills*[32] (the Australian courts follow *Davie*) where an employee was injured by a defective tool. It was noted that had the tool been carelessly manufactured by an employee then the employer would have been vicariously liable and it would have been no defence that the employer had taken reasonable care to select a competent workman. What if the employer had taken reasonable care to buy from a reputable manufacturer? In the Court of Appeal Jenkins LJ (dissenting) had held this made no difference. The obligation to supply safe plant was personal to the employer and could not be delegated. Such a conclusion was a natural consequence of *Wilson* and, additionally, was justifiable on policy grounds:

> an employee has to use the tools provided by the employer and has no voice in the selection of the tools or as to the manufacturer or supplier from whom they are obtained. If he is injured through a defect in one of the tools provided by his employer, it is surely not unreasonable that the employer should be held liable if the defect was due to the negligent manufacture of the tool, whether by the employer himself or by somebody else.[33]

The House of Lords rejected the approach of Jenkins LJ. The mooted extension was not required by *Wilson* and, more fundamentally, ran counter to the governing principles of fault liability. Viewed in the open-textured terms of assumption of responsibility the decision of the House of Lords is undoubtedly capable of justification. As has been seen, the undertaking of such an assumption would be wholly compatible with restricting responsibility to an obligation to take reasonable care to ensure that the tools come from a reputable manufacturer. An enterprise liability perspective may point to a different conclusion.[34]

A further way in which inconsistency might be thought to arise is in connection with the provision of safe premises. The duty on an employer

[31] *Leichhardt*, n. 2 above, 709. [32] [1959] 1 All ER 346. *Kondis*, n. 8 above.

[33] [1958] 1 All ER 67, 81.

[34] In the UK this particular instance of common law inconsistency has been rendered irrelevant given that the impact of the decision in *Davie* was reversed by the Employer's Liability (Defective Equipment) Act 1969.

to take all reasonable steps to ensure the safety of employees applies whether the premises where an employee is directed to work are occupied by the employer itself or by a third party. The law here is in a state of some confusion, reflecting, the author would suggest, the lack of theoretical underpinning. On the one hand, it is said that the duty cannot be delegated. On the other, it was said in the Court of Appeal in *Cook v Squares*[35] that where an employee is injured on premises in the occupation of a third party, the extent of the employer's responsibility depends upon what is reasonable in all the circumstances. For example, in *Cook* it was said that 'where a number of employees are going to work on a foreign site or where one or two employees are called upon to work there for a very considerable period of time, an employer may be required to inspect the site and satisfy himself that the occupiers are conscious of their obligations concerning the safety of people working there'.[36] The amelioration in favour of the employer in *Cook* gives rise to an unsatisfactory hybrid whereby a non-delegable duty is imposed unless that would be unreasonable.

The differing judicial views over the implications of *Wilson* should there be defective equipment or unsafe premises are not surprising. *Wilson* provided a pragmatic deviation from the general applicability of fault-based norms but failed to furnish any wider explanation. Why, though, should an employee who works away from the employer's premises (or who uses a tool not made by the employer) be in an inferior position? In both cases the risk of injury is run for the benefit of the employer and, therefore, the employer should bear the financial consequences should that risk materialise (leaving the employer to recover against third parties).[37] The fact that the injury was caused by the condition of another's premises is irrelevant. The injury arose because the employee was required to be at those premises in furtherance of the employer's business.

Enterprise liability and the law of employer's liability

The contention of this chapter is that enterprise liability provides a sound and convincing theoretical underpinning of the law of non-delegable duties in the employment context. If that contention is well

[35] [1992] ICR 262. [36] Ibid., 271.

[37] Stevens, n. 11 above, points out at 355 that the decision in *Wilson* 'appears anomalous not only in relation to other cases of an employer's liability to ensure his employee's safety but also in relation to the duties of those who rent tools'.

founded there are further implications for the law of employer's liability. It is arguable that enterprise liability dictates that vicarious liability should be extended to cover the acts of independent contractors (see Chapter 7). It is also arguable that the three-pronged statement of the employer's duty to employees set out in *Wilson* is underdeveloped in situations where the staff of a number of employers are working together on a particular project, e.g. a construction site.[38] Recourse to enterprise liability may assist in determining the proper extent of an employer's common law responsibilities in that context. The employer's duty to employees set out in, and rendered non-delegable by, *Wilson* is premised on a rather atomised model. The law's vision of the working environment is seen through the eyes of an individual employer working independently and relying on its own workforce (which may or may not be employees) to perform the work. Frequently, of course, in fields like construction and engineering, the position is very different. The common law's failure to take full account of this gives rise to several issues. First, and more prosaically, the safety of workers involved in multi-employer activity is compromised because insufficient attention is paid by the common law to the interaction of the different employing entities. Second, the employer's responsibilities in law fall short of those that would be compelled by an enterprise liability analysis.

In general, in the UK, the obligations imposed by the law of employer's liability are not owed to the employees of other enterprises who interact with the employer's business.[39] A dictum of Lord Keith in the employer's liability case of *Ferguson v Welsh* is often cited in this context:

> It would not ordinarily be reasonable to expect an occupier of premises having engaged a contractor whom he has reasonable grounds for regarding as competent, to supervise the contractor's activities in order to ensure that he was discharging his duty to his employees to observe a safe system of work. In special circumstances, on the other hand, where the occupier knows or has reason to suspect that the contractor is using an unsafe system of work, it might be reasonable for the occupier to take steps to see that the system was made safe.[40]

[38] In *Wilson*, n. 14 above, at 645 Lord Maugham noted that there was a duty on the employer to take reasonable care, and to use reasonable skill: first, to provide and maintain proper machinery, plant, appliances, and works; secondly, to select properly skilled persons to manage and superintend the business; and thirdly, to provide a proper system of working.

[39] A more general *Donoghue v Stevenson* [1932] AC 562 type of duty may arise.

[40] [1987] 1 WLR 1553, 1560.

The general rule has recently been reaffirmed by the Court of Appeal in *Makepeace v Evans Bros.*[41] It must be admitted that there are exceptions, e.g. the employer may come under a duty of co-ordination.[42] It is, however, not entirely clear when the latter duty arises. In *McArdle v Andmac Roofing* the main contractor was obliged when it employed two firms of subcontractors in circumstances 'which inevitably involved that they should work in close proximity to each other and in close proximity to this dangerous hole in the roof, to take reasonable steps, or to see that Andmac and Newton took reasonable steps, to prevent the workmen from coming to harm'.[43] It is difficult to discern from the judgments when such a duty would otherwise arise and what weight, for example, should be placed on factors such as the existence of 'close proximity'. The fact that the subcontractors were small concerns may have counted against the defendant. Given the way work is organised in contemporary society one might have thought that the employer's responsibilities should be more all embracing. Exceptions, such as the rule in *McArdle*, might be thought to form the basis for a reformulation of the general rule. In this regard the Australian position is somewhat different and merits careful consideration.

Over twenty years ago, in *Stevens v Brodribb Sawmilling*,[44] the High Court of Australia took the view that where the work being carried out for the main contractor involves interdependent activities safety can only be assured if it takes on a co-ordination role. The undertaking of that role was in turn compelled by the duty said to be owed in negligence, Mason J stating that:

> If an entrepreneur engages independent contractors to do work which might as readily be done by employees in circumstances where there is a risk to them of injury arising from the nature of the work and where there is a need for him to give directions as to when and where the work is to be done and to co-ordinate the various activities, he has an obligation to prescribe a safe system of work.[45]

Mason J was of the view that interdependency of activity gave rise to a responsibility to co-ordinate. However, he also regarded it as relevant that the contractors involved were hired 'to do work which might as readily be done by employees'. The focus of concern may therefore be in the realms of 'disguised employment'. Where an employer exploits its superior bargaining power to structure the relationship as self-employment (when

[41] [2001] ICR 241. [42] *McCardle v Andmac Roofing* [1967] 1 All ER 583.
[43] Ibid., 589. [44] (1986) 160 CLR 16. [45] Ibid., 31.

it might just as readily have been one of employment) it will thereby avoid the duties set out in *Wilson*. Mason J, perfectly understandably, may have been anxious to avoid this conclusion. In *Balesfire v Adams* he expressed concern about working relationships which give rise to 'a vulnerability that was capable of exploitation with immunity from the consequences that flow from an employment relationship'.[46] Similar concerns over disguised employment were evident in *Rockdale Beef v Carey*.[47] There the claimant had been employed by the defendant as a stockman for a number of years. In 1997 he ceased being an employee and was engaged as an independent contractor. The change in the contractual arrangements included a pay increase, but the New South Wales Court of Appeal also noted the advantages that accrued to the employer: 'It no longer needed to take out workers compensation insurance cover in respect of his employment and there must have been opportunities for savings resulting from a number of administrative tasks, imposed by law on employers, no longer being necessary.'[48] There was, however, no change in the nature or methods or extent of his work. The conclusion was reached that the claimant was, in effect, an employee due to the degree of control the employer exercised over the work site and system of work. The claimant was viewed as being as reliant on the defendant for his safety as any employee. The substantive content of the relationship was what mattered. As a result the defendants owed a duty to take reasonable care to provide a safe system of work. The obligations owed to agency workers by end-users have also come under scrutiny and again the Australian courts may impose the sorts of duties that would be owed by employer to employee. In *TNT Australia v Christie*[49] the plaintiff was employed by an employment agency (Manpower) who assigned him to work at a brewery operated by TNT. The plaintiff had been assigned there for almost nine months at the time of the accident. He used to report to the TNT warehouse manager who gave him his daily duties. He worked alongside four permanent employees of TNT and was the sole casual worker, but his duties did not differ from those of his fellow workers. The plaintiff was injured when a 'pallet jack' he was using to pick up beer orders malfunctioned and moved backwards over his foot. The plaintiff sued both Manpower and TNT. Manpower were found to have breached their non-delegable duty of care by failing to adequately instruct and provide proper assistance to the plaintiff in the performance of his duties. The trial judge also found

[46] [2006] NSWCA 112, para. 31. [47] [2003] NSWCA 132.
[48] Ibid., para. 20. [49] (2003) 65 NSWLR 1.

that TNT owed duties to the plaintiff analogous to those duties. This conclusion was upheld on appeal given that TNT exercised day-to-day control over the plaintiff's work activities, treating him to all intents and purposes in the same manner as its employees as regards work on the factory floor. It was noted that employees of TNT told him what time to come to work, what work he had to do each day, what hours he would work and the specific jobs that he would have to do. The view was taken that the plaintiff and TNT had placed themselves in a relationship, day in and day out, which was indistinguishable from that of employee and employer. The extent of the control existing in practice was crucial to this finding.

The approach of Mason J in *Brodribb* may take an unduly narrow view of the situation given that interdependence might be thought to bring about risks which go beyond concerns over disguised employment. Further issues in respect of multi-employer activity were taken on board in *Brodribb* by Brennan J, who formulated the duty at issue somewhat differently: 'An entrepreneur who organizes an activity involving a risk of injury to those engaged in it is under a duty to use reasonable care in organizing the activity to avoid or minimize that risk, and that duty is imposed whether or not the entrepreneur is under a further duty of care to servants employed by him to carry out that activity.'[50] Brennan J states the obligation in broader terms and does not seek to differentiate in any way between different categories of subcontractors. Discharge of that obligation may require both supervision and co-ordination: 'the circumstances may make it necessary for the entrepreneur to retain and exercise a supervisory power or to prescribe the respective areas of responsibility of independent contractors if confusion about those areas involves a risk of injury'.[51] It is submitted that the approach of Brennan J is to be preferred to that taken in the UK in that it is much more attuned to the myriad of ways in which work is organised. It is also much more closely aligned to the demands of public policy as reflected in the requirements imposed by modern health and safety legislation.[52]

[50] *Brodribb*, n. 44 above, 47. Brennan J added, with reference to *Sutherland Shire Council v Heyman* (1985) 59 ALJR 564, 587, that the entrepreneur's duty arises simply because he is creating the risk and his duty is more limited than the duty owed by an employer to an employee.

[51] Ibid.

[52] For example, see the duties placed upon the principal contractor in the UK by virtue of Regulation 22 of the Construction (Design and Management) Regulations 2007 (SI 2007/320).

The position in *Brodribb* may be justifiable on policy grounds simply because it furthers the safety of workers. It may be correct that the burden on the main contractor be increased. He will often be best placed to ensure that safety measures are taken; indeed it may be impracticable for anyone else to assume that role. Such pragmatic considerations are reinforced by the logic of enterprise liability which, as we have seen, seeks to attribute responsibility to the enterprise for activities which it has undertaken that carry risks. The pursuit of any particular activity may require the services not just of an entity's own employees but also those who contract on a different basis. As a result it was submitted in Chapter 7 that a contractor should be seen as a constituent part of the enterprise. It is further submitted that it follows from this that the duty of care owed to the subcontractor's employees should be in line with that owed to the enterprise's actual employees. Both groups of staff encounter risks created by the enterprise whilst furthering its aims. It would seem equitable that parity of treatment in terms of safety obligations exists. Recent cases suggest that the Australian courts are moving in this direction in that the main contractor may be found to have 'quasi-employer' responsibility towards the employees of a subcontractor depending upon the control exercised over those staff. The extent of control retained and exercised by the main contractor gave rise to such a duty in *Maricic v Dalma Framework*.[53] The main contractor was obliged to ensure that those working for the subcontractor were not exposed to unreasonable risks to their safety.

Conclusions

Enterprise liability can provide a theoretical justification for the law of non-delegable duties in the employment context. The approach of Brennan J in *Brodribb* is also highly attractive. However, it might be said that such a modification of the present position would not go far enough because it permits of delegation in a way that vicarious liability and non-delegable duties do not. *Brodribb* itself stipulates that the employer, depending on the circumstances, may avoid liability provided reasonable care was taken over the selection of independent contractors:

> If there is no failure to take reasonable care in the employment of independent contractors competent to control their own systems of work, or in not retaining a supervisory power or in leaving undefined

[53] [2006] NSWCA 174.

> the contractors' respective areas of responsibility, the entrepreneur is not liable for damage caused merely by a negligent failure of an independent contractor to adopt or follow a safe system of work either within his area of responsibility or in an area of shared responsibility.[54]

This suggests that, to be consistent with enterprise liability, alignment with *Brodribb* is insufficient because, in terms of the obligations that would thereby be imposed by a revised law of employer's liability, disparate treatment of workers would still arise. Those working for the subcontractor would have less protection. As matters stand the employer cannot delegate the provision and operation of a safe system of work in respect of those directly employed. Why should it be permitted to do so in respect of other workers who are hired to further the aims of the enterprise? Enterprise liability would suggest that the employer should not be able to delegate the provision and operation of a safe system of work where the employees of subcontractors are concerned. Failure to so extend non-delegability means that employment of a subcontractor and consequent access to his employees allows for contracting-out of the employer's responsibilities. This position can only be maintained as long as subcontractors and their staff are not viewed as part of the employer's undertaking. It is the author's contention that they should be so viewed – to be consistent with enterprise liability the law of negligence must go behind the contractual arrangements entered into by the employer. This would result in an extension of the employer's non-delegable duty.

[54] *Brodribb*, n. 44 above, 48.

12

Fundamental obligations

Enterprise liability has the potential to have a significant impact on the obligations which govern the relations of employer and employee; so far it has not done so. Should it do so we might expect to see changes in the way that risk is allocated between the parties to the employment relationship (as discussed in Chapters 8, 9 and 10). Despite this the common law of employment has evolved very considerably in recent years and displayed far greater recognition of the interests of employees. Through the medium of the employment contract rather than the law of tort, the courts in all the jurisdictions under review have, through mechanisms such as implied terms, strengthened the rights of employees. The philosophical imperative has not been tort law's vision of enterprise liability. Instead a different conception of corporate responsibility has been arrived at through a judicial articulation of the key values which underpin the employment relationship. It is now judicially recognised that: 'Work is one of the most fundamental aspects in a person's life, providing the individual with a means of financial support and, as importantly, a contributory role in society. A person's employment is an essential component of his or her identity, self worth and emotional well-being.'[1] It follows from this that it is hugely important that the obligations of the employment contract serve to promote the dignity of the employee and ensure he/she is treated with respect. Traditionally, the common law has disregarded the imbalance of power that is the hallmark of employment relations. That is no longer the case and recognition of this is no longer the prerogative of the academic community. In *Slaight Communications v Ron Davidson* the Canadian Supreme Court endorsed the following passage from Sir Otto Kahn-Freund's seminal work, *Kahn-Freund's Labour and the Law*: 'The relation between an employer and an isolated

[1] *Reference Re Public Service Employee Relations Act* [1987] 1 SCR 313, 368. The dictum was quoted with approval in *Wallace v United Grain Growers Ltd* [1997] 3 SCR 701, per Iacobucci J, 742.

employee or worker is typically a relation between a bearer of power and one who is not a bearer of power.'[2] In a similar vein, in *Malik v BCCI* it was said that: 'An employment contract creates a close personal relationship, where there is often a disparity of power between the parties. Frequently the employee is vulnerable.'[3] The combined acknowledgement of the fact that the worker's interest in employment extends beyond pecuniary considerations and that there is almost always a significant disparity in bargaining power has proved pivotal. This dual recognition has prompted resort to a variety of devices such as the creation of implied terms as a means of protecting and promoting fundamental values. In the UK the implied obligation of mutual trust and confidence provides a means of translating employees' aspirations to be treated with dignity and respect into a primary legal obligation. It has also proved to be an effective tool with which to police employer discretion. The Australian courts have agonised over whether the contract of employment contains such a term; in *Burazin v Blacktown City Guardian Pty Ltd*[4] the full Federal Court left the question open. In the last few years the courts seem increasingly inclined to accept its existence.[5] It was accepted by the Supreme Court of South Australia in *McDonald v State of South Australia*, where Anderson J observed that there:

> are so many examples in the workplace where, without such an implied term, an employer could capriciously and unreasonably prejudice an employee in the workplace without any sanctions. On the face of it, if the term were not to be implied, it would allow employers to make unreasonable and unfair decisions without consultation with the employee and with consequences affecting the employee's enjoyment of their job.[6]

The decisions are not all one way.[7] Nevertheless, the term is steadily gaining greater and greater acceptance. Riley points out that its existence

[2] [1989] 1 SCR 1038. And see P. Davies and M. Freedland, *Kahn-Freund's Labour and the Law*, 3rd edn (London: Stevens & Sons, 1983).

[3] *Malik v Bank of Credit and Commerce International SA* [1998] AC 20, 37, per Lord Nicholls of Birkenhead.

[4] (1996) 142 ALR 144.

[5] *Easling v Mahoney Insurance Brokers* [2001] SASC 22; *Thomson v Orica Australia* (2002) 116 IR 186; *Morton v Transport Appeal Board* [2007] NSWSC 1454; *Downe v Sydney West Area Health Service (No. 2)* [2008] NSWSC 159.

[6] [2008] SASC 134, para. 388.

[7] The existence of such a term was rejected in *Walker v Citigroup* (2006) 226 ALR 114 and *Van Efferen v CMA* [2009] FCA 597.

was assumed by the High Court in *Koehler v Cerebos*.[8] In any event, there are other indications that current Australian judicial attitudes are broadly in line with those in the UK (see below for discussion of the legislation in New South Wales).

The Canadian courts have also been extremely active in extending the protection afforded by the common law. Whilst they have not adopted an obligation of mutual trust and confidence as such, they take the view that there is a fundamental implied term of the employment relationship which requires that the employer treat the employee with civility, decency, respect and dignity,[9] an approach endorsed by the Court of Appeal for Ontario in *Shah v Xerox Canada*.[10] The case is also notable in terms of judicial technique. A fundamental breach, allowing the employee to resign and claim constructive dismissal, might arise where the employer's behaviour made it 'intolerable' for the employee to remain in employment. Of course it might be said that such a state of affairs arises where the employee was not treated with decency, but what is particularly striking about *Shah* is that the employee was not required to identify a specific term of the contract that had been breached provided that the 'employer's treatment of the employee makes continued employment intolerable'. It is difficult to see how this approach is reconcilable with general contractual principles, but it conveys the strength of the judicial desire to promote a civilised working environment. The court in *Shah* cited with approval the judgment in *Whiting v Winnipeg River Brokenhead Community Futures Development Corp.*, where the trial judge had concluded that an employee had been constructively dismissed because of a series of incidents culminating in the imposition of probation where the employer had unjustifiably criticised the employee, levelled vague and unfounded accusations against her, and created a hostile and embarrassing work environment.[11] *Whiting* demonstrates the practical importance of the implied term of decency to the employee.

The unwelcome practices associated with a relationship founded upon unequal bargaining power can often be readily predicted. It comes as no surprise to find that numerous decisions have focused upon the issue of

[8] (2005) 222 CLR 44. And see J. Riley, 'What About the Worker?! The Move Toward Establishing a System of Rights for Employees' [2008] UNSWLR 64.

[9] *Lloyd v Imperial Parking Ltd* [1997] 3 WWR 697; *Morgan v Chukal Enterprises* (2000) BCJ (QL) No. 1563 (BCSC).

[10] 2000 Can. L. Il 2317 (ON. CA).

[11] (1998) 159 DLR (4th) 18.

abuse of discretion. At common law, in developing the obligation of trust and confidence, where the employer possesses discretionary powers under the contract of employment the courts have sought to guard against abuse of power. Indeed, one of the most significant consequences of the advent of the term has been in respect of control over employer prerogative. It appears to be the case that all aspects of the employer's prerogative are subject to the implied obligation (or in some instances other fundamental implied terms), though the precise extent of the restraint on the employer's discretionary powers may vary. This remains the case even where an express power is clear and unambiguous. This body of case law is steadily growing. The employer must therefore now assume that all discretionary clauses and, more generally, prerogative powers will be read subject to such fundamental implied terms that can be regarded as expressing the essence of the contract. The courts acknowledge that, while the parties to an employment contract are likely to have conflicting interests, where 'the provisions of the contract effectively place the resolution of that conflict in the hands of the party exercising the discretion, it is presumed to be the reasonable expectation and therefore the common intention of the parties that there should be a genuine and rational, as opposed to an empty or irrational, exercise of discretion'.[12] The role of mutual trust in patrolling the exercise of the employer's discretionary powers has been explored in a variety of contexts. Many of the decisions (including some of the most interesting) have arisen where remuneration is at issue. The courts are concerned to ensure that the employee gains the 'full' entitlement from the remuneration package. The failure to impose an implied restraint would risk removing from a term 'any contractual value or content in respect of the employee whom it is designed to benefit and motivate. It would fly in the face of the principles of trust and confidence which have been held to underpin the employment relationship.'[13] It should be stressed that this remains the case even where the wording of a clause dealing with the award of pay or bonus is highly discretionary in nature. Contracting-out of the obligation of trust and confidence is, at least in theory, feasible but decidedly difficult to accomplish given contemporary judicial attitudes.[14] Writing extra-judicially after the decision of the House of Lords in *Johnson v Unisys*,[15] Lord Bingham has said that attempts may 'be

[12] *Horkulak v Cantor Fitzgerald International* [2004] IRLR 942, 948.

[13] Ibid., 950. [14] And see 'Contracting-out' below. [15] [2003] 1 AC 518.

made to relax the obligations by express terms set out in a contract of employment, but I would not expect such terms to be sympathetically interpreted'.[16] In the recent case of *Commerzbank v Keen* the clause in dispute stated: 'You are not eligible to participate in the [bank's] discretionary bonus scheme. The decision as to whether or not to award a bonus, the amount of any award, and the timing and form of the award are at the discretion of the [bank].'[17] The very wide drafting notwithstanding, it was accepted that the exercise of the clause was subject to implied limitation.

The values underpinning the obligation of mutual trust and confidence and the obligation of decency can be said to be concerned in particular with questions of dignity and respect. These values are now seen as fundamental in employment relations and are consistent with the contemporary judicial view that the employee's interest goes beyond purely pecuniary concerns.

Core values

The pervasiveness of contemporary judicial attitudes is powerfully illustrated by the approach adopted under the statutory framework established in New South Wales by the Industrial Relations Act 1996. The 1996 Act bestows the Industrial Relations Commission with extensive powers where unfair contracts are concerned.[18] The definition of such contracts is very open-textured and includes those that are unfair, harsh or unconscionable, or against the public interest.[19] The Commission can determine that an unfair contract is void, in whole or in part.[20] It also has power to vary the terms of a contract. Section 106(2) is worthy of note in that it allows for account to be taken of the dynamics of employment relations. A contract, fair at the point of formation, may

[16] 'From Servant to Employee: A Study of the Common Law In Action' 13 SAcLJ 253, 266.

[17] [2007] IRLR 132. Similarly in *Horkulak*, n. 12 above, payment of bonus was said to be at the 'sole discretion' of the employer. Again in *Mallone v BPB Industries* [2002] ICR 1045 there was said to be an 'absolute discretion' to determine the 'appropriate proportion' of the number of shares comprised in an option granted to the claimant under a company's senior-executive share-option scheme.

[18] Industrial Relations Act 1996, s. 106. The legislation has been amended so that it now has an extremely limited scope and is said to have been reduced to a narrow jurisdiction for a special group of workers. Nevertheless it remains an extremely interesting model. For further discussion, see C. Sappideen, P. O'Grady and G. Warburton, *Macken's Law of Employment*, 6th edn (Sydney: Lawbook Co., 2009), p. 545.

[19] Industrial Relations Act 1996, s. 105. [20] Industrial Relations Act 1996, s. 106.

become unfair by reason of the conduct of the parties. This allows for control of the way in which the contract operates. As well as being able to vary or void the contract the Commission has the power to make a consequential order for the payment of such a sum of money as is just in the circumstances of the case. In addition, section 107 looks to prevent abuse in the future and allows for the making of an order against the employer to prevent it entering into unfair contracts – whether with the claimant or someone else. Where the common law is concerned the judges have a great deal of scope to develop the law as they see fit but, if anything, there is even greater scope for judicial creativity under the 1996 Act. It has been said that:

> the test of unfairness of a contract or arrangement or understanding has been found to be determinable by the application of common sense and sense of justice and the common sense approach of a juryman and that it is a moral and not a legal issue. Also, in applying that test, it is not simply a case of applying standards which appear to provide a proper balance or division of advantage or disadvantage between parties who have made a contract or arrangement. What has also to be born (sic) in mind is the conduct of the parties, their capability to appreciate the bargain that was made and the comparative bargaining positions when entering into the contract or arrangement. Further, the legislation's massive power makes it imperative that it should be exercised with proper restraint and should not become a refuge for those who are merely disgruntled with a bargain entered into on even terms.[21]

The NSW regime and the common law one are in some ways very different but both allow the judiciary to paint on a very broad canvass. It is striking, given the extraordinary degree of discretion conferred, that cases decided under the statutory scheme display the same desire to promote key values such as dignity and respect. Again NSW decisions seek to promote natural justice and ensure that discretion is exercised in an equitable manner. Mutual trust and confidence performs the same functions. The commonality of values arises despite the fact that one regime is statutory and the other is an expression of the values of the common law. Nevertheless both allow aggrieved employees to challenge the express terms of a contract dictated by the employer with a view to improving procedural protection or substantive terms. In *Cukeric v David Jones*,[22] for instance, the Industrial Relations Commission sought to improve procedural protection for employees and thereby promote

[21] *Reilly v TDG Logistics Pty Ltd* [2001] QIR Comm. 52.

[22] [1997] NSWIR Comm. 172.

the values of natural justice. In the context of a restructuring it was held that an employee was entitled to expect fair consideration to be given to whether there was a position available for him in the new structure. Such an assessment would involve regard being had 'to perfectly ordinary considerations, such as Mr Cukeric's past performance, the experience and skills which he possessed, the skills the Company required in the various positions available under the new structure and, of necessity, some adequate discussion of those matters with him'. At the point of termination, the NSW scheme provides that the employee benefits from natural justice-type protection. A contract of employment might be held to have become unfair because the employer acted unreasonably in failing to give the employee warnings in the event that performance was so inadequate as to put the employment in jeopardy.[23] Mutual trust also requires that detrimental action should not be taken against an employee unless they have been made aware of the case against them and had the opportunity to respond. This may be illustrated by *Harris v TSB*,[24] where a reference revealed that seventeen complaints had been made against the employee, of which four were upheld and eight were outstanding. The content of the reference was such that a prospective employer was not prepared to offer the employee a position. The employee had only ever been informed about two of these complaints by her existing employer. It was accepted that there 'is no legal duty . . . to refer complaints to employees at the point of time when no disciplinary action is contemplated'. However, failing to reveal complaints which were later used against the employee amounted to a beach of mutual trust and confidence: 'Implicit in the decision of the tribunal is the finding of a breach of contract in having a process of unrevealed complaints, knowing that they may be used for a reference, and then using them as a reference so as, in this case, to terminate the career . . . of an able employee.'[25] A significant limitation in the scope of common law protection arises because, in *Johnson v Unisys*, the House of Lords held that the employer's capacity to dismiss is not restrained by the implied obligation of mutual trust and confidence. A decision for the plaintiff in that case would have created inappropriate duplication with the statutory remedy of unfair dismissal.[26] The '*Johnson* exclusion' aside, the role

[23] *Westfield v Sidney Helprin* [1997] NSWIR Comm. 36.
[24] [2000] IRLR 157. [25] Ibid., 166.
[26] [2003] 1 AC 518. An approach which has found favour elsewhere: *New South Wales v Paige* (2002) 115 IR 283.

assumed by mutual trust and confidence in regulating the disciplinary process demonstrates the term's affinities with the principles of natural justice. Returning to the statutory scheme, abuse of discretion is again seen as a problem and, once more, there is a willingness to intervene. Indeed in *Adams v Westfield* it was apparent that the structure of the scheme was inherently unfair: 'The way in which, particularly in a situation of redundancy where all prior performance levels had been met, the respondent reserved unto itself the absolute discretion whether a bonus became payable, but in the absence of any published or available criteria by which that could be measured, represents to me a fundamental unfairness in the scheme.'[27]

The comparison of common law decisions with those arrived at under the statutory framework in New South Wales is of interest. It demonstrates that even though the context may be very different the judiciary are determined to promote and protect certain key values. Crucially, their understanding of the balance of power in employment relations leads them to regard judicial intervention as a matter of necessity.

Contracting-out

There are two major differences between the common law and the statutory model that has been enacted in New South Wales. The latter scheme allows the bargain entered into by the parties to be completely rewritten. Should the contract be held to be unfair, judicial discretion is at large when it comes to varying the obligations originally entered into. The Industrial Relations Commission, unlike a court exercising a common law jurisdiction, is not restricted in its mission by what can be achieved by interpretation or the implication of terms. The issue of contracting-out reveals a far more significant difference and one where the NSW legislation serves to highlight fundamental limitations in the common law armoury. The most direct, and often highly effective, way for the employer to contract-out of the obligations of the employment contract is to elect for a different form of contractual relation. The courts, in applying the common law tests to determine the existence of the employment contract, have a limited capacity to prevent inappropriate use of other types of contract. The values that underpin the general principles of the law of contract very much restrict what might be achieved. The ideology of freedom of contract that informs the common

[27] [2000] NSWIR Comm. 112.

law is obviously sympathetic to contracting-out. For example, in *Stevedoring and Haulage Services v Fuller*[28] the employer had, in effect, been able to set aside the obligations he would otherwise have owed by imposing express terms inconsistent with mutuality of obligation existing between the parties. Mutuality of obligation is a precondition of a contract of employment coming into being. The key issue was whether casual workers were employees other than when they were actually working. The contractual documentation included a clause which provided that: 'You are not an employee of the company; your services being utilised only when mutually agreed, with no obligation by either party other than to honour a specific pre-agreed period of engagement.' This meant that the workers were regarded as being employed under a series of individual engagements. The difficulty for the employee in all of this is that the employer, given its far greater bargaining power, is in practical terms free to choose to structure relations through a series of discrete contracts. It is important to note that third parties' rights may also be adversely affected. As Sedley LJ pointed out in *Dacas v Brook Street Bureau* the danger is that the use of workers who are not employees can circumvent the law of vicarious liability: 'An employer is vicariously liable for injury to others caused by an employee's carelessness, and is required by statute to insure against it; but an enterprise will have no such liability for harm done by somebody working for it who is not an employee.'[29]

The NSW scheme tackles these difficulties in a very different way. It combines a wide-ranging and highly inclusive statutory definition with very considerable judicial discretion. The scheme applies to any 'arrangement whereby a person performs work in an industry, that is, a transaction which directly leads to the performance of work in an industry'.[30] The width of definition means that the scheme has the potential to be over-inclusive in that it is capable of embracing contracts that would be widely regarded as purely commercial in nature. Much in the way of difficult demarcation decisions is then left to the Industrial Relations Commission and the courts:

> Notwithstanding the wide language of s. 88F,[31] I have found difficulty in becoming convinced that it was within the contemplation of the

[28] [2001] IRLR 627. [29] [2004] IRLR 358, 368.

[30] *Reich v Client Server Professionals* (2000) 99 IR 69.

[31] Section 88F was an earlier version of the current section 106.

> legislature that agreements for business ventures, of which the present may be a specimen, freely entered into by parties in equal bargaining positions, should be so far placed within the discretion of the Industrial Commission as to be liable to be declared void. However, I have come to the conclusion that the language of s. 88F of the Act is intractable and must be given effect according to its width and generality. The legislature has apparently left it to the good sense of the Industrial Commission not to use its extensive discretion to interfere with bargains freely made by a person who was under no constraint or inequality, or whose labour was not being oppressively exploited.[32]

The effectiveness of the scheme is heavily contingent upon judicial interpretation and elaboration of the key policy imperatives. In this respect we find that worker protection is furthered in that a broad interpretation has been given to the phrase 'performs work in any industry' and the coverage of the legislative scheme has been held to extend clearly beyond employment contracts.[33] The legislation and its predecessors enabled the Commission to go to the substance of an arrangement made for a person to perform work and 'to do so in disregard of the legal dress in which the arrangement has been clothed'.[34] This statutory framework has led to a wide variety of contractual arrangements being scrutinised. *Majik Markets v Brake and Service Centre*,[35] for example, dealt with a franchise agreement. Whilst commercial in form the substance of the agreement could be seen as akin to an employment relationship:

> The form of agreement requires the franchisee to perform work in the retail industry either personally or through employees and therefore it leads directly to the performance of work in that industry. The franchisor has a real interest in the performance of that work ... While the franchisees, if not natural persons, are working for themselves, they are also in a very real sense working for the franchisor. If the business was not operated by some franchisee, the franchisor would either have to employ staff of its own or sell or lease the site to an independent purchaser or lessee.[36]

Majik demonstrates that one of the merits of a wide definition is that the adjudicator can react very quickly to the use of new types of

[32] *Stevenson v Barham* (1977) 136 CLR 190, 201.
[33] J. Riley, 'Regulating for Fair Dealing in Work Contracts: A New South Wales Approach' (2007) 36 ILJ 19.
[34] *Brown v Rezitis* (1970) 127 CLR 157, per Menzies J, para. 2.
[35] (1991) 28 NSWLR 443. [36] Ibid., 465.

contractual arrangements intended to circumvent the protection afforded by the contract of employment. Where franchise agreements are concerned protection may be essential on grounds of social policy given that franchising may involve an extensive degree of bureaucratic control by the franchisor whilst simultaneously transferring the risks of business failure to the franchisee.

The width of the jurisdiction is illustrated by *Mitchforce v Industrial Relations Commission*[37] where the position in respect of a commercial lease fell to be considered. The boldness of the legislative scheme is confirmed by the fact that, in principle, a contractual relationship of this type falls within the Commission's jurisdiction. However, in the particular circumstances arising in *Mitchforce* the Court of Appeal held that a long-term lease of a hotel was not a contract whereby work was performed in an industry. The Industrial Relations Commission had found to the contrary. The tenants were working proprietors who applied to the Commission for relief under section 106 on the ground that the lease was a contract whereby work was performed in an industry. Hungerford J upheld the claim, varied the lease to reduce the rent and declared that the tenants were entitled to a renewed lease. He found that the lease gave rise to an ongoing relationship with the clear purpose that the applicants would conduct the business of a hotel for the duration of the lease and that necessarily contemplated the performance of work. The Court of Appeal were concerned that relationships which were, in truth, commercial would be caught. They were of the view that the applicants entered into the lease to allow them to conduct a business on their own account. The tenants were not viewed as working for the landlord. In an interesting dissent, Handley JA was of the view that the impact of the rent variation clause meant that over time the position changed: 'The lease was unsaleable, they were locked in, and they had been reduced to the role of managers because the landlord was taking all the profits of the business and leaving them with a loss. They continued to live off the business but in economic terms they were working for nothing because their losses must have substantially exceeded their drawings.'[38]

The approach adopted is therefore to be over-inclusive by way of legislative formula and rely on judicial discretion and development of sub-rules through precedent to determine the appropriate extent of

[37] (2003) 57 NSWLR 212. [38] Ibid., para. 192.

control under the statutory scheme.[39] Barwick CJ acknowledged in *Stevenson v Barham* that the statutory formulation is wide enough to encompass relationships between parties of equal bargaining power: 'The legislature has apparently left it to the good sense of the Industrial Commission not to use its extensive discretion to interfere with bargains freely made by a person who was under no constraint or inequality, or whose labour was not being oppressively exploited.'[40]

The focus in the preceding paragraphs on contracting-out through the use of alternative contractual relations provides one means of circumventing judicial norms. Clearly where one is dealing with an employment contract the employer may seek to contract-out of a particular term. Where specific contractual obligations are concerned the courts again have a decidedly limited capacity at common law to control contracting-out. In extreme situations a term may be voided on grounds of public policy. It would be open to the courts to determine that an implied term was mandatory on the basis of public policy.[41] This, though, is a technique which it seems that the courts are unlikely to deploy other than in exceptional circumstances. *Johnston v Bloomsbury HA* concerned the interaction of an express term on working hours with the implied term in respect of reasonable care.[42] In the context of striking-out proceedings it was said to be 'a matter of grave public concern that junior doctors should be required to work such long hours without proper rest that not only their own health may be put at risk but that of their patients as well'. The court found for the applicant on the basis of section 2 of the Unfair Contract Terms Act 1977. Nevertheless, it appears that, at common law, the Court of Appeal would have declined to render the implied term mandatory. The policy considerations at issue were perceived to be too daunting. It was said that:

[39] In *Mitchforce*, n. 37 above, it was said at para. 12 that: 'It seems to me that the legislature was concerned to empower the industrial tribunals, more recently the Commission alone, to examine contracts and arrangements which led directly to the employment of persons and the performance of work in any industry, not simply because the contract or arrangement in a commercial sense involves the provision of goods and services, with a consequent performance of work in an industry, but rather because the impugned agreement or arrangement itself directly envisages the employment of a person or persons in industry and has a recognizable impact upon the conditions of that employment, and, whether or not it envisages that a contracting party will perform the work, discloses a purpose that by the adoption of the arrangement the industrial objectives of the legislation will be more or less defeated.'

[40] *Stevenson*, n. 32 above, 192.

[41] *Lee v Showmen's Guild* [1952] 2 QB 329, 342.

[42] [1992] QB 333. And see Chapter 9 under 'The contractual matrix'.

> The courts should be wary of extending the scope of the doctrine beyond the well recognised categories ... They should be even more reluctant to embark upon a wide ranging enquiry into matters of public debate where it is plain that there are two views bona fide and firmly held, and where complex considerations of capacity of the NHS and public funding are involved.[43]

Where entrenchment of common law norms is at stake, such conservatism continues to prevail. In *Johnson v Unisys*,[44] for example, none of the Law Lords were willing to hold that mutual trust and confidence was a mandatory term on grounds of public policy. At root the ideology of the common law dictates that implied terms in law remain 'default rules'. In the absence of legislative fiat the autonomy of the parties is allowed to prevail. In *Johnstone* the matter was viewed as 'more appropriate for negotiation between the professional bodies ... or for Parliament, than for resolution by the courts'.[45] This is to be regretted. Implication follows from an assessment that certain obligations are inherent in a particular type of relationship. The framework of the relationship is diminished in their absence. In contracts where there is greater equality of bargaining power between the parties it is appropriate that implied terms operate merely as default rules. In contracts of employment, on the other hand, core rights within employment relations may be dependent on judicial implication. To allow an employment contract to be formed without the benefit of the implied terms in law, or at least some of them, may significantly diminish the social protection afforded to employees by the law. The NSW scheme is well-equipped to meet those concerns. The width of the wording allows, in effect, the contract to be remade: 'this can be done either by omitting parts and retaining the rest, or by adding new terms. Thus, destruction, dilution, renovation and patching are all weapons in the section's arsenal.'[46] It is apparent, for instance, that any attempt to contract-out of mutual trust and confidence could be readily dealt with.

The NSW legislation has the merit that it can review all clauses falling within contracts of a particular type. Unlike say, the Unfair Contract Terms Act 1977 in the UK, it is not limited in its scope to terms of a particular type which are specified and defined in the legislation. This makes it harder for employers to avoid the impact of the legislation

[43] *Johnstone v Bloomsbury HA* [1992] QB 333, 346–7.

[44] [2003] 1 AC 518. [45] *Johnstone*, n. 43 above.

[46] *Davies v General Transport Development Pty Ltd* [1967] AR (NSW) 371, 373.

through astute drafting. It also means that the courts do not become entangled in issues which are more about semantics than the underlying policy. For example, section 3 of the Unfair Contract Terms Act 1977 is only engaged where there is an exclusion clause and not where there is a clause which simply defines the extent of the relevant obligation. Such a distinction may not be easy to draw. In *Brigden v American Express*[47] the contract provided that 'an employee may be dismissed by notice and/or payment in lieu of notice during the first two years of employment, without implementation of the disciplinary procedure'. It was held that the clause was not an exemption clause but, instead, simply defined the parties' obligations. The judgment contains little by way of justification for this stance. Certainly, in cases of this sort it will be very much a question of semantics as to whether or not a clause is caught by the Unfair Contract Terms Act. This bestows a great deal of power on the party drafting the contract. There is admittedly judicial authority to the effect that the courts should look to the substance of a clause:

> In applying section 2(2), it is not relevant to consider whether the form of a condition is such that it can aptly be given the label of an 'exclusion' or 'restriction' clause. There is no mystique about 'exclusion' or 'restriction' clauses. To decide whether a person 'excludes' liability by reference to a contract term, you look at the effect of the term. You look at its substance.[48]

Conclusions

Enterprise liability ensures that key or fundamental obligations owed to third parties are, to a large extent, non-derogable. Particularly where the parties are not in a pre-existing relationship, the tortfeasor's ability to exclude or restrict liability by the use of devices such as disclaimers is limited. Legislation such as the Unfair Contract Terms Act 1977 in the UK may make matters even more problematic for the tortfeasor. Whilst the concept of enterprise liability has yet to impact on the obligations which exist at the level of employer/employee, there have, nevertheless, been significant judicially imposed changes in the content of the employment contract. These changes have promoted a judicial vision

[47] [2000] IRLR 94.

[48] *Phillips Products Ltd v Hyland (Note)* [1987] 1 WLR 659, 666, and cited with approval by Stuart-Smith LJ in *Johnstone* (n. 43 above), 346. Again in the Inner House decision in *Chapman v Aberdeen Construction Group* [1991] IRLR 505 it was said that the proper question is whether the 'true effect' of a term of a contract is to exclude liability.

of the core values of the contract of employment. They embody a vision of corporate responsibility which furthers the interests of employees to a much greater extent than previously. Enterprise liability has the potential to generate further changes in the law of the employment contract and extend the scope of employer's responsibility. However, the potential for contracting-out is very considerable and it is far from clear that the common law is capable of addressing this problem. Statutory intervention may be the only answer. At common law the capacity to contract-out of obligations in tort owed to third parties is limited and therefore this impacts on the employer's capacity to avoid the judicial reforms driven by enterprise liability. The position is different where the contract of employment is concerned as, given that the employer normally sets the terms of the contract, matters are very much within the employer's control and the common law finds it difficult to respond. The employer can exploit its role as drafter of the contract to cast aside unwanted obligations. Lack of recognition of inequality of bargaining power would, at one time, have stood in the way of judicial intervention. The problem is now much more one of limitations in common law technique, and statutory intervention may be called for. The NSW scheme is designed to thwart employers who seek to contract-out by resort to a contractual relationship other than employment. This stance is notable for the width of definition which by being, prima facie, over-inclusive renders evasion extremely difficult. This is attractive in that it combats very effectively a popular means of avoiding the import of employment protection legislation.

13

Concluding remarks

Bazley has without doubt been a hugely influential decision. In an age where increasing focus is placed upon corporate social responsibility the decision of the Supreme Court can be seen as the common law's response. Enterprise liability undoubtedly strikes a chord in a period where there is tremendous debate on the role and responsibilities of corporations. The decision has contributed to the expansion of employer responsibility through the doctrine of vicarious liability. As between two innocent parties decisions are more likely to favour third parties rather than employers than would previously have been the case. It would be easy to assume that enterprise liability will continue to further this expansion, but I am not convinced that this will come about. The reception of *Bazley* has not been uncritical – in particular there has been considerable criticism of the core concept of enterprise risk, the latter being the tool through which enterprise liability fashions new legal rules and reshapes existing ones. The criticism is likely to temper the desire to utilise the concept to bring about further significant change. Controversy centres upon whether the concept of enterprise risk is based upon a false dichotomy. Can one really distinguish between situations where the enterprise has created or increased the risk and not merely provided the opportunity for harm to arise? Equally problematic have been the attempts to arrive at a test which would allow judges at first instance to arrive at decisions in a manner consistent with the concept of enterprise liability. The close connection test appears to be no more than a convenient way of describing a situation where liability has arisen. Two more difficulties arise here. The decision in *E. B. v the Order of Oblates of Mary Immaculate*[1] means that the tort must be sufficiently connected to the tortfeasor's assigned tasks before it can be regarded as a materialisation of the risks created by the enterprise. This serves as a means of restraining the logical impact of the doctrine of enterprise liability and thereby

[1] [2005] 3 SCR 45.

shields the enterprise. Were attention to be focused upon the enterprise rather than the individual the boundaries of liability might be much more extensive. Who is to say that this would not be more equitable? Certainly greater consideration of empirical evidence would introduce new perspectives. The courts have also identified employments which confer 'job-created authority' as giving rise to a much higher degree of risk. It is again questionable whether this position would be maintained were regard to be had to empirical evidence.

Enterprise liability has yet to impact upon internal relations within an employing organisation. There is, though, huge potential for the concept to act as a catalyst for change in the employee/employer relationship. The law on non-delegable duties provides a good example in that at present we have a set of rules which are not underpinned by a policy justification. By classifying the employer's duty to take reasonable care for the health and safety of employees as non-delegable the law says very plainly that the obligation concerned is fundamental. However – as was recently confirmed by the Court of Appeal in *Farraj v Kings Healthcare NHS Trust*[2] – it is not clear why the employer's obligation of reasonable care is viewed in this way. As a result there is a danger that the rule appears to be an anomalous exception to the general principles of fault liability and principled evolution becomes more difficult. There is an absence of contemporary justification, and it is the author's contention that enterprise liability can supply this. Harm arising from a breach of the employer's obligation of reasonable care would not be suffered but for the employer's desire to pursue activities necessitating the involvement of employees for gain. Enterprise liability can explain existing rules and also provide a theoretical platform for reform. The concept could, with profit, inform the rules of employer's liability and allow the common law to address current concerns such as multi-employer activity. It can also point to a reconfiguration of rules on allocation of risk within the law of the employment contract. Were that to happen the position on matters such as the employer's right of indemnity and recovery in respect of psychiatric injury suffered in the course of employment might change. At the same time it must be acknowledged that core common law obligations imposed by the contract of employment have been reformed of late – with considerable benefit to the employee. The burden on the employer by virtue of

[2] [2009] EWCA Civ 1203.

entering into a contract of employment is now considerably greater. The emergence of obligations such as the implied term of trust and confidence are of real significance. It may therefore seem churlish to criticise on the basis that enterprise liability has not benefited employees in the way that it has third parties. Clearly a different conception of corporate social responsibility is operating where the employment contract is concerned. However, the fact that the contract has developed in the way that it has does not mean that the current rules on allocation of risk within the employment relationship are equitable. As between the enterprise and the employee risk allocation remains undisturbed. The contrast with the position of the third party is stark. For example, the employer's right of indemnity remains in place and could not look more anachronistic. La Forest J's view that vicarious liability should not be viewed simply as a means of ensuring that an employee's liability to a third party was capable of being discharged seems to be utterly in accord with enterprise liability. The law should seek to facilitate 'the broader function of transferring to the enterprise itself the risks created by the activity performed by its agents'.[3] The contrast between the position of the employee and the third party may be due to a reluctance to alter the nature of the bargain struck by employer and employee where allocation of economic resources is concerned.

It has been necessary to explore what is meant by an enterprise for the purposes of enterprise liability. This has allowed a number of questions concerned with corporate structure to be addressed, such as the responsibilities owed to employees where a group of companies is involved. It has also been necessary to determine for whose activities an enterprise should be liable. For instance, where an employer operates through the medium of independent contractors, should it be responsible (whether through the medium of vicarious liability or on the basis of non-delegable duties) for their tortious acts? Where contractors are concerned it would seem that the weight of tradition may present an insuperable barrier in the path of reform at common law. Recourse to enterprise liability impacts on the classification of a worker's status in a number of ways. In general in tort cases a decision in favour of employment is probably more likely. In addition, there are some indications, admittedly rather tentative, that enterprise liability may prompt a revival

[3] *London Drugs v Kuehne* [1992] 3 SCR 299, 339.

of the integration/organisation test in determining whether a contract of employment exists. Were that to happen the author would suggest that classifications of working relationships as ones of employment would be more likely to be arrived at. It is difficult to predict just how influential enterprise liability will continue to be, but without doubt, the potential for change is huge.

INDEX

For EU product safety concerns, contact us at Calle de José Abascal, 56–1°, 28003 Madrid, Spain or eugpsr@cambridge.org.

www.ingramcontent.com/pod-product-compliance
Lightning Source LLC
LaVergne TN
LVHW011814200926
848484LV00005B/1196